Engineers of Jihad

ENGINEERS OF JIHAD

The Curious Connection between Violent Extremism and Education

DIEGO GAMBETTA AND STEFFEN HERTOG

PRINCETON UNIVERSITY PRESS

Princeton and Oxford

Copyright © 2016 by Princeton University Press
Published by Princeton University Press, 41 William Street, Princeton, New Jersey 08540
In the United Kingdom: Princeton University Press, 6 Oxford Street, Woodstock,
Oxfordshire OX20 1TR

press.princeton.edu

Jacket art: "Terror by Hacking" © Brian Stauffer

Library of Congress Cataloging-in-Publication Data

Names: Gambetta, Diego, 1952– author. | Hertog, Steffen, author.
Title: Engineers of Jihad : the curious connection between violent extremism and
education / Diego Gambetta and Steffen Hertog.
Description: Princeton : Princeton University Press, [2016] | Includes bibliographical
references and index.
Identifiers: LCCN 2015037056 | ISBN 9780691145174 (hardback : alk. paper)
Subjects: LCSH: Radicalism—Islamic countries. | Extremists—Education—Islamic
countries. | Terrorists—Education—Islamic countries. | Engineering students—Political
activity—Islamic countries. | Violence—Religious aspects—Islam. | Terrorism—Religious
aspects—Islam. | Jihad.
Classification: LCC HN768.Z9 R343 2016 | DDC 303.48/4091767—dc23 LC record
available at http://lccn.loc.gov/2015037056

British Library Cataloging-in-Publication Data is available

This book has been composed in Sabon and DIN 1451

Printed on acid-free paper. ∞

Printed in the United States of America

10 9 8 7 6 5 4 3 2 1

CONTENTS

PREFACE

TO EVEN THE MOST CASUAL OBSERVER, KEY MOMENTS IN THE LAST TWO centuries demonstrate the disproportionate impact that the violent actions of a handful of extremists can have in shaping the course of events in the Western world. Not all extremists' acts have had momentous effects of course, but memorable cases come readily to mind. The attacks of September 11, 2001, for example, whose nefarious consequences have been and will remain with us for a long time, and the assassination of Archduke Ferdinand and his wife by a Serbian nationalist in Sarajevo in 1914, which unleashed World War I. The Spartacists whose revolutionary zeal contributed to the rise of the right in Germany in 1919 and the Baader-Meinhof Gang which, fifty years later, shook the stability of the young West German democracy. Or the anarchists who rocked the European monarchies at the turn of the twentieth century, and Sendero Luminoso in Peru and FARC in Colombia who held their countries hostage for decades. Bearing in mind all of these, the Islamist extremists, who have been the salient threat for the last two decades and who are the focus of this book, are but the latest in a long line.

Violent extremists may have abruptly changed the course of history, both nationally and internationally, but often not in the way they intended. The outcome of their actions depends more on the response of the establishment that is targeted than on the nature of the actions themselves. Who could have anticipated the reaction of the Bush administration to Al-Qaida's 9/11 attack, a disastrous war on Saddam Hussein's Iraq that had nothing to do with the attack, to say nothing of the mad carnage of World War I, which broke out following the assassination of the Austrian archduke?

To make their opponents feel threatened, extremists do not need to be well armed, or rational, or even very numerous. But their extreme risk-taking behavior makes the question of what kind of individuals become extremists all the more pressing. What kind of people embark on a violent, radical course when their chances of success are low and the fight they pick is so asymmetrical in terms of force? Only a few violent groups develop social roots, sowing the seeds of broader militant movements and larger insurgencies, and fewer still succeed in gaining power. Most are ultimately crushed and disappear. So what makes some people form or join groups of violent extremists?

Answering this question has been difficult for social scientists for obvious reasons. Extremists are few in number, operate underground, and are hard to reach not least because they tend to die young. Whatever they communicate to the outside world is tainted by their strategic aims—they let us know only what they believe serves their purposes, and it is hard to separate truth from obfuscation. Trying to understand their motivation from afar through introspection does not help either, as the very fact that they are extremists makes them difficult to identify or empathize with.

The powers under attack, too, strive to impose their narrative on events, and demonizing extremists is an inevitable part of that process. The very use of the label "terrorist" is part of the ubiquitous tactic of belittling the enemy's ends while magnifying their means. State enforcement agencies and armies are wary of allowing independent scholars access to information that might undermine their official rhetoric. It is not even clear whether state agencies, under pressure from the paranoia and political impatience that typically inform "counterterrorism" policies, can afford the time and mental energy to turn the wealth of information that they possess about extremists into a deep understanding of the phenomenon. It is striking that even at a safe historical distance from particular conflicts with extremists, no insightful reports from government agencies seem to surface. The truth could be the first victim of conflict not so much because it is censored, manipulated, or strategically kept from public view for reasons of "national security," but because it is never reached in the first place. There continues to be a yawning gap between what violent extremists can do and what we, the public, really understand about them.

The difficulty of researching violent extremism has not deterred people from writing about the phenomenon, and the literature is as copious as it is inconclusive. While there are peaks of high-quality research, with which we shall engage in the book, much of it is based on speculation and armchair theorizing. When there is any evidence at all it is often anecdotal and distorted by selection biases or prejudices.

In this book we take a different and unusual approach. Our point of departure is a surprising fact: *engineers are overrepresented among violent Islamist extremists*. This puzzling correlation, the existence of which we establish beyond a reasonable doubt in the first chapter, offers a vantage point from which to understand the nature of Islamist extremism and the mechanisms behind its emergence.

Relying on education as our key variable has several advantages. The level of education and, for those who attended university, the discipline of the degree pursued are types of biographic information that are *not very difficult to obtain*; because they are considered irrelevant for governments' counterterrorism operations, they are unlikely to be classified or strategically manipulated. Data on education are also, in this case, preferable to data on occupation, since *everyone* receives some education and does so *early in life*; in addition, education usually does not change or progress after an individual has gone through the education system, while occupation does. So these are types of information that we can potentially acquire about everyone, even extremists, many of whom are old enough to have gone to university but are too young to have had a significant career. Lastly, education level and types are fairly comparable across the educational systems of different countries.

But there is more to education level and type: their greatest advantage for our purposes is that they reflect actual *behavior* rather than (self-) reported attitudes, and, unlike other biographical data that are often available—such as gender, age, or place of birth—they are at least to some extent the result of the subjects' *choice*. As such they carry a wealth of information that can help us uncover important socioeconomic circumstances as well as personal dispositions. The *discipline* of the degree attained in particular has the potential to contain information about personal characteristics. Individuals' preexisting traits and motivations may determine how they choose among similarly demanding and rewarding but otherwise incommensurable areas of study, such as medicine, engineering, economics, and law. For those who can afford to select among equivalent courses, their choices are likely to be less constrained by social or economic factors and thus be a proxy of personal propensities.

These features of education made it both possible and worthwhile for us to put together data sets on the level and type of education of five categories of Islamist activists.

(1) Three large and diffuse groups: militant individuals born and active in a variety of Muslim countries in peacetime; militants born or raised in Western countries; and nonviolent Islamists from across the Muslim world.

(2) Two more specific groups: Islamist extremists in Iran before the revolution; and Islamist extremists from around the world who defected and abandoned the ways of violent politics.

We do not include in the main sample larger Islamist insurgent groups such as Boko Haram in Nigeria, the Shabab in Somalia, the Taliban in Afghanistan, and ISIS in Iraq and Syria. Even though they now represent a salient threat to Western interests, we believe that they are significantly different from the smaller clandestine groups. They operate in less asymmetric conflicts and engage in more traditional warfare; they have a territorial basis and strategy; and they build up a governance of sorts in the territories they hold, with rich interactions with local communities. What we know about them indicates that both their recruitment mechanisms and people's motivations for joining are likely to be very different.[1]

While we focused on smaller groups rather than full-blown insurgencies, we pursued as wide-ranging comparisons across ideologies as we could. We collected data on the education of nine types of right- and left-wing extremists active both before and after World War II: the early Nazi and Italian fascist movements; the neo-Nazis in Germany and Austria; U.S. and Russian white supremacists; members of the Spartakusbund, of the Rote Armee Fraktion and of the Brigate Rosse; and a collection of anarchists active around the world. In total, we collected biographical data on more than four thousand individuals.

A second, more general advantage of our approach lies in the type of reasoning that results from starting research with a causal puzzle. Research on complex topics can easily drown in a sea of conjecture. Bad research is littered with unnervingly long lists of potential causes of whatever it is the researcher is trying to explain: asking, for example, "What are the causes of suicide?" is not likely to be of much help in identifying any of them. By contrast, following a method Emile Durkheim put to systematic use, asking, "Why do Protestants commit suicide more often than Catholics or Jews?" and thus restricting the range of what differentiates one group from another, can help isolate some of the causes of suicide.

Similarly, our puzzle compels us to recast the grand questions concerning extremism within circumscribed limits: whatever conjecture we put forward must be compatible with the basic finding that engineers are much more likely (and, as we will see, students of certain other disciplines much *less* likely) to pursue the violent route of Islamist extremism. Conversely, any inference we draw from this basic fact, by being narrower and well-defined, offers greater scope for being testable. Engaging in this exercise opens up unexpected implications for extremism of other kinds, both right and left wing, which we compare with Islamist extremism in the last three chapters.

There are four classic questions that surround extremism that the correlation at the core of our book will help us frame in a new and clearer light.

What are the socioeconomic conditions that explain why people join extremist groups?

---

1 We decided to include Hamas because it is a hybrid group that, on the one hand, uses many conventional "terrorist" tactics and that for long periods of its existence lacked a territorial basis but, on the other, is larger and more embedded in local society than typical "terrorist" groups. Leaving it out of the sample would not materially change results.

With respect to Islamist extremists alone, scholars have produced an "almost inexhaustible lists of precipitating factors, including the failure of secular modernization projects, blocked social mobility, economic malaise, Arab defeat in the 1967 war with Israel, the legacy of colonialism and cultural imperialism, and political alienation" (Wiktorowicz 2004b: 3). When taking a broader view to include other kinds of extremists, the list becomes even longer. Poverty is often invoked, though its presence is uneven at best; in some cases it seems to matter but not in others, or if it does it is not with first movers but with second-generation rebels (see, e.g., Hertog's review [2010] of Krueger 2007). In fact, the opposite effect has also been detected: there is evidence of a *positive* correlation between *level* of education and militancy both among Islamist and left-wing radicals (Russell and Miller 1977; Krueger and Maleckova 2003; Krueger 2007; Berrebi 2007).

To deal with these contrasting predictions, social movement theories have invoked "political opportunity structures" and "political entrepreneurs" able "to frame discontent" (Snow et al. 1986; Tarrow 1998; Tilly 2004; Wiktorowicz 2004a, 2004b). Still, concepts such as these are too abstract to distinguish between cases with precision, and it is not apparent how they can generate testable hypotheses that can explain why, among larger dissatisfied populations, certain agents were the first to become radicalized or were more prone to join. Social movement theorists themselves have advocated a move away from global theories to more mechanism-based explanations (McAdam, Tarrow, and Tilly 2001). Some important results have been achieved in this direction, for instance, by studying how social networks matter in mobilizing certain individuals rather than others (McAdam 1986; Sageman 2004).

By taking the general question to the specific microlevel of mobilization we aim to contribute to this more focused research agenda: we do not look for any general mobilizing factor but for factors that are consistent with Islamic *engineers* rebelling to a greater extent than graduates of other disciplines. Can we identify the socioeconomic conditions to which engineers are particularly exposed relative to other graduates that could explain their radicalization? And could these conditions be the same ones that contribute to mobilization generally?

Do some people more than others have a mind-set susceptible to the lure of extremism?

The idea that, given the "right" socioeconomic conditions, *anyone* can end up an extremist is widespread among social scientists. We are wary of believing that there could be *types* of individuals whose hardwired traits make them more likely to become extremists. This is not just because it seems contradictory for a *social* scientist to focus on factors other than "the social." Many among us also hold deep-seated beliefs that are hostile to psychological explanations—for example, that humans are born tabula rasa or that it is morally wrong to assume that there are innate predispositions to embrace certain political ideas.

But there are better justifications for the social scientists' skepticism. These lie in the weakness of the existing psychological studies. While we know that violent extremists are more likely to be male and young, no other feature has consistently emerged. No one has been able to construct a profile of *the* archetypal extremist. A thorough review of the psychological studies of "the mind of the terrorist" by Victoroff (2005), a psychiatrist, ends with somewhat vague statements such as "terrorists are psychologically extremely heterogeneous" and "terrorist behavior is probably *always* determined by a combination of innate factors, biological factors, early developmental factors, cognitive factors, temperament, environmental influences, and group dynamics" (34–35).

If everything explains then nothing does. Many social scientists thus understandably think that the "terrorist mind" is a chimera and that by and large extremists are "normal people" (Kruglanski and Fishman 2006; Ruby 2002; Silke 1998). Still, it may be premature to come to that conclusion. As Victoroff (2005) writes, "the much-cited claim that no individual factors identify those at risk for becoming terrorists is based on *completely inadequate research*" (34, emphasis added). Furthermore, an increasing amount of empirically grounded research in political psychology, which we review in chapter 6, shows that political preferences in general are grounded in personality types and even in genetic dispositions.

The puzzling correlation at the core of our book carries implications that offer a good opportunity to evaluate the extent to which personality traits matter. Once we control for socioeconomic conditions that lead engineers to rebel we can measure the extent to which engineers are still overrepresented; and if they are, we can infer that character traits must matter, given that character likely influences choice of education and vice versa.

There are theoretical grounds to suggest that certain political and ideological orientations can be either promoted by the discipline one chooses to study or be the reason why certain individuals are attracted to a discipline in the first place. As for being promoted, both the Marxist and the Weberian traditions would predict that professional socialization shapes, respectively, one's economic interests and one's beliefs about the causal and moral order of the world. As for the attraction hypothesis, there are plausible reasons to expect that the choice of different disciplines will be driven by different preexisting talents, tastes, and dispositions.

To what extent is the question of who ends up becoming an extremist a matter of "supply"— different types of people choosing particular types of extremism—or a matter of "demand"—groups searching for and selecting suitable recruits?

There is a particular mechanism that could explain engineers' overrepresentation and weaken our inferences that socioeconomic circumstances or personality matter and which speaks to another general question concerning extremists. Theoretical work on the economics of terrorism (Bueno de Mesquita 2005; Benmelech, Berrebi, and Klor 2010) points to recruitment strategies to explain why some well-known "terrorists" come from relatively privileged backgrounds: of all the individuals that at any given point are clamoring to commit violent political acts, organizations select those who seem most likely to succeed, and these people are more likely to be found among the elites.

This explanation of violent extremists as demand driven seems particularly suited to the case of engineers, who possess technical skills that make them prized recruits among all kinds of extremist groups. This conjecture can be tested by looking in depth at how and why engineers end up becoming extremists—for instance, whether engineers are found in greater than expected numbers among other types of extremists who have as much interest as Islamist radicals in employing the skills of engineers; and, regardless of the type of extremists, whether engineers occupy roles in the organizations that best exploit their technical skills.

Does ideology matter in determining which types of people join certain groups?

The strategic recruitment hypothesis may not work if different types of people are attracted to different types of groups, in which case regardless of how groups select, groups would receive different types of people: "It is plausible but yet to be proven that different types of terrorism disproportionately attract individuals with specific temperaments. Future research should attempt to determine the most likely psychological types among terrorists in groups with different political orientations" (Victoroff 2005: 35). We take up this challenge through the focused lens of our puzzling correlation. Are there particular traits among engineers that cause them to be more attracted to the Islamist radical ideology, and if so what are these? And do we find that engineers are also attracted by ideologies that have features in common with the Islamist ideology?

In chapter 1 we examine the distribution of engineers and graduates from other disciplines among Islamist radicals active in Muslim countries. In chapter 2 we explore to what extent the rather neglected theory of relative deprivation as a source of radicalization is supported by the data on education of Muslim world extremists. In chapter 3 we probe how robust and exhaustive an explanation relative deprivation really is by analyzing (1) the educational distribution of extremists in countries in which engineers have not been particularly deprived, for instance, in Western countries, and (2) whether engineers stand out relative to other graduates even when we vary factors—use of violence, group religiosity, and propensity to defect—that should make no difference as far as relative deprivation is concerned. In chapter 4 we investigate whether the ideology of Islamist extremists—covering an ensemble of beliefs, values, and tastes—has any parallel with that of groups of non-Islamist political extremists: in other words whether Islamist extremists' ideology is more akin to that of the extreme right or the extreme left. In chapter 5 we detail the education of a long list of non-Islamist extremists, both on the right and the left of the political spectrum. Lastly, in chapter 6, we try to discover what might be the character traits and dispositions that distinguish the various types of extremists.

ACKNOWLEDGMENTS

When we first posted a paper on the web in 2008 describing the puzzle that lies at the core of this book, many people who read it superficially or even just heard about it took it either as a chance to attack and ridicule engineers in general or took exception to what we wrote as if we did attack engineers in general. These responses were regrettable and unwarranted: we write about a fringe of engineers who, while much more likely than people from other disciplines to join some extremist groups, remain a tiny minority. It is no larger than graduates of the humanities and social sciences who are as overrepresented in other types of extremist groups as we shall show in chapter 5. Our first thanks should therefore go to the many other engineers who wrote to us or about our puzzle fairly and offered perceptive comments, as for instance Susan Karlin in *IEEE Spectrum* (http://spectrum.ieee.org/telecom/security/extremist-engineers, posted on 1 September 2008), the magazine of the largest professional association of engineers in the world.

Over the several years it took us to complete this book many friends and colleagues have generously helped us in various ways and at different points in the process. We wish to thank Peter Bergen, Rohan Gunaratna, Thomas Hegghammer, Roberto Franzosi, Shiraz Maher, and Swati Pandey for sharing their data with us and, for their help with various detailed pieces of information, Angel Alcalde, Francisco Herreros, Stephane Lacroix, Stephen Lukes, André Mazawi, Thomas Pierret, Josh Pollack, Valeria Pizzini Gambetta, Pedro Riera Sagrera, Melanie Smith, Maria Sobolewska,

Larry Wright, and several Gulf2000 listserv members. We are very grateful to Becky Kahane, Martin Lestra, Janto McMullin, Jane Roberts, Neil Rudisill, Moritz Schmoll, Marina Tsvetkova, and Karsten Wekel for their invaluable research assistance, to Heike Naumann from Hochschul-Informations-System Gmb H in Hanover, Germany, for her generous assistance on European higher education data, and to Riaz Hassan for sharing his survey data on the Islamic world. Finally, we are indebted to Michael Biggs, Annalisa Cristini, Jon Elster, Nils Petter Gleditsch, Elisabeth Iversflaten, Ekaterina Hertog, Elisabeth Longuenesse, Rick Ludkin, Tiziana Nazio, John Owen, Andrea Patacconi, Roger Petersen, Valeria Pizzini Gambetta, Tom Snijders, Anna Zimdars, and the participants in the several venues at which we presented our findings for comments on earlier drafts.

The Education of Islamist Extremists

ON CHRISTMAS DAY 2009, UMAR FAROUK ABDULMUTALLAB, A TWENTY-three-year-old Nigerian man, arrived from Ghana into Amsterdam's Schiphol airport where he boarded Northwest Airlines Flight 253 to Detroit. As the airplane approached its destination, Abdulmutallab disappeared for twenty minutes into the lavatory. Back in his seat, he started fumbling around with his underwear. Neighboring passengers saw his trousers on fire and Jasper Schuringa, a Dutch film director, jumped on Abdulmutallab and subdued him, while flight attendants rushed to the scene with a fire extinguisher. The explosive device he had hidden in his pants failed to detonate and Abdulmutallab was arrested. Authorities discovered that he had been in contact with Al-Qaida elements in Yemen. Just a year earlier Abdulmutallab had received a degree in mechanical engineering from University College London.[1]

Two months before Abdulmutallab's attempt, on 13 October 2009, Mohamed Game, a thirty-seven-year-old Libyan living in Italy, blew himself up with two kilos of nitrate at the entrance of the Caserma Santa Barbara, an army barracks in Milan. This was the first and thus far only suicide attack attempted in Italy, and Game might have been a "lone wolf" operator, at most a member of a small local network. Game—who lost his right hand in the attack and is now serving a fourteen-year sentence—has a degree in electronic engineering.

Exactly three months before Game's failed attack, on 13 July 2009, a German court sentenced forty-seven-year-old German Pakistani Aleem Nasir to eight years in prison for his role as an Al-Qaida facilitator in Europe. Nasir had been traveling regularly to the tribal areas in Pakistan, supposedly to trade in semiprecious stones but apparently to transfer money to, and coordinate European recruitment for, Islamist militant groups. Nasir is said to have been enlisting a number of German Muslims for jihad, among them German Moroccan Bekkay Harrach, who would become infamous—also in 2009—for his videotaped threats of jihad against the German government, apparently recorded in a hideout in Pakistan. Nasir holds a degree in mechanical engineering while Harrach had

---

1 *BBC News*, 7 January 2010.

begun college studies of laser technology and mathematics before dropping out to take a part-time job in a mosque in Bonn.[2]

Apart from being male and of Islamic faith, these four men have little
in common. They vary in terms of nationality, age, the Western country
with which they had most contact, and even the extremist network they
were part of. They also differ in marital status: Game, Nasir, and Harrach
had wives and children; Abdulmutallab did not.

Their careers vary greatly, too. Nasir had worked at an energy research institute in Karlsruhe before being fired for supposed extremist
statements, after which he worked as a gem trader. Game, despite his
degree, had a history of underemployment and was in debt, while Harrach
lived off odd jobs. Abdulmutallab never even began a career, jumping
straight from his studies into extremist activities.

The only thing they have in common is having studied engineering.

As one would expect there are militant Islamist university or college
graduates who have not had successful careers after graduation: Faisal
Shahzad, the Pakistani man who left an SUV packed with explosives near
Times Square in Manhattan on 1 May 2010, is said to have been "unemployed and bankrupt at the time of his arrest," though it is not clear
whether his progressive radicalization was the effect or the cause of his
unemployment.[3] Wadih El-Hage, a Lebanese man who is serving a life
sentence in the United States for his involvement in the 1998 bombings of
U.S. embassies in Africa, held minimum-wage jobs in the United States as
a city custodian and auto mechanic, despite having university training as
an urban planner.[4]

However, other extremists abandoned successful careers to devote
themselves to the cause. Abdul Subhan Qureshi, leader of the Students
Islamic Movement of India, who is wanted in India for various attacks,
including the ones on the Mumbai trains on 11 July 2006, left his wife,
three children, and a thriving occupation. Qureshi joined Radical Solu-
tions, a computer firm in South Mumbai, in November 1996. According
to his coworkers, Qureshi was an exceptional worker: "He handled several major independent projects, including an intranet for Bharat Petro-
Chemicals carried out by Wipro in 1999, and then joined Datamatics." In
just three years, his salary quadrupled. In a letter dated 26 March 2001
he resigned, stating, "I wish to inform you, that I have decided to devote

2 *New York Times*, 23 September 2007; *Der Spiegel*, 6 April 2009; *Frankfurter Allge-
meine Zeitung*, 20 September 2009; Raffaello Pantucci, "Bekkay Harrach: The Face of
German Terror," *Terrorism Monitor* (Jamestown Foundation), vol. 7, no. 30.
3 *New York Times*, 4 May 2010.
4 PBS *Frontline*, "A Portrait of Wadih El-Hage," www.pbs.org/wgbh/pages/frontline/
shows/binladen/upclose/elhage.html.

one complete year to pursue religious and spiritual matters."[5] For other extremists their careers mattered less because they came from very privileged backgrounds: underpants bomber Abdulmutallab is the youngest of the sixteen children of Alhaji Umaru Mutallab, former chairman of First Bank of Nigeria and former Nigerian Federal Commissioner for Economic Development, and lived in a luxury apartment in Marylebone while studying for his engineering degree in London.[6]

And yet, despite their deeply dissimilar employment histories, Shahzad, El-Hage, and Qureshi all have engineering degrees, just like Abdulmutallab and the others. Shahzad "enrolled at the University of Bridgeport, where he received a bachelor's degree in computer science and engineering in 2000, followed by a master's in business administration in 2005."[7] El-Hage studied urban planning at the University of Southwestern Louisiana in the 1980s, interrupted by spells of jihadist training in Afghanistan.[8] Qureshi for his part "obtained a diploma in industrial electronics [in 1995], and landed a part-time job at String Computers in Mazgaon. Later, in 1996, he went on to earn a specialised software maintenance qualification from the CMS Institute in Marol."[9]

Socioeconomic background, age, country of origin or relocation, group of affiliation, employment and family situation—all these features vary among the men discussed thus far. The only feature they share is a degree in higher education, in particular a degree in engineering. This is doubly puzzling when set against commonsense expectations. While we readily accept that the dispossessed are natural candidates for extremism, we are at a loss to comprehend why well-off, educated men should join the ranks of jihad. And why would individuals with a technical mind and training in modern technology have a penchant for a movement at once violent, religious, and in many cases, as we will see in chapter 4, permeated by antiscientific beliefs?

At the Origins

Evidence of this link is not limited to recent cases. It spans three decades and three continents and appears in connection with notorious attacks. Mohamed Atta (Egyptian) and Khalid Sheik Mohammed (Kuwaiti), leading figures in the 9/11 plot, both studied technical subjects: one urban

5 Praveen Swami, "The Hunt for the Indian Mujahideen's 'al-Arbi,'" *The Hindu*, 13 September 2008, www.hindu.com/2008/09/13/stories/2008091355761100.htm.
6 *Wall Street Journal*, 29 December 2009.
7 *New York Times*, 4 May 2010.
8 "A Portrait of Wadih El-Hage."
9 *The Hindu*, 13 September 2008.

planning in Hamburg, the other mechanical engineering in the United States. In fact, of the twenty-five individuals directly involved in the 9/11 attacks, eight were engineers. Engineers are, moreover, found right at the beginning of modern Islamist militancy. In 1970s Egypt, three groups considered part of the beginning of modern jihadism had been started or were led by individuals who had a technical education. Al-Takfir wal-Hijra, which was involved in the assassination of a cabinet minister, was founded in 1969 by Shukri Mustafa, an agricultural engineer and former member of the Egyptian Muslim Brotherhood. Shukri was radicalized during his incarceration in the Tura prison and Abu Zabal concentration camp in Egypt. The second group—known as the Military Academy Group for its violent occupation of the Egyptian Technical Military Academy in April 1974, from where it launched a failed attempt to march on the ruling party's headquarters—was founded in the 1970s by Salih Siriyya, a Palestinian with a doctorate in the teaching of science (Ibrahim 1980; Kepel 1985). Siriyya, too, had been imprisoned. Finally, an electrical engineer, Muhammad Abd al-Salam Faraj, played a pivotal role in the group al-Jihad, which was responsible for the assassination of President Sadat in 1981 and became the most notorious successor to the earliest Egyptian groups (Nesser 2004; ICG 2004). Saad Eddin Ibrahim, an Egyptian sociologist who was the first to study the early violent Islamists, interviewed thirty-four members of two of these groups, the Military Academy Group and Al-Takfir, who were imprisoned in the late 1970s. Twenty-nine of them were either university graduates or students, and of the twenty-five for whom he reports their area of study, nine were engineers, seven were doctors, five were agronomists, two were pharmacists, two were studying technical military science, and one was studying literature (Ibrahim 1980, 1982).

Engineers were also members of radical student groups in Egypt in the 1970s called Gama'at Islamiyya. Ayman al-Zawahiri, who later gained worldwide notoriety as bin Laden's partner and successor at the helm of Al-Qaida, was a member of one of them. Abdallah Schleifer, an American Jew who is now a professor of media studies at the American University in Cairo and converted to Islam in the 1960s, made Zawahiri's acquaintance in 1974 when working for NCB news in Cairo. When they first met, Zawahiri, then at medical school, gave Schleifer a tour of the campus: "during the tour, Zawahiri proudly pointed out students who were painting posters for political demonstrations, and he boasted that the Islamist movement had found its greatest recruiting success in the university's two most élite faculties—the medical and engineering schools. 'Aren't you impressed by that?' he said" (Wright 2002).

Indications of the link between radical Islamism and engineering are also found beyond the Middle East. We have already mentioned Abdul Subhan Qureshi, the Indian computer engineer. Two of the three men who in 1987 founded Lashkar-e-Taiba, a Sunni fundamentalist Pakistani group that fights against India's sovereignty over the State of Jammu and Kashmir, were professors at the University of Engineering and Technology of Lahore, albeit not engineers themselves.[10] While appealing to madrasa students and the disenfranchised, Jemaah Islamiya in Southeast Asia also recruited "many technical faculty members, including architects, engineers, geophysicists, chemists, and robotics engineers" (Abuza 2006: 78). The three leading suspects in the September 2004 bombing of the Australian Embassy in Jakarta had an engineering background. According to a Tunisian professor of the history of Islam, 60 percent of salafi-jihadists in his country are trained as engineers.[11]

While the groups mentioned thus far are made up of Sunnis, the phenomenon extends to Shiite Islamists too: engineers were prominently represented in Mahmoud Ahmadinejad's radical 2005 cabinet,[12] and the former Iranian president himself trained as a civil engineer. While he is not a militant, his rhetoric as well as his biography reflect radical leanings: he was among the many engineering students at the University of Science and Technology in Teheran who played a very active role in the 1979 Islamic revolution.[13]

Hezbollah, the Lebanese Shiite group, also has a strong link with engineers. Soon after it was founded in 1982, Hezbollah established Jihad al-Binaa ("construction jihad"), an organizational branch devoted to the reconstruction of civil infrastructure and private housing. According to Hezbollah expert Judith Palmer Harik, "this is an interesting organization because it is chock-full of professionals—contractors, engineers, architects, demographic experts."[14] Representatives for Jihad al-Binaa estimate that more than two thousand of their engineers and architects have been involved in the reconstruction of Lebanon since the war with Israel in August 2006, which, considering that the estimated total Shiite male labor force in Lebanon likely lies below three hundred thousand, is a large number indeed.[15]

10 Zafar Iqbal and Hafiz Mohammad Saeed founded Markaz Dawa Al Irshad, which is Lashkar-e-Taiba's political wing. The third founder was Abdullah Azam of the International Islamic University: http://en.wikipedia.org/wiki/Markaz_Dawa-Wal-Irshad; www.hinduonnet.com/businessline/2001/01/05/stories/040555ra.htm.
11 Mohamed Lahmar, "Tunis: Les djihadistes sont aux 2/3 des ingénieurs," *African Manager*, 24 May 2013, www.africanmanager.com/151248.html.
12 http://secularcaniranik.blogs.com/scaniranic/2005/08/whos_who_in_ahm.html.
13 Goudarz Eghtedari, personal communication with the authors, July 2006.
14 www.finalcall.com/artman/publish/article_2940.shtml.
15 This estimate is obtained considering that the total Lebanese male labor force is, according to the World Bank, about 700,000 (2004) and that Shiites are about 40 percent of the Lebanese population. See http://devdata.worldbank.org/genderstats/genderRpt.asp?rpt=profile&cty=LBN,Lebanon&hm=home.

A SYSTEMATIC TEST

Several scholars have mentioned the link between radical Islam and science and engineering[16] but more as an oddity than as anything that could help us understand the phenomenon. A few have speculated about what might explain it,[17] but no one has attempted to find a systematic confirmation of the phenomenon. In fact, no one since Russell and Miller (1977) has published any research on the type of higher education extremists, whether Islamist or otherwise, receive. The few studies that document levels of education are limited and include only small or partial samples.[18]

To discover whether the overrepresentation of graduates in general and engineers in particular can be confirmed by more than anecdotal evidence, we compiled a list of 497 members of violent Islamist groups in the Muslim world active since the 1970s. It includes almost exclusively men for the simple reason that they are the overwhelming majority of extremists.[19] We drew from a variety of sources. We took lists of names included in academic literature, we asked colleagues, we combed through government documents, and we visited websites of radical organizations themselves. Then we conducted research on each person to gather additional biographical data in news archives in several languages, online sources, and further official documentation.[20] We mainly sought data on each person's level and type of education but also gathered information on age, socioeconomic background, international mobility, function within groups, and other qualitative biographical information. We supplemented this data-gathering effort with a daily survey of major international and Middle Eastern newspapers from 2004 to early 2010 to record, verify, and research new names as they appeared.

---

16 Bergen and Pandey 2005; Hoffman 1995; Huntington 1996: 112; Sageman 2004: 76; Schulze 1990: 22; Wickham 2002: 1; Wright 2006: 301.

17 Abuza 2006; Bergen and Pandey 2005; Sageman 2004: 76; Schulze 1990: 22; Waltz 1986.

18 Bergen and Pandey 2006; Krueger 2007; Berrebi 2007; Hegghammer 2006. See also chapter 2.

19 We found two women: Aafia Siddiqi, an MIT-trained biochemist working as an Al-Qaida courier who was tried and convicted in the United States in early 2010 and sentenced to eighty-six years in prison, and Hila al-Qusair, an alleged fund-raiser for Al-Qaida in Yemen.

20 We searched for biographical information on these individuals in Lexis Nexis and Factiva news databases and on Google. We also searched many other news media in various languages, as well as a series of online databases, such as Global Jihad and Global Security. All websites were consulted between September 2009 and January 2011.

The list of names includes individuals who grew up in countries that have either a Muslim majority or an indigenous Muslim minority, all of which are non-Western.[21] The list does not include violent members of groups born or bred in a Western country, which we investigate in a separate sample in chapter 3.[22] The median year of birth of the three hundred cases whose ages we could establish is 1968. This implies that the median year in which those who went to university started their courses is 1986–87, with a spread ranging from the mid-1950s to the late 1990s.

Our sample consists of members of groups that manifest an Islamist ideology of some kind *and* that employ violence in pursuit of their aims. In cases in which the involvement of a given individual was not certain, we erred on the side of caution. For instance, we did not include prisoners at Guantanamo with the exception of the few among them whose involvement in violent groups was confirmed by other sources.[23]

Our list is not a random sample of the Muslim world's Islamist extremists, and it does not cover all areas with a presence of Islamist militancy. It leaves out or underrepresents groups in South Asia and North Africa, for instance. It also excludes larger insurgent groups like Boko Haram in Nigeria, the Shabab in Somalia, and the Taliban in Afghanistan, which operate in a different strategic context of less asymmetric conflict.

However, the sample spans three continents and three decades, allowing us to investigate how far the phenomenon reaches in both space and time. The list includes individuals from thirty-five nationalities from a dozen larger groups and almost twice as many smaller groups, which injects ideological and organizational variety. The sample includes locally oriented groups struggling against authoritarian regimes (such as Egyptian Takfir wal-Hijra) or foreign occupation (such as Hamas), as well as global jihadists pursuing a millenarian anti-Western struggle (such as Al-Qaida and its franchises).[24] The list includes members of both small cells

---

21 By Western we mean North American and Western European.

22 Group affiliation of radicals is the primary criterion we used for selecting individuals into the two samples, so as to avoid dividing cohesive groups into different subsamples. In some cases, group membership straddles the Islamic and Western worlds, yet all of these are still primarily anchored in one or the other.

23 We excluded individuals whose culpability remains unclear as well as individuals without educational information who are not clearly linked to any group. We also left out groups for which we failed to find educational information on any single member. The latter two categories amount to 124 cases; with the progressive widening of our search, we were increasingly focusing on badly documented groups. Including these cases in our estimations of education levels and engineers' overrepresentation in the sample would not materially change the results. As soon as educational information was found on at least one member, we included the whole group concerned, even if that meant adding many cases with missing data.

24 For a classification of different types of Islamist militancy, see Hegghammer 2009a.

(such as the October 2004 Sinai bombers in Egypt) and larger clandestine networks (such Jemaah Islamiya in Southeast Asia). Many of these groups are well-known in the West, but others, such as the Indian Mujahedeen, are known mostly to specialists. Variation in geography, group strategy, and ideology are important because they allow us to put the link between extremism and higher education in general and engineering in particular through a stricter test—to see whether it holds independently of the groups' specific makeup or whether it is more common in some types of groups than in others.[25]

Education Levels

Out of the 497 individuals in our sample, we found some biographical information for 436 and educational information for 335 (figure 1.1). Of these, only 28 had less than a secondary education and 76 had completed secondary education (including madrasas).[26] Two hundred thirty-one had undertaken higher education, whether finished or unfinished, and of these at least 40 studied in Western countries.

The share of individuals who undertook higher education is remarkable: 69 percent, if we consider only those in the sample whose education we know about (231/335). And even if we assume that *none* of the individuals whose education is unknown had higher education, the share of those with higher education would still be a hefty 46.5 percent (231/497).[27] The well-known cases of highly educated individuals who carried out violent acts—for example, the master bomber of the 2004 and 2005 Bali attacks, Azahari Husin, was an engineer with a PhD from the University of Reading and a lecturer at the Technical University of Malaysia, while Ramadan Abdullah Shallah, a leader of Palestinian Islamic Jihad, received his PhD in economics at the University of Durham—are just the tip of a well-educated iceberg.

We cannot, however, rule out the possibility that even the lower percentage is an overestimate because proportionally more graduates might have ended up in our sample. Who is included in our list *and* the information we found on these individuals are a function of the public avail-

25 Hezbollah is one important group where we found practically no individual-level data on the education of its members. Given the organization's size, this might seem odd, but the secrecy of its governance structures and leadership makeup is a well-known and frustrating fact among Lebanon specialists.
26 In cases in which only "secondary education" was mentioned in our sources, we assumed it had been completed.
27 If the denominator included members of all groups on which we found no information at all (see footnote 23), the share would still be 37.2 percent.

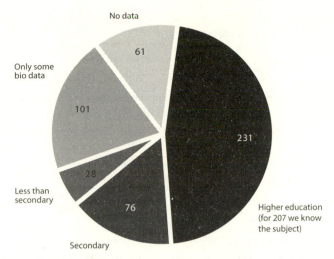

Figure 1.1: Levels of education in the Muslim world sample (497 individuals).
Source: Muslim world sample.

ability of data. This in turn depends largely on whether the individuals came to the attention of the authorities and media because they were killed, captured, or investigated. Since university graduates may hold positions that might expose them to a greater risk of detection than do nongraduates, they may also be more likely to enter the sample.

We were able to establish that at least 169 members of our sample exerted a leadership role in their organization or group—no less than 34 percent of the total sample, making this a plausible bias. It may obtain particularly among bigger groups in the sample, such as Jemaah Islamiya in Indonesia or Hamas in Palestine, whose total membership is much larger than the number of individuals in our records. In the case of smaller groups, however—such as the 1970s Egyptian groups and the international jihadi cells we have included—the majority of actual members *are* in our sample, somewhat mitigating the bias. If educational levels are broken down by group (see table 1.7), the members of the more exhaustively documented groups have similar levels of education as the members of the partially sampled ones.

The difference between the levels of education in the populations from which the sample is drawn and the levels of education in the sample itself is so dramatic that even a marked selection bias could not plausibly explain it: the rate of tertiary enrollment in all countries in the sample in 1987—

when the median case in our sample would have entered university—was 11.3 percent (weighted average).[28] The odds of being educated are thus, at the very least, more than six times higher in our sample than they are in the relevant population.

Although we cannot say by how much with precision, there is little doubt that violent Islamist radicals outside of mass insurgency and civil war settings are vastly more educated than their compatriots. Previous studies have highlighted the high levels of education among specific groups of Islamist militants.[29] The data presented here confirm the phenomenon in a much larger and diverse sample. Although in recent years radical Islamist movements seem to have undergone a process of "proletarization,"[30] looking at the last three decades one finds a strong overrepresentation of the highly educated almost wherever one chooses to look.

Considering the view often taken of such rebels—that they are poor, ignorant, or have nothing to lose—it is surprising to find that so many individuals with university degrees should join militant Islamist movements, given both the personal costs involved and the supposed backwardness of Islamist ideologies. We will come back to this in chapter 2.

Education Types

Of those who attended university, who studied what? Before revealing our results we need to mention that throughout this book we use the same *seven disciplinary groupings* when presenting the types of education for all extremists—Islamist extremists in this and the next chapters and left-wing extremists, anarchists, and right-wing extremists in chapter 5. Our categories include, first, the "big four" degrees, which rely on established knowledge and whose holders typically apply it to professional fields: engineering; medicine; law; and economics, business, and administration. We then further group other disciplines into three clusters. These disci-

---

28 UNESCO 1990, section 3-2. The rate of enrollment was calculated by weighing the national averages by the number of cases per country in our sample.
29 Ibrahim 1980; Krueger 2007; Krueger and Maleckova 2003; Bergen and Pandey 2005; Berrebi 2007; Benmelech and Berrebi 2007.
30 Ibrahim (1996) documents the declining share of the college educated among Egyptian violent Islamists. The tourist resort bombings in Egypt in 2005 and the subsequent jihadi campaign on the Sinai Peninsula were linked to radicalized Bedouins, a new phenomenon (*Christian Science Monitor*, 24 May 2006). In Morocco, Al-Qaida recruiters have focused on poor slum-dwellers (*International Herald Tribune*, 11 April 2007). Similarly, levels of education among broader-based and relatively recent Islamist groups like the Taliban in Afghanistan and Pakistan, the Shabab in Somalia, and Boko Haram in Nigeria appear to be quite low. On the intellectual shifts accompanying Islamist "lumpenization," see Roy 1994: 84ff.

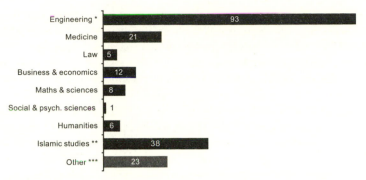

Figure 1.2: Islamist extremists by discipline of study (207 individuals).

   * "Engineering" includes computer science and architecture. The latter was included because it is commonly part of engineering faculties in Middle Eastern countries, as it is in European countries.

   ** "Islamic studies" includes various Islamic subjects such as "Islamic law," "Quranic studies," and "religion."

   *** "Other" includes agriculture, education, English, food sciences, pharmaceutical science, social services, and technical military science.

   Source: Muslim world sample.

plines, while not having clearly corresponding professions, share methods and core concerns (and often buildings): math and science; social and psychological sciences; and humanities. Unlike the "big four," these disciplines, albeit with greater or lesser rigor, focus on creating knowledge rather than learning how to apply it. When relevant we provide information on additional specific subjects, such as Islamic studies for the sample discussed in this chapter or history for right-wing groups in chapter 5.

In the Islamist sample we were able to find the discipline of study for 207 of the 231 individuals who at some point had full or partial exposure to higher education (figure 1.2).[31] Unsurprisingly, the second most numerous group comprises 38 individuals who pursued Islamic studies. But the largest group among the Islamist extremists is that of the engineers: 93 out of 207 individuals, or 44.9 percent of those whose type of degree we know, studied this subject. The engineering group is followed at some distance by medicine (21 individuals), economics and business studies (12), and math and science (8). On the whole, the individuals who pursued what we might call "elite degrees"—engineering, medicine, and science—make up 58.9 percent of the total. The elite degrees are universally more demanding and have stricter admission criteria in the countries

31 For the few individuals who enrolled in more than one discipline, we registered the one first studied or, if that was not clear, the one first mentioned in order to avoid problems of double accounting.

in our sample than do the other degrees. If we add economics and business studies, which in some countries such as Egypt is also a selective degree (Moore 1994: 46), to the elite category, we reach 64.7 percent. Militant Islamists are not only highly educated but have some of the most prestigious degrees available in their societies. Zawahiri had good reason to feel proud.

The engineers' birthdates (based on the 65 cases for which we could determine them) range from the 1930s to the late 1970s, with the median date of birth in 1966—two years older than the overall median (based on the 300 cases for which we know the date of birth). The oldest, born in 1936, is Hamas spokesperson Ibrahim Ghousheh, who graduated with a degree in civil engineering from Cairo University. The youngest one is underpants bomber Umar Abdulmutallab, followed by Youssef Mohamad Al-Hajdeeb and Jihad Hamad, two Lebanese nationals born in 1985 who moved to Germany to pursue engineering degrees but were caught attempting to bomb German trains in 2006 before they finished their course of study.

With regard to specific fields of study, three types of engineering predominate for the 56 cases for which we have that information: civil, electrical, and computer-related (figure 1.3). We do not know whether the distribution across engineering fields means anything or simply faithfully reflects the distribution found in the population of the relevant countries; we could not find systematic data on this. What we do know is that several illustrious individuals are from these three subdisciplines. Dokka Umarov, the most prominent Chechen Islamist military commander and self-proclaimed emir of the unrecognized Islamic state of Caucasus Emirate from 2007 until his death in 2013, had a degree in construction engineering.[32] The one-eyed, hook-armed Abu Hamza Al-Masri, notorious for his firebrand preaching at London's Finsbury Park mosque and whom a UK court sentenced to life in prison without parole in January 2015, has a civil engineering degree. A particularly strong battalion of jihadi VIPs is made up of electrical engineers: Muhammad Abdul-Salam Faraj, prominently involved in the Sadat assassination; Pakistani Ramzi Yousef, a leading figure in the first attack on the World Trade Center in New York in 1993 who went on to concoct the "Bojinka Plot" with Khalid Sheikh Mohammed (himself a mechanical engineer) to simultaneously blow up twelve airplanes in midair between Asia and the United States in 1995; 9/11 support staff Said Bahaji and Mounir al-Motassadeq; and Yahya Ayyash, Hamas's master bomb-maker in the 1990s. Computer and electronic engineers include the above-mentioned Abdul Subhan Qureshi of Mumbai

32 www.chechenpress.co.uk/english/news/2006/06/23/01.shtml.

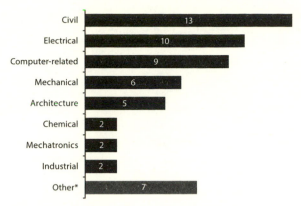

Figure 1.3: Types of engineering disciplines (56 individuals).
* "Other" includes urban planning, telecommunication electronics, industrial electronics, thermal energy engineering, medical technology, shipbuilding, and aeronautical engineering.
Source: Muslim world sample.

train-bombing fame, as well as Qatari national Ali Saleh Kahlah al-Marri, for many years the only foreign enemy combatant held on U.S. soil.

How Truly Overrepresented Are Engineers?

A bias in reporting the type of degree is implausible: we see no reason why the sources we used should be more inclined to report an engineering degree than any other degree. Still, the high proportion of engineers could be the result of "battlefield" selection: more engineers, we could conjecture, might have fallen into the investigative net, and hence ended up in our sample, because they took greater risks or had more visible leadership roles. This would be an important finding in its own right: even if engineers did not form a disproportionate share of jihadists as a whole, they would be the group that played the most significant role and paid the price for it.

However, this bias is unlikely. We were able to identify individuals who had held a leadership function within their militant group and had pursued higher education and found that the engineers were no more likely to be in a leadership role than were those who had studied other subjects at the university level (table 1.1). They were also no more likely to be bomb-makers, as we shall see shortly.[33] These data indicate that

33 Moreover, if there was a bias that makes engineers more visible whenever they engage in extremist activities then, all things being equal, they should be more visible in non-

TABLE 1.1
Leaders among Islamist extremists by discipline

Education	Leaders	Total in sample	%
Engineering	38	93	40.9
Medicine	5	8	62.5
Business & Economics	5	12	41.7
Math & Science	7	21	33.3
Islamic studies	19	38	50.0
Other degrees	15	36	41.7
Unknown degrees	5	23	21.7
Total	94	231	40.7

Source: Muslim world sample.

engineers are not taking on more exposed roles than are students of other disciplines.

The skeptical reader, however, might remain unconvinced for a different reason. Suppose the extremists come from countries in which scores of youngsters study engineering, a common career to aspire to in developing countries. This would then simply be reflected in the composition of the extremists. We would still have to explain why there are so many university graduates among the extremists, but the type of degree would simply follow from the distribution of graduates in the countries of origin. To see whether there is any truth in this, we looked at the number of engineers among the extremists relative to the number of engineers in the general population and then among the number of university graduates overall.

General Population

The share of engineers among the total male working population in the countries of origin of the individuals in our sample, weighted by the number of extremists we identified as coming from each country, is 1.3 percent. By contrast, even if we include all missing cases in the denominator,

---

Islamist militant groups, too. And yet, as we shall see in chapter 5, very few engineers are found among many non-Islamist groups. In the most extreme case the few engineers found in non-Islamist groups might still be an overestimate of the actual share of militant engineers, but for this to be the case they ought to be drastically underrepresented relative to other graduates.

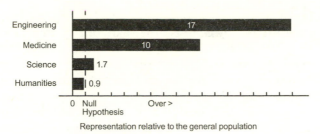

Figure 1.4: Representation of disciplines of study among Islamist extremists relative to presence of the same disciplines in the general population (odds ratio).
   Source: Muslim world sample.

the share of engineers among our extremists is 18.7 percent (93/497). These figures allow us to calculate the ratio between the odds of being an engineer in the general population and the odds of being one in our sample of extremists. The odds of finding an engineer in the sample is *seventeen times greater* than what we would expect if engineers were as likely to radicalize as the male adult population in general.

Doctors, too, are overrepresented by ten times. The odds of finding scientists, by contrast, are only slightly higher than what the null hypothesis predicts, while humanities students appear slightly less frequently in our sample than they do in the general population.

Population with Higher Education

This massive overrepresentation of engineers among Islamist extremists does not tell us to what extent engineers are also overrepresented among the militants with higher education. How many engineers could we expect to become radical if they did so at the same rate as graduates in any other subject? To address this question we compare our results with enrollment rates in higher education. Again, the data are for *males*, since all the individuals with higher education in our sample are males with the exception of U.S. citizen Aafia Siddiqui. We were able to obtain higher education data for all of the countries with a substantial number of cases in our sample for 1987, the median year in which the men in our sample went to university.

As table 1.2 shows, the overrepresentation of engineers in our sample is very pronounced for all nationalities (Saudi Arabia is an exception, which we will explore in the next section). The average share of engineers among the total number of male students of the 19 countries in our sample is 11.6 percent (individual country averages are weighted by the number of men per country in our sample who had pursued higher education). In our sample, by contrast, the share of engineers among those with known higher education is 44.9 percent.[34] The odds of being an engineer are more than *six times greater* than we would expect, a result that is highly statistically significant. For some of the countries in our sample the overrepresentation is even greater. In Egypt the proportion of engineers among male students was 10.9 percent in 1987 (dropping to 8.3 percent by 1995–96),[35] while among the 53 Egyptian cases in our sample whose subject of study we know 35.8 percent (19) are engineers. For Palestinians the enrollment rate was 5.9 percent, and out of 62 cases with known subject of study 35.5 percent (22) are engineers. (The differences between expected and actual ratios are highly significant for both countries in a chi-square test.)

To be accurate, we have to take into account 40 cases in our sample who studied in Western countries, 27 of whom (67.5 percent) studied engineering. To use the overall engineer ratio in the sample as the term of comparison, therefore, is not entirely correct, as Muslims studying in the West might have a higher propensity to choose an elite subject like engineering or medicine. But even if we remove this group we still have a ratio of 39.5 percent engineers (93–27/207–40), which makes the odds of being an engineer in our sample still five times larger than they would be if the likelihood of radicalization were the same across subjects. The difference remains highly statistically significant.

But what about the other disciplines? Table 1.3 compares weighted null hypotheses for four subjects with their actual presence in the sample. We find that there are more than twice as many doctors in the sample as we would expect—and out of 9 cases with known specialization, 5 are surgeons, arguably the most engineering-like type of medicine. Scientists, however, though they are often lumped together with engineers when scholars discuss the link between extremists and technical education, are in fact significantly *underrepresented*. More dramatic still, we find the almost total absence of humanities students. While we would expect on average 31 of them to appear in a randomly drawn sample of 207 male

---

34 The difference of the two ratios is significant in a chi-square test at $p < .001$. Engineering enrollment data were not available for a few countries, but these represent less than 5 percent of all cases with known higher education in the sample. We have detected some fluctuation over time in engineering enrollment relative to total tertiary enrollment in a few of the cases where more than one data point was available, but there appeared to be no systematic biases.

35 This share is estimated using aggregate enrollment figures (Arab Republic of Egypt 1996) and assuming the ratio of female students has remained constant.

TABLE 1.2
Islamist extremists with higher education, finished or unfinished, and share of engineers compared with the share of male students studying engineering, by country of origin

Country of origin	Total in sample	With higher education	% with higher education	Subject of higher education known	Engineers In sample N	Engineers In sample % *	Engineers % of male students in 1987 — 1987
Palestine	128	68	53.1	62	22	35.5	5.9
Egypt	88	59	67.0	53	19	35.8	10.9
Indonesia	53	12	22.6	7	1	12.5	15.3
India	36	10	27.8	9	7	77.8	14.4
Singapore	31	5	16.1	5	4	80.0	67.0
Saudi Arabia	33	14	42.4	12	2	16.7	10.2
Morocco	13	6	46.1	6	4	66.7	1.8
Yemen	12	3	25.0	2	0	0	4.1
Jordan	11	5	45.5	5	3	60.0	16.4
Malaysia	10	8	80.0	8	6	75.0	19.1
Pakistan	10	7	70.0	7	4	57.1	29.1
Algeria	9	3	33.3	3	1	33.3	14.3
Lebanon	7	6	85.7	6	4	66.7	11.0
Kuwait	4	3	75.0	1	0	0	10.1
Afghanistan	5	4	80.0	4	2	50.0	11.1
Syria	4	2	50.0	2	2	100.0	21.9
Sudan	4	2	50.0	2	1	50.0	11.1
Libya	4	0	0	0	0	0	–
U.S.	4	3	75.0	3	3	100.0	13.1
Canada	3	0	0	0	0	0	14.8
U.K.	2	2	100.0	1	0	0	30.2
Tanzania	2	0	0	0	0	0	12.1
Kenya	2	0	0	0	0	0	19.7
Philippines	2	0	0	0	0	–	31.8
Other**	12	8	66.7	8	7	87.5	–
Unknown	8	1	12.5	1	1	100.0	–
Totals	497	231	46.5	207	93	44.9	11.6 (weighted average)

* The share is calculated on the number of those whose degree we know.

** Belgium, Comoros, UAE, Germany, Guyana, Iraq, Ireland, Mauritania, Nigeria, Qatar, Somalia, Spain.

Sources: For the first 6 columns, Muslim world sample; for the last column, UNESCO 1990 (architecture counted as part of engineering); the figure for the United States is from 2005.

TABLE 1.3
Expected and actual shares of Islamist extremists in select disciplines (N in parentheses)

	Humanities		Science		Medicine		Engineering	
	yes	no	yes	no	yes	no	yes	no
Expected	14.9% (31)	85.1%	10.2% (21)	89.8%	4.8% (10)	95.2%	11.6% (24)	88.4%
Actual	2.9% (6)	97.1%	3.9% (8)	96.1%	10.1% (21)	89.9%	44.9% (93)	55.1%
Odds expected vs. actual	0.18 vs. 0.03		0.11 vs. 0.04		0.06 vs. 0.11		0.13 vs. 0.82	
Representation	5.9 times under		2.9 times under		2.0 times over		6.2 times over	

Source: Muslim world sample.

students from the countries in question, there are in fact only 6,[36] a finding almost as striking as that of the engineers' dominance.

Data on students in teaching colleges are not available for many of the countries in our sample. We know, however, that in Palestine and Egypt about 20 percent of all students are trained as teachers, while the share in our sample is only 2.8 percent: a mere 6 cases. Teachers have played only a marginal role in post-1970s Islamist militancy. This is true even though some of the highest-profile figures among the first generations of post–World War II militant Islamists were teachers, including Hassan Al-Banna and Sayyid Qutb of the Egyptian Muslim Brotherhood and Sheikh Yassin of Palestine's Hamas. But for some reason, the days of the schoolteacher-turned-revolutionary seem to have passed (see chapter 2).

The situation is similar for lawyers: constituting only 2.4 percent of the militant graduates in our sample, they are clearly underrepresented. Although no good data are available across all cases, in Egypt, for instance, we know that law students are about 15 percent of the total student body. Finally, in our sample we have only one individual trained in a social or psychological science, Ali Mohamed, an American of Egyptian origin who was involved in the bombings of U.S. embassies in Africa in 1998 and holds a BA in psychology (in chapter 5 we will show that left-wing extremists have studied social sciences and psychology much more frequently).[37]

36 Chi-square tests comparing actual and expected distributions were highly significant ($p < .01$).
37 UNESCO statistics unfortunately combine business, law, and social sciences into one category, preventing us from calculating precise null hypotheses.

If all university students were similarly likely to end up in radical groups, there *should* be many more scientists, teachers, and humanities students and graduates among Islamists and many fewer engineers. The data we've presented indeed show that the overrepresentation of the highly educated in the sample is largely driven by engineering and, to a lesser extent, medicine. It does not, however, disappear if we remove these two categories: we have at least 93 individuals in the sample known to have studied fields other than engineering and medicine. If we take out the special case of Islamic studies (38 cases), there are still at least 55 individuals with other types of university education, which is still at least three times as many as expected relative to the general population.[38]

THE SAUDI EXCEPTION

A closer inspection of the distribution of degrees by nationality (table 1.2) reveals that among the countries with a substantial number of graduates, Saudi Arabia does not have an engineering overrepresentation.[39] Scattered across several groups there is a contingent of 33 Saudis, 12 of whom have higher education, but only 2 are engineers. The paucity of Saudi engineers is also visible in the educational background of the extremists who perpetrated the 9/11 attacks: among the 25 individuals involved, there were 8 engineers and 15 Saudis. Seven of the 10 non-Saudis were engineers, but only 1 Saudi was an engineer—one of the two in our sample. These low numbers have increased significance when we consider two other sources. One is a sample of Saudi Islamist militants collected by Hegghammer. Out of a "core" of 70 violent Islamists active in the post-2003 domestic insurgency in Saudi Arabia (not overlapping

---

38 In our sample 104 individuals are known to have education that is less than tertiary. Given the levels of education and distribution of degrees in the relevant background populations, we would in fact only expect 9 individuals with "other degrees" in a randomly drawn sample of which we only know that it contains 104 cases without higher education. If we add to the 104 all 101 cases in our sample for which we have no information, and assume that they also have no higher education, we would still expect only 18 individuals with "other degrees" to complement them in a randomly drawn sample.

39 Indonesia might also appear as an exception with its small number of engineers. However, the numbers of graduates in our sample are small, and complementary research seems to show that they do, in fact, have a considerable presence of them: Noorhaidi Hasan, who interviewed 125 members of the militant Indonesian salafi group Laskar Jihad in various parts of the country, states that "almost half are students, dropouts and graduates from a dozen universities in Indonesia" and that "these students are generally enrolled in science and engineering departments" (2006: 159–60).

TABLE 1.4
Islamist extremists with higher education, finished or unfinished, and engineers in Saudi Arabia by source, compared to other countries of origin

	Total	With higher education		Known discipline of higher education	Engineers	
		N	%		N	%
Saudis in our sample	33	14	42.4	12	2	16.7
Saudis in Hegghammer's sample	36	17	47.2	11	1	9.1
All others in our sample	464	217	46.8	195	91	46.7

Sources: Muslim world sample; Hegghammer 2006.

with our sample), he found educational data on 36, 17 of whom had a degree or college exposure. Among the 11 of these for whom the subject of study is known, 5 pursued religious degrees but only 1 was an engineer (not the one in our sample).

The second source is a database of foreign Islamist militants who went to fight (and often died) in Iraq from all over the Arab world in the mid-2000s, put together by organizers affiliated with Al-Qaida. The U.S. military found it in a computer in a jihadi safe house in the border town of Sinjar, which they raided in October 2007, and declassified it in December of the same year. The Sinjar records include 590 short biographies of volunteers. The records are incomplete, providing educational information on only 88 individuals, and they represent a type of insurgency that is not part of our main sample. This, however, means that they constitute an "out of sample" check on our results that is independent of our other sources. As far as we know, the information has been released unfiltered.

According to the original Arabic records, 73 of the 88 militants were exposed to some kind of higher education, the subject of which is known for 46 cases (figure 1.5). Only 9, one-fifth of the total, are engineers. This is only somewhat higher than what we would expect given the distribution of disciplines among male Arab students. Ten individuals were trained as teachers—a marginal group in our main sample. Both facts, however, are only an apparent contradiction of the findings in our main sample—in fact the Sinjar data are much in line with our previous results: once we break the group of 10 teachers down by nationality, we find that 8 of the 10 are Saudis; the other 2 are from Libya, another oil-rich coun-

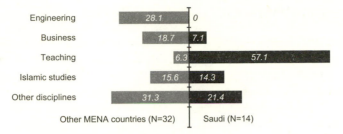

Figure 1.5: Distribution of nationalities and discipline of study among Sinjar individuals with higher education (%).
Note: MENA stands for Middle East and North Africa.
Source: Sinjar records (2007).

try. Among the 23 cases from Arab countries other than Saudi Arabia and Libya, 35 percent (8) are engineers, which is close to the proportion we have in our sample. The Sinjar data, however imperfect, match both the general finding of a surfeit of engineers as well as the Saudi exception.

What we are to make of the Saudi exception is a question we address in chapter 2.

SELECTION EFFECTS

The proportion of graduates in general and engineers in particular among Islamist extremists appears to be genuinely significant. It requires explanation—but what exactly is to be explained first needs to be established. There are two processes that could generate these findings: one is a greater propensity among graduates and engineers to become jihadi and the other is a selection mechanism by which more graduates and more engineers are admitted to the ranks of jihad, regardless of propensity. The two processes could of course also work in combination.

The first filter, in other words, is individuals' willingness to join jihad, and to determine the extent to which the *over*representation of graduates and engineers is a reflection of an extra willingness on their part, the explanation must address the substantive question of why graduates are more willing than nongraduates to join and why engineers are the most willing graduates of all. But how faithful a reflection it is depends on the force of the second filter.

The second filter (which does not apply to founders and first movers) is extremist organizations' recruitment of certain types of militants rather than others. In so far as they exercise a choice rather than simply going after anyone available, they might prefer more able and hence more educated people—especially those with technical skills—because such individuals would be better able to fulfill the organization's goals.[40] If the supply of militants is larger than the demand, organizations could fill their ranks to capacity by first choosing highly qualified people even though these are not necessarily more frequently available, that is, more willing, than the lesser qualified people among the supply. So, in an extreme case, the composition would seem to reflect a greater willingness on the part of the highly educated or of engineers to join, while in reality it merely reflects the fact that as members of the most desirable group they were being recruited in larger numbers, while all others, though equally willing, were being recruited in smaller numbers.

A number of reasons, some of which we will discuss at length in chapter 3, incline us to think that selection on the basis of educational level cannot explain away the high proportion of university graduates in our sample. We believe that the high number raises substantive questions concerning the motivations of graduates who join jihad. We do know that there is selection: for instance, Sageman (2004: 121) reports that only 10–30 percent of trainees in Al-Qaida camps in Afghanistan were formally accepted into jihad, although we do not know whether these trainees were accepted because their level of education correlated with the skills the organization sought. Moreover, Al-Qaida is perhaps the organization that faced the starkest trade-off between quality and quantity, and for which an upper limit of membership size is plausible. But it is not clear whether all groups systematically privilege quality over quantity—in some strategic contexts, it may be useful to simply maximize membership. Next, we know from historical sources (see chapter 2) that radicalization in places like Iran, Egypt, Palestine, and Indonesia was student driven or initiated by educated elites. Also, even if there was a general bias toward recruiting the better educated, there are large differences between the education levels of extremists in different regions that require an explanation (see table 1.2 as well as our data on the West in chapter 3).

In this chapter, we can use our existing sample to test for selection based on technical skills such as bomb-making or communication management. This allows us to evaluate whether engineers rather than graduates in other disciplines are overrepresented because they are overrecruited for their technical abilities. Below we will also test for a kind of selection that can affect both the university-educated in general and engineers in particular: this is the case in which organizations happen to be formed in

---

40 For conjectures along these lines, see Bueno de Mesquita 2005 and Benmelech, Berrebi, and Klor 2010. Note, however, that even these authors include the supply of would-be militants in their argument: while groups select their operatives among a larger pool, the quality of the larger pool shifts as a function of economic development, resulting in a shifting of the quality of the operatives over time.

certain domains, as for instance a university, and this original "accident" influences the "types" of people who are subsequently recruited through local social networks.

Bomb-making Skills

If attendance at a man's funeral is a measure of his success in life, few Arabs have been more successful than Yahya Ayyash. Tens of thousands of angry Hamas supporters showed up at his funeral in January 1996 in the Gaza Strip (Kahana 2007: 69)—two days after Israeli Intelligence had assassinated him.[41] Among his admirers, Ayyash was known as "the Engineer," an honorific that had more to do with his fabled skill at bomb-making than with his degree in electrical engineering from Bir Zeit University. Ayyash had orchestrated a lethal campaign of suicide bombing, taking the lives of no fewer than ninety Israelis and making him Shin Bet's most wanted target. He was killed by another feat of engineering: a modified mobile phone, given to him by way of a mole, blew away most of his head.

In December of the same year, Samar Alami, a Lebanese banker's daughter of Palestinian extraction, and Jawad Botmeh, a Palestinian Jordanian businessman, avoided a funeral but were still sentenced by a British court to twenty years in jail for the bombings of the Israeli embassy and of a Jewish charity in London in the summer of 1994. Alami held a BS in chemical engineering from University College London—the same school that underpants bomber and fellow engineer Umar Abdulmutallab attended two decades later—and an MS in chemical engineering from Imperial College. Botmeh had electrical engineering degrees from the University of Leicester and King's College London.[42]

Azahari Husin, the Indonesian "master bomb-maker" of the 2004 and 2005 Bali bombings, was killed in 2005 in Batu, near Malang in East Java, during a protracted shoot-out with the police who had surrounded his hideout. Nicknamed "demolition man" by Malaysian newspapers, he trained as a mechanical engineer in Australia in the 1980s before taking a doctorate at the University of Reading in 1990.[43]

Different in social background, biography, and theater of activity, Ayyash, Husin, and the imprisoned pair had two things in common: their training as engineers and their bomb-making skills. This may lead us to conclude that violent groups deliberately recruit individuals with a technical

41 *New York Times*, 7 January 1996, www.nytimes.com/1996/01/07/world/palestinians -vow-vengeance-at-gaza-funeral-of-terrorist.html?src=pm.
42 www.freesaj.org.uk/.
43 *The Scotsman*, 3 October 2005, http://thescotsman.scotsman.com/world/Demolition -Man-and-Money-Man.2666376.jp; *International Herald Tribune*, 2 July 2006.

education to make bombs or to maintain clandestine communications, or that individuals with those skills might be more inclined to form or join radical groups. This explanation for the strong presence of engineers among violent Islamist radicals[44] appears further corroborated by the fact that some groups overtly value technical skills: on Hamas websites, admiring references to bomb-building and technical skills of activists abound, and "engineer" is used as a general honorific title (although only Ayyash was "*the* Engineer"). The technical skills hypothesis is intuitively appealing—it is the immediate explanation proffered by most colleagues when we first tell them about the overrepresentation of engineers among extremists. It is also the explanation offered with some degree of professional pride on many of the engineers' blogs in which our puzzle has been discussed: they claim that it is obvious that only engineers have the necessary skills to carry out a technically sophisticated insurgency. And yet there is compelling evidence to suggest that technical ability does not really account for this phenomenon.

The first piece of evidence is found in a British intelligence dossier, which reports that "a network of 'extremist recruiters' is circulating on campuses targeting people with 'technical and professional qualifications', particularly engineering and IT degrees."[45] Abuza reports a similar recruitment practice for Indonesia's Jemaah Islamiyah (2006: 78).[46] But it does not appear to be technical skills that recruiters are after. The dossier states that Islamist "extremists are known to target schools and colleges where young people may be very *inquisitive* but *less challenging* and more susceptible to extremist reasoning/arguments" (emphasis added). The choice of adjectives is interesting: we can find people who are inquisitive and challenging or supine and unchallenging, but the combination of a sharp mind with a loyal acceptance of authority may be rare, especially among those ready to choose extreme paths. A training manual for jihadists lists the traits to look for in potential recruits: "discipline and obedience, patience, intelligence" (p. 18), "caution and prudence" (p. 19), and the ability "to observe and analyze" (p. 20).[47] These traits could be

44 For instance, Bergen and Pandey (2006) refer to this hypothesis to explain the strong presence of technically educated in their sample.

45 *Sunday Times*, 10 July 2005.

46 In July 2014, Abu Bakr al-Baghdadi, the Islamic State's self-styled caliph, called for "judges, doctors, engineers and people with military and administrative expertise" to migrate to ISIS territory (www.bbc.com/news/world-middle-east-28116846). At the time, however, ISIS was engaged in a broader project of state-building rather than just small-scale insurgency.

47 "Military Studies in the Jihad against the Tyrants," used in court in the trial, held in New York from January to May 2001, against four men charged in the 1998 embassy bombings in East Africa. Identified in the trial files as "Government Exhibit 1677." Date and author are unknown.

more likely to be found among engineers, and recruiters might be aware of this. In years of research we have never encountered any evidence of recruits being selected because of their *technical* skills. Personal trust and dedication seem a far more important criteria (Sageman 2004: 107–12).

Second, bomb-making is the task of a few specialists in a group, a fact that makes the high proportion of engineers among many organizations, especially larger ones, puzzling. In Hamas, many engineers hold prominent positions in senior management that have no technical component (while among Hamas suicide bombers, the majority pursued religious degrees; Berrebi 2007: 28n51). If Hamas leaders are selected based on their skills, they are not technical ones.

Third, the technology involved in carrying out most of the violent attacks by Islamist extremists does not require great expertise. It is harder to obtain good-quality explosives than it is to put them to use. And electricians, mechanics, and ex-army officers have shown themselves to be just as good at making bombs as (if not better than) engineers. Dulmatin, the other mastermind of the Bali bombings—nicknamed "the Genius" for his prowess with explosives and who was killed in a shootout in March 2010—was an auto mechanic.[48] His bomb-making colleague Noordin Mohammad Top, who was killed in 2009 in a police raid, had a degree in accounting.[49] In the UK-based plot to blow up transatlantic jets in 2006, the quartermaster in charge of explosives and logistics, Assad Sarwar, had studied sports science. The one engineer in the group, Ahmed Abdullah Ali, who had a computer systems engineering degree, was the leader of the cell rather than its bomb-maker.[50] Fathur Rahman al-Ghozi, key operative and bomb-maker of the Islamist militant Jemaah Islamiya group in Southeast Asia, had trained at Abu Bakar Bashir's religious school. Ahmed Ghailani, bomb-maker for the devastating 1998 bombings of the U.S. embassies in Tanzania and Kenya, had taken electronics courses in vocational school.[51]

Fourth, the destructive capacity of these violent groups does not seem to increase with the proportion of engineers among their members. Consider, for instance, the Saudi insurgency, which, with almost no engineers in its ranks, still mounted devastating bomb attacks in 2003 and 2004;

48 *The Times*, 9 March 2010, www.timesonline.co.uk/tol/news/world/asia/article7054952 .ece.
49 *Sydney Morning Herald*, 18 September 2009, www.smh.com.au/world/terror-kingpin -dies-in-siege-20090917-fttc.html.
50 *The Telegraph*, 7 September 2009, www.telegraph.co.uk/news/uknews/terrorism-in -the-uk/6024777/Airlines-bomb-plot-profiles.html.
51 *Financial Times*, 26 January 2002, www.singapore-window.org/sw02/020126ft.htm; *New York Times*, 24 January 201, www.nytimes.com/2011/01/24/nyregion/24ghailani .html?pagewanted=all.

or, for non-Islamist cases, consider the LTTE in Sri Lanka, or the IRA and ETA separatist movements, whose members were largely poorly educated and working class (Hudson 1999: 47, 50; Iribarren 1998: 47).

Fifth, "hands-on" knowledge is not always acquired in engineering classes. Being an engineer may make someone more likely to try their hand at bomb-making than it would someone with a nontechnical degree, but this may be the result of unwarranted self-confidence: in recent years a string of five attempted attacks, all aimed at Western targets, involved engineers *and* failed. It is not surprising that the likes of Richard Reid, an uneducated man with a troubled past of abuse and petty crime who went from convict to convert, should have failed to carry out even his technically unsophisticated plot. In December 2001, he was overpowered by other passengers and crew while trying to detonate with a match his shoe laced with explosives during American Airlines Flight 63 from Paris to Miami. It *is* surprising, however, to go through a list of abysmal failures at the hands of technically educated extremists that came to our attention within just a few years. Their exploits are summarized in table 1.5 (some of them were carried out by militants who grew up in the West who are part of a second sample we present in chapter 3).

For instance, Times Square bomber Faisal Shahzad, whose explosive contraption of firecrackers, a pressure cooker, fertilizer, gasoline, and gunpowder fizzled out without doing any damage, holds a BA in computer science and engineering. Kafeel Ahmed, one of the two jihadists who tried to drive a Jeep Cherokee loaded with propane canisters into a Glasgow Airport terminal in June 2007 but got stuck on security bollards, was studying for a PhD in computational fluid dynamics and held degrees in mechanical and aeronautical engineering.[52] While five bystanders were slightly injured, he and his partner in the attack, Bilal Abdullah, a medical doctor, sustained severe injuries and Ahmed died a month later (in that he was more successful than Abdullah, if belatedly so: a joint suicide note showed that the two had actually intended to die in the attack).[53] The duo had previously deposited two bombs in London, which were defused by the police, one of which could not have exploded because it lacked an oxidizer.[54]

---

52 *Wall Street Journal*, 4 May 2010, http://blogs.wsj.com/dispatch/2010/05/04/faisal -shahzads-life-in-america-and-path-to-citizenship/; *Hindustan Times*, 6 October 2007, www.hindustantimes.com/Bangalore-cleric-tells-how-Kafeel-Sabeel-changed/Article1 -235277.aspx; BBC News, 6 July 2007, http://news.bbc.co.uk/1/hi/northern_ireland/ 6278858.stm; www.timesonline.co.uk/tol/news/uk/crime/article5352923.ece.

53 *The Australian*, 6 July 2007, www.theaustralian.com.au/news/world/glasgow-suspects -left-suicide-note/story-e6frg6so-1111113898104.

54 *The Register*, 29 June 2006, www.theregister.co.uk/2007/06/29/more_fear_biscuits _please/.

TABLE 1.5
Failed engineer-led attacks against Western targets, 2007–10

Name	Degree	Year	Location	Attempted attack
Kafeel Ahmed	Mechanical and aeronautical engineering	2007	Glasgow Airport, UK	Drove a Cherokee SUV loaded with gas canisters into a terminal but got stuck on security bollards, slightly injured five innocent people, and died of his wounds.
Hicham Doukkali	Civil engineering	2007	Meknes, Morocco	Blew himself up near a tourist bus armed with a butane canister; killed no one but lost an arm.
Mohamed Game	Electronic engineering	2009	Milan, Italy	Blew himself up with two kilos of nitrate near Caserma Santa Barbara; killed no one while barely surviving his injuries.
Umar Abdulmutallab	Mechanical engineering	2009	Northwest Airlines Flight 253 Amsterdam to Detroit	Tried to detonate explosive he had hidden in his underwear but was overpowered by other passengers.
Faisal Shahzad	Computer science and engineering	2010	New York City	Left an SUV packed with a homemade cocktail of explosives in Times Square. It failed to explode, but he was identified and arrested.

Sources: Press archives.

To test the bomb-making skills hypothesis systematically, we were able to identify the functions that individuals performed within their militant group for 228 of the 497 cases in the sample (table 1.6). Two results stand out. First, bomb-makers are a minority among the overall staff (15 percent); many more individuals seem to be tasked with organizational and

TABLE 1.6
Functions within groups by discipline (individuals can have more than one function)

Education	Founder		Leader		Bomb-Maker		Media and outreach		Total functions (individuals)	
	N	%	N	%	N	%	N	%	N	%
Engineering	5	9	38	72	8	15	14	26	65 (53)	100
Medicine	0	0	5	63	3	38	3	38	11 (8)	100
Business & Economics	2	33	5	83	1	17	3	50	11 (6)	100
Math & Science	4	40	7	70	0	0	6	60	17 (10)	100
Islamic studies	5	21	19	79	2	8	6	25	32 (24)	100
Other degrees	3	13	20	83	2	8	2	8	27 (24)	100
No higher ed. or unknown ed.	4	4	75	73	19	18	16	16	114 (103)	100
Total	23	10	169	74	35	15	50	22	277 (228)	100

Source: Muslim world sample.

propaganda duties. Second, of those with engineering degrees, only 15 percent were bomb-makers, which is no more than the average share across all types of disciplines.[55]

A Random Event Amplified through Networks?

Could our findings be explained by a different kind of selection process, one that is essentially accidental? Illegal groups are set up in clandestine fashion, and to diminish the chances of detection their existence is advertised along networks of preexisting social bonds. Their opportunities for expansion are constrained within circles of friends, colleagues, and kin.

---

55 Among the Western-based groups we investigate in chapter 3, engineers appear more frequently among the groups that are formed independently of larger organizations (table 2.6). This indicates that if skills matter, they matter for self-recruitment at least as much as they matter for recruitment.

If the prime movers were, even accidentally, engineers or engineering students, their network would be more likely to expand within the faculty in which they work and socialize, among like-minded people with whom they interact on a daily basis. Whether for recruits or recruiters, the opportunities would follow network lines. Observations in our sample would hence not be "independent" from each other with regard to education; a combination of historical accident and network-based selection with no deeper meaning could thus explain the engineers' overrepresentation. A similar reasoning could be extended to the overrepresentation of graduates in general.

This might indeed be true for the early Egyptian groups in which, as Ibrahim has written, "three recruitment mechanisms were employed: kinship, friendship and worship" (1980: 437ff.). However, the more we find graduates in general and engineers in particular to be overrepresented in extremist groups in different countries and in different networks, the less likely it is that their dominance is due to a historical contingency and its network effects.

To test this hypothesis, consider the distribution of degrees both by country of origin and by group. As we have already seen (table 1.2), university graduates in general and those with engineering degrees in particular are not clustered in any one country of origin but spread across most of them—with the exception of Saudi Arabia, which we have just discussed. The same obtains when we consider the distribution across groups (table 1.7). Strikingly, the proportion of engineers is even more evenly distributed across groups than is the proportion of individuals with higher education, especially among the groups with more cases in the sample, giving further support to our finding that engineers are overrepresented.

Our sample of jihadists contains at least four clusters that grew independently of each other—North Africans, Southeast Asians, Palestinians, and core Arabs—and both graduates in general and engineers in particular are strongly represented in all of them. The idea that the technically educated were able to connect with each other via the Internet and thus likely to form a virtual network—as suggested, for instance, by Abuza (2006: 79–80)—does not apply to the individuals in our sample, most of whom radicalized before the Internet became available. (For example, as late as 1998, even in a developed country like the UK only 4 percent of households had an Internet connection.)

Moreover, in broad-based movements such as Hamas, network effects should become less important with the growing scale of mobilization. Also, mosques and radical preachers—often the focus of initial radicalization and recruitment—are loci where in principle students of different faculties can mix. In so far as places of worship functioned as recruitment

TABLE 1.7
Islamist extremists with higher education, finished or unfinished, and share of engineers, by militant group or attack

Group / Attack	Total in sample	Level of education known	With higher education	% with higher education over total cases	% with higher education over known cases	Discipline of higher education known	Engineers	
							N	% of known higher education
Hamas	92	73	55	60%	75%	50	19	38%
Core Arab cluster*	36	14	7	19%	50%	5	1	20%
Indian Mujahedeen	35	10	9	26%	90%	8	6	75%
Ibrahim sample	34	34	29	85%	85%	26	9	35%
Palestinian Islamic Jihad	32	11	9	28%	82%	9	1	11%
Jemaah Islamiyah Singapore	31	31	6	19%	19%	6	5	83%
Various Al-Qaida	30	17	14	47%	82%	14	6	43%
Central Qaida*	27	15	13	48%	87%	9	5	56%
11 September 2001	24	24	17	71%	71%	14	8	57%

Group							
Jemaah Islamiyah (Indonesia, Malaysia)	24	20	7	29%	35%	3	3	100%
Bali bombings	22	14	6	27%	43%	6	3	50%
African embassies	16	13	6	38%	46%	6	3	50%
Southeast Asian cluster*	12	4	2	17%	50%	1	0	0%
World Trade Center 93	12	12	12	50%	71%	11	5	60%
Islamic Jihad (Egypt)	10	7	5	25%	67%	5	3	50%
GSPC Algeria	8	3	2	71%	100%	2	1	20%
Al-Gama'a Al-Islamiya (Egypt)	7	5	5	60%	96%	5	1	52%
Sundry cases	45	28	27	60%	75%	27	14	38%
Totals	497	335	231	46%	69%	207	93	45%

* These groups are taken from Sageman 2004. If cases overlapped with the event-based categories of Bergen and Pandey (who kindly shared their data on individuals involved with several violent events), they are included in the Bergen groups; Sageman's categories hence are residual sets including individuals from the same network who were not directly implicated in the events.

Sources: Muslim world sample; Sageman 2004; Bergen and Pandey 2006.

vehicles, it must mean that graduates in general and engineers in particular were already attracted by them.

Network ties cannot explain why certain networks radicalize while others do not, or why certain individuals in a network radicalize first while others leave the network once it radicalizes. All that network effects can explain is why individuals who lacked the "right" network ties failed to radicalize even if they had a predisposition to do so. Sageman, who makes the strongest case for preexisting network ties to explain the expansion of salafi-jihadists, claims that "in-group love" more than "out-group hate" drove these movements and that "social bonds came first, and ideology followed" (Sageman 2004: 136, 133). To warrant such a conclusion, however, we would need a stringent test, namely to know how many of those who had network ties with individuals or groups that *subsequently* radicalized *failed* to radicalize and abandoned or remained at the margin of their groups. The fewer the people who left, the stronger the network effects would be. Conversely, the more the people who left, the more other traits and factors must have been involved in such decisions. But in the absence of this crucial data one cannot say.

This does not imply that the *size* of the engineering contingent within each independent cluster is unaffected by network effects—it very probably is. What we cannot explain by network effects is the greater propensity of engineers to become prime movers and their greater willingness to stay in or join a radical network. For an explanation of these factors we will need to look elsewhere. In chapter 2, we start by taking another look at their biographies for inspiration.

Conclusions

The puzzling phenomenon with which we started has been confirmed: engineers are indeed overrepresented among violent Islamist radicals. Relative to their presence in the male population in their countries of origin, the number of engineers among extremist groups is fourteen times what we would expect; and relative to graduates with other degrees they are four times more numerous than we would expect. Furthermore, the overrepresentation is evenly distributed across all groups and across all countries of origin, strongly suggesting that the correlation is not the result of a historical contingency amplified by network diffusion. The only notable exception to the engineering phenomenon is Saudi Arabia, where engineers are only weakly present among extremists. The findings are further confirmed by the Sinjar database of jihadists who went to fight in Iraq.

The hypothesis that the overrepresentation could be the result of selective recruitment based on technical skills in bomb-making and communications does not stand up to scrutiny for a host of different reasons, the most important of which is that the ratio of bomb-makers among engineers is identical to that among jihadists with other degrees.

Over and above the engineering puzzle, we found that university students and graduates generally are vastly overrepresented among Islamist radicals. Overall, our results suggest that the higher the level of education the greater the likelihood of joining a violent group, and furthermore that among those with higher education, students with more demanding professional degrees have a greater likelihood of joining. These results provide the first wide-ranging systematic confirmation that the core of the Islamist movement emerged from would-be elites, not from the poor and the dispossessed.

The factors that might explain our double finding—the overrepresentation of graduates in general and of engineers in particular—will be explored in the following chapters.

Relative Deprivation in the Islamic World

EDUCATION IN THE DEVELOPING WORLD, MORE SO THAN ELSEWHERE, IS a means to social advancement—at least for those without special privilege. At the same time, many Muslim countries have suffered development crises and have failed to create decent jobs for university graduates. This is true especially for countries with high shares of graduates like Egypt and Palestine. We might speculate that political rebellions grow out of the frustrated expectations of the educated. If acquiring a degree in higher education is a reflection of high hopes and ambition, does thwarted ambition produce militants among university graduates? Can this help us explain the patterns we documented in chapter 1?

FRUSTRATED AMBITIONS AND RELATIVE DEPRIVATION

The link between frustrated ambitions and political radicalization, known as relative deprivation theory, has a venerable tradition—a classic explanation of the onset of rebel movements dating back to Aristotle and Tocqueville. The theory is not about absolute deprivation or poverty as such, factors that are not necessarily linked to militancy (Krueger 2007). It is about expectations of social advancement—both individual and collective—that first are raised and then disappointed. When disappointment follows a phase of progress, which raises hopes high, rebellion is triggered.

This is an individual-level explanation that has been out of fashion for more than two decades. Political scientists have traditionally tried to use it to account for the onset of rebellions and revolutions in certain countries and not others, producing at best ambiguous empirical findings (Berman et al. 2011; Davies 1962; Gurr 1970; Salert 1976; Finkel and Rule 1986; Piazza 2006). In our case, however, we are not concerned with explaining the emergence of Islamist militancy as a whole but rather with the internal composition of groups within each country's radical sector. Relative deprivation could explain why more graduates became radicalized, specifically in the poorer Islamic countries that have gone through development crises since the 1970s.

The process might not be limited to individual economic failure but could also involve "group relative deprivation," a concept originally proposed by sociologist W. G. Runciman as "fraternal deprivation" (1966). This occurs when an individual feels that the group he belongs to is collectively deprived—vis-à-vis other groups, elites, or outside powers. Social psychologists have found that group relative deprivation is more likely to lead to collective action than is individual relative deprivation and have linked it to anti-immigrant prejudice as well as rejection of affirmative action for other groups (King and Taylor 2011; Pettigrew et al. 2008; Leach, Iyer, and Pedersen 2007; Smith and Ortiz 2002). Moghaddam (2005) mentions it as a potential first stage of political radicalization.[1]

Because relative deprivation has a dynamic component, it yields more fine-grained predictions than the simpler "poverty breeds terrorism" theory. It leads us to look for specific triggers, to trace the timing of radicalization, and to look for different types of actors within countries.

Unfulfilled Promises: Egypt

In our reading of relative deprivation, individuals with above-average skills, who have been selected for their university studies on merit, are particularly susceptible to frustration and a sense of injustice when they find their professional future hampered by a lack of opportunities. At least in the Middle East and North Africa (MENA)—heavily represented in our sample—economic development failures have indeed led to mobility closure on a large scale and exactly when we would expect it. After an initial phase of quick economic advancement, infrastructure expansion, and middle-class growth following independence, MENA countries largely failed to develop advanced industries or technological capacities (UNDP 2003a: 97–109; Carvalho 2009). Since the mid-1970s they have progressively fallen behind economically relative to the rest of the developing world. It is from this point on that militant Islamist groups populated by students and graduates appeared across the region.

Egypt, where our puzzle first emerged, perfectly epitomizes the story of militancy rooted in frustrated ambitions. During Nasser's "socialist years," from 1960 to 1966, the Egyptian university system was opened to lower-class students and enrollment greatly increased. Nasser offered

---

1 Our hypothesis also resembles recent arguments in the conflict studies literature that "horizontal inequalities" between social groups can breed resentment and conflict (Østby 2008; Cedermann, Weidmann, and Gleditsch 2011). Our causal mechanism, however, is the differential strength of subjective relative deprivation across groups in a society, while the "horizontal inequalities" literature focuses on intergroup envy within societies that is caused by objective economic inequalities. The target of resentment and violence in our explanation is typically the West or, in some cases, local government, not another social group in the same society. Even those with relative material privileges can feel acute deprivation as their expectations are unmet.

state employment to all new graduates (Longuenesse 2007: 41). By 1969, the state employed virtually all Egyptian engineers, scientists, and agronomists, more than 87 percent of physicians, and two-thirds of lawyers. Nasser's regime created a generalized expectation of universal upward mobility (Moore 1994: 66–73; Kepel 1993: 11).

When development sputtered and Egypt lost the 1967 war against Israel, students, who had been socialized and mobilized into Nasser's ideology like no other group, were the most disillusioned. Protests occurred regularly, first dominated by leftist slogans but turning to Islamic rhetoric in the 1970s. This proved particularly attractive to young migrants from the countryside who held conservative values and felt socially marginalized (Wickham 2002: 122). Despite the surfeit of graduates and the scarcity of workers with vocational training (Wickham 2002: 25–27; Moore 1994: 6ff.), under Nasser's successor, Sadat, the provincial intake into Egyptian higher education in the 1970s further increased. For a while he even supported Islamist students against their urban leftist rivals (Kepel 1993: 129–71).

Ibrahim, in his early study of 1970s radicals, noted that most activists in his sample ranked "decidedly high in both motivation and achievement."[2] He linked the emergence of radical movements in Egypt to the decrease in social mobility in the 1970s, which hit the middle classes the hardest (1980: 447). (Zawahiri, who read Ibrahim's study in prison, later told him: "You have trivialized our movement by your mundane analysis. May God have mercy on you" [quoted in Wright 2002]).

In the 1980s, with the bureaucratic ranks crowded by previous generations, the opportunities for social mobility decreased further. The Nasser-era state job guarantee weakened, while real salaries in the public sector plummeted; by 1987, bureaucratic wages had fallen to 55 percent of their 1973 level in real terms, forcing employees to "moonlight" in side jobs (Wickham 2002: 47).

With the 1985–86 oil price crash, labor markets in the Gulf states, which had provided a safety net for the educated Egyptian workforce, shrank drastically (Moore 1994: 126–30, 214ff.; Henry and Springborg 2001: 36–38; Abdel Jabber 1993: 155). The official rate of unemployment in Egypt increased from 7.7 percent in 1976 to 14.7 percent in 1986, and unusually in international comparison, joblessness was particularly concentrated among young job seekers with secondary or higher education (Owen and Pamuk 1998: 146). Among unemployed new labor

---

2 In Ibrahim's sample, 14 of the 18 students were majoring in subjects with small enrollment numbers and high admissions requirements: medicine, engineering, pharmacy, and military technical science (1980: 440).

force entrants in 1986, 91 percent had at least an intermediate-level degree (Wickham 2002: 38).

Many graduates preferred joblessness even to relatively well-paying menial jobs, and for numerous young Egyptians marriage became unaffordable. Making a virtue out of necessity, many graduates tried to restore their dignity by adopting an austere Islamic morality to compensate for their material deprivation (Hoffman 1995: 208).

With the liberalization of the economy, initiated in the 1970s and accelerated subsequently, inequality between classes increased (Carvalho 2009: 32–37). While living standards for the middle class declined (Longuenesse 2007: 133), a newly rich, ostentatious bourgeoisie emerged, dominated by friends of the Mubarak regime. The crony capitalists sent their children to expensive private universities such as the American University of Cairo, while public universities were resource starved and left to rot. The gradual marginalization of the middle classes, previously the bedrock of regime support, became increasingly obvious. The dearth of opportunities was made all the more grating by the corrupt allocation of jobs by the state, whereby elites channeled the country's few well-paying jobs to their own offspring. Without personal connections, it became almost impossible to find employment commensurate with one's education (Waltz 1986: 662; Moore 1994: 217; Wickham 2002: 54–55; Tourné 2005). The perception that after a degree was achieved on merit, professional success depended on connections rather than on skills and personal sacrifice was particularly galling, especially for the highly qualified at the top of the educational pyramid: "For the [Egyptian] graduates who had been socialized to view themselves as a meritocratic elite, perhaps the greatest source of bitterness was what they perceived as an erosion of the link between merit and reward" (Wickham 2002: 159).

The Islamist opposition was able to provide an organized focus to this discontent, as documented by Wickham in her seminal study of grassroots Islamist mobilization. Appealing to religious laws, Islamist movements rode economic dissatisfaction by promising accountability and fairness, so sorely lacking in these regimes. Muslim Brothers found strong support among lower-middle and middle-class students. Young people were accorded prominence in Islamist movements, which gave them a sense of importance and mission they could not otherwise obtain in such a patriarchal, nepotistic, and immobile system (Wickham 2002: 2, 62, 84, 115, 140).

Inequality and job prospects for graduates outside the networks of privilege further worsened in the 1990s (Longuenesse 2007: 190). In 1993, the government had still not assigned jobs to graduates of the post-1984 cohorts (Moore 1994: 215). At least one case of mobility closure had momentous consequences: in the late 1990s Mohamed Atta, the leader of the 9/11 hijackers, wanted to return from his technical studies in Germany to work in Cairo but faced dire job prospects as his family lacked the "right connections."[3] When he left Germany for good in summer 2000, it was not to return to his home country but to enroll in a flight school in Florida on orders of Osama bin Laden. The rest in this case is, truly, history.

Beyond Egypt

Some authors have argued that there is evidence of a link between economic failure and radicalization in other countries. Willis reports that the economic crisis in Algeria pushed young men, particularly students, toward Islamist movements in the 1980s and 1990s (1996: 85, 109). According to Sageman—who briefly mentions relative deprivation as a necessary condition of radicalization—many Al-Qaida members, although academically gifted, did not have full-time jobs (2004: 92, 95).

Benmelech, Berrebi, and Klor (2010) show that high levels of unemployment enable militant Palestinian organizations to recruit more educated and experienced suicide terrorists, who in turn attack more important Israeli targets. They reject the theory that militancy is caused by poverty, arguing instead that poverty influences the *quality* of militancy, that is, who becomes involved in it. Meyersson Milgrom and Jasso (2004) demonstrate that higher levels of education are associated with lower support for the Roadmap to resolve the Israeli-Palestinian conflict, while higher levels of income among Palestinians are associated with greater support. In other words, highly educated but low-income individuals appear the most rejectionist and potentially radical. This means that what drives radicalization is the gap between economic and educational status; it would be hard to think of a better "material" measure of relative deprivation.

The post-1970s development path of Algeria, Jordan, Lebanon, Morocco, Palestine, Syria, and Yemen—all represented in our sample—closely resembles the Egyptian one. Overstretched university systems produced large numbers of graduates whom local job markets were unable to absorb in the face of a deepening development crisis (Carvalho 2009; Hoffman 1995: 208; Richards and Waterbury 1996: 118–23; Longuenesse 1990). The education systems in most Arab countries produced many more graduates than their underdeveloped economies could absorb (see figure 2.1).[4]

---

3 Lappin 2002; see also McKay 2009.
4 Even Yemen is only an apparent exception: as an extremely poor country, it produced more graduates than similarly poor peers in the developing world.

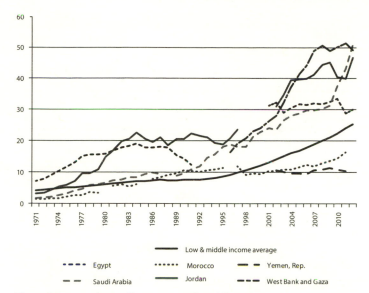

Figure 2.1: Tertiary enrollment rates of Middle East countries with more than 10 cases in our sample (%) vs. all low- and middle-income countries. *Source:* World Bank, World Development Indicators.

While the newly minted, postindependence middle class often enjoyed considerable social mobility up to the 1970s, this plateaued soon after (Longuenesse 2007: 81). Carvalho applies the relative deprivation argument to the Islamic world at large, which underwent "a growth reversal which raised aspirations for upward mobility and subsequently left aspirations unfulfilled among the educated middle class." The lower-middle class, he argues, has been particularly hard hit by rising inequality and pauperization, leading to a broad Islamic revival (Carvalho 2009).

While Middle Eastern growth rates in the 1950s and 1960s had been impressive, the whole region fell behind in terms of per capita income compared to other developing economies from the mid-1970s on (see figure 2.2), exactly the time when Islamist opposition and, in most cases, militancy emerged as a major phenomenon across the region (Yazbeck Haddad, Esposito, and Voll 1991; Hunter 1988; Kepel 2002; Roy 1994).

Elisabeth Longuenesse—who has written the foremost study of the social and educational history of the professional middle class in Egypt, Jordan, Lebanon, and Syria—provides a rich description of the emerging "discrepancy between expectations and possibilities" for graduates in the 1970s and 1980s and of the tensions "between a self-conception as

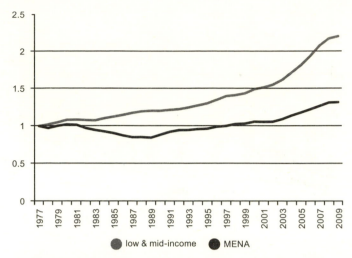

Figure 2.2: GDP per capita, Middle Eastern and North African
countries vs. all low- and middle-income countries (constant values,
standardized at 1 for both in 1977).
Source: World Bank, World Development Indicators.

an elite and a reality of social shifts and loss of status" (2007: 67).[5] The
gap between the social and symbolic status of diplomas and their economic value widened progressively. Labor markets organized through
patrimonial and personal networks revealed that the official rhetoric
about education, social progress, and meritocracy was patently false
(ibid., 86–87). Longuenesse seems to describe a classic case of relative
deprivation—which is all the more revealing as she does not mention this
concept.

While much of the literature on the decline of the educated middle
class in the Arab world is qualitative, there are some hard data that illustrate the limited mobility chances of average graduates in 1980s and
1990s Arab countries: private returns to higher education—the amount
of extra earnings per year of education—in Egypt, Jordan, Morocco,
and Yemen were considerably lower than they were in Latin American
and Asian countries (see figure 2.3). Average returns in Arab countries
remain about half of what they are in other low- and middle-income
countries (Tzannatos 2011: 12n19). And returns seem to have decreased
over time (see also World Bank 2008: 63, 217).

5 Longuenesse 2007: 67 : "entre representation de soi comme une élite, et réalité des
recompositions, et declassements professionnels." The descriptive subtitle of her book is
"Decline of Elites, Crisis of the Middle Classes."

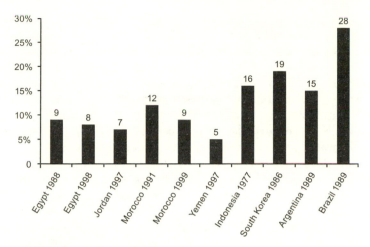

Figure 2.3: Private returns to higher education in %, select countries (per year of education).
Source: World Bank 2008: 63.

In Palestine, the size of the educated labor force increased dramatically from 1981 to 1987 while income differences between secondary school and university graduates fell by half, meaning that a university degree paid off progressively less (Angrist 1995). As wages in general declined from 1981 to 1987, the educated were doubly squeezed. Like their Arab brethren, young Palestinians were ever more likely to attain degrees, and ever more likely to then face mobility closure on the labor market. The first intifada broke out in 1987, also the year in which the Islamist resistance movement Hamas was founded. On the Hamas websites we consulted, we found numerous cases of "martyrs" who could not pay for or had to drop out of university because of economic hardship or who were forced to find employment at a young age to contribute to their family's income. Hamas itself seems to draw an implicit link between such frustrations and their militancy. Islamist militancy across the region emerged from the 1970s on and strengthened in the 1980s, reflecting the region's arc of economic stagnation.

There is one further prediction we can make using the relative deprivation hypothesis that is borne out by our data. If mobility closure for the highly educated explains their overrepresentation among militants, then Islamic countries with more successful economies should have fewer radicalized graduates than Arab countries. There are several countries in our sample where graduates have not encountered mobility closure: Singapore, Indonesia, and India have not undergone economic crises as pronounced and protracted as those in the Arab world, and their output of university graduates is also more aligned with their level of development.[6] These are the same countries that have the lowest presence of graduates in our sample (22.5 percent). The share is the lowest in Singapore (6 of 31 cases),[7] which is the most successful economically, despite much higher levels of education in the population at large.[8] Even if we might have generally "oversampled" individuals with higher education in our database, the difference in education between radicals from different countries still corroborates the theory of relative deprivation.

In conclusion, attempts to substantiate the hypothesis that mobility closure for a would-be middle class has driven young graduates into radicalization have thus far been largely anecdotal, and at best based on single-country case studies. Our study documents for the first time individual education levels of Islamist extremists across different countries, demonstrating that militants are indeed for the most part well educated—and showing that relative deprivation is consistent with much of the observed variation across time and space. Comparative international research has shown that a larger share of adults who have attained some level of higher education makes democratic revolutions more likely (Kurzman and Leahey 2004). We show that if coupled with development crises, attaining a degree in higher education can lead people to all forms of mobilization, not all of which are pro-democratic.

ARE ENGINEERS ESPECIALLY DEPRIVED?

This all accounts for one important finding—the strong role of the university educated among Islamist extremists—but why should engineers stand out further among already overrepresented militant graduates? As we researched educational systems in the Islamic world, one prominent feature of engineering consistently stood out: along with medicine, engineering is considered the most prestigious university degree and the requirements to enter into an engineering course of study are consistently high (Moore 1994: 45ff., 214; Cornand 1990: 192; Sonbol 1988: 26ff.;

6 Indian tertiary enrollment has stayed below the average for low- to middle-income countries in past decades, while Indonesia's has broadly followed it (World Bank Development Indicators). Singapore has, if anything, had lower university enrollment levels than have other rich countries.

7 Abuza (2003: 130) also points out that extremist recruitment in Singapore focused only on moderately educated individuals.

8 Malaysia is the only fairly successful economy with a high share of graduates. But the number of cases there—only 10—is too small to draw any strong conclusion. The share of graduates in Pakistan (7 out of 10 cases) in turn is in line with our expectations, given the country's troubled economic record.

Kepel 1993: 136ff.; Abrahamian 1989: 229ff.). Enrolling in a course of study to pursue an engineering degree is a strong sign of above-average talent and ambition. Unlike many other selection processes in the region, university admission to demanding programs of study seems to be based on merit.

In the MENA region, a degree in engineering carries more than mere technical status (Cornand 1990; Wickham 2002), and many students choose it as much because of their interest in the subject as because of the prestige it confers (Hanafi 1990: 173). Many Arab managers in government and business put their title of engineer—"muhandis"—on their business cards. Both "muhandis" and "duktur" continue to be highly respected titles in the region (Longuenesse 2007: 95; Moore 1994: 21). In Iran, Pakistan, India, and Southeast Asia, too, engineering and medicine are the most prestigious degrees one can obtain (Abdollahyan and Nayebi 2009; Zaidi 1986; Rhines Cheney, Brown Ruzzi, and Muralidharan 2005: 8).[9] All across the Islamic world, enrollment in engineering and medical programs appears to be a good proxy for talent and social ambition. Mobility failure for these students at the top of the educational pyramid must be all the more galling.

Could it be that engineers and, to some degree, doctors are subject to relative deprivation like everyone else—but more intensely so? Could the explanation be embedded within the larger relative deprivation argument?

Early Engineering Elites

As early as the 1820s, Egypt's modernizing regimes under the Muhammad Ali dynasty glorified science and industry as a means of catching up with the West (Longuenesse 2007: 174). Engineers and doctors in Egypt and Syria were a small, highly regarded elite, trained in Europe or in local colleges that governments set up on the European model (Longuenesse 2007: 45, 52). This trend continued throughout the twentieth-century colonial period, as higher education remained the preserve of a small elite (Reid 1974: 36; Longuenesse 2007: 76).

The early postindependence period provided a further boost to the social status of engineers. Whether in conservative monarchies or in "progressive" republican regimes, governments embarked on ambitious programs of modernization, aiming to close the gap with the West. MENA regimes entertained a technocratic rhetoric of development and encouraged the growth of technical faculties. The 1950s and 1960s were two

9 See also personal communications with Shoibal Chakravarty (on India) and Professor M. Naseemullah (on Pakistan).

decades of rapid, state-driven growth in which engineers played a vanguard role in planning and executing state-led modernization that was to be implemented with scientific certainty. Medicine and engineering were "at the core of a socio-political project characterized by the idea that scientific and technical development is the source of social progress" (Longuenesse 2007: 13; see also Moore 1994: 12).[10]

Under the Nasserist regime in Egypt and Ba'athist rule in Syria in the 1960s, the "hegemony of modernist scientism became total" (Longuenesse 2007: 68). The state-employed engineer was the epitome of this ideology: "Equipped with a solid technical toolkit and an acute sense of duty towards the nation, [French-trained engineers in Algeria, Morocco, Tunisia, Vietnam, Iran, and Lebanon] saw themselves as entrusted with the economic destiny and the wealth of their countries" (Karvar 2003: 209).[11]

Engineers were in many cases well represented among the ruling elite. Among Egypt's Nasserist technocrats, engineers had a heavier and more visible presence than any other category of graduates (Moore 1994: 9, 13,166ff.). In Syria, too, engineers rose to all levels of administration; the profession has supplied most of the country's prime ministers since 1971 (Longuenesse 2007: 71).

No Politics among the Engineering Aristocracy

Arab engineers were apolitical for most of their history, primarily focused on serving governments in the interest of technical modernity (Longuenesse 2007: 60, 101). Compared to their dominant role in post-1970s Islamist militancy, they are strikingly absent from previous political movements.

Early nationalist and socialist leaders and even early Islamists overwhelmingly came from other professions; many of them were lawyers and teachers. While doctors were involved in nationalist parties in significant numbers from the 1920s on, engineers were rare (Longuenesse 2007: 60, 120). Syrian engineers in fact even collaborated with their colonial superiors in the interwar period, taking an ostensibly apolitical view of their "public service" role, while remaining in a position of local privilege (Longuenesse 2007: 74–75).

Michel Aflaq and Salah al-Din al-Bitar, the two founders of the secular-nationalist Ba'athist movement in Syria, were teachers, as was Zaki al-Arsuzi, the leader of a parallel movement that joined forces with the Ba'ath in 1947. It was in turn a triumvirate of medical doctors that led

10 "au coeur d'un projet sociopolitique caraterisé par l'idée que le developpement scientifique et technique est source de progres social."
11 "Munis d'un bagage technique solide et d'un sens aigu du devoir envers la nation, ils se sont vus confier la destinée économique et les richesses de leur pays."

the takeover of the Syrian leadership by a radical wing of the Ba'ath party in 1966 (Longuenesse 2007: 70). Engineers appeared later, as functionaries, not revolutionary leaders.

In Egypt until the 1970s journalists and lawyers were at the forefront of mobilization against Sadat's regime (Wickham 2002: 188). Springborg (1978) describes the political mobilization of the lawyers', doctors', and journalists' syndicates from the 1950s to the 1970s but does not mention engineers. The smaller population of engineers in earlier periods does not account for their absence from politics, as there were also proportionally fewer lawyers, teachers, and journalists in Arab countries.[12] The only account we found of engineers' political activity in the pre-1970s period was outside the Arab world, in Iran, where their professional society was involved in the activities of the nationalist party (Chehabi 1990: 113, 120–21).

Professionals were already present in Egypt's Muslim Brotherhood in the 1940s and 1950s,[13] but most of the leading Islamist activists in the 1950s and 1960s in Egypt and North Africa came from second-tier faculties like education. An early survey of wanted and arrested Muslim Brotherhood members in Egypt in the 1940s and 1950s shows a strong presence of white-collar workers, yet of 180 cases, only 2 are listed as engineers, 1 as an architect, and 1 as a doctor, while there are 18 teachers (Mitchell 1969: 328–29). Among the well-known early Islamist leaders across the Arab world, there is not a single engineer. This pattern is visible in our own sample of extremists: if we take only those born before 1947—18 individuals, 13 of whom had some form of higher education—we find only 1 engineer but 7 trained in Islamic studies.

Among early Islamists, teachers had the leading positions that engineers occupy today: the prime mover of twentieth-century Islamist organization, Hassan Al-Banna, founder of the Muslim Brotherhood in 1928, was a teacher at Dar Al-Uloum school in Cairo, an institution that tried to combine Western and Islamic education. Isam Attar, leader of Syria's Muslim Brotherhood after 1957, was a teacher of Arabic literature. The Shabiba Islamist movement in Morocco was set up by an educational inspector in 1972, a job also held by the leader of the Moroccan justice and charity movement, Abdessalam Yassine (b. 1928, d. 2012). Teacher and educational inspector were also the occupations of Sayyid Qutb, the godfather of the radical spinoffs of the Muslim Brotherhood who was executed under Nasser in 1966. Sheikh Ahmed Yassin, spiritual leader of

12 For Egypt, see syndical membership figures in Wickham 2002: 82 and graduation statistics in Reid 1974: 36. In Syria, numbers of engineers did grow disproportionately but from a basis in 1960 that was only one-third smaller than that of doctors and lawyers and had overtaken doctors by 1965; Longuenesse 2007: 72, 81.
13 Munson 2001.

Palestinian Hamas until his assassination in 2004—born in 1937 and hence a generation senior to most of his peers in the organization's leadership—also trained as a teacher in Cairo and taught Arabic in the Palestinian territories.[14] Abbassi Madani, born in 1931 and former president of the Algerian Islamic Salvation Front, holds a doctorate in educational psychology.

A Turn for the Worse, and toward Radicalization

During the golden age of engineer-led state planning from the 1950s to the 1970s, the Arab world witnessed tangible infrastructural, social, and educational progress (Longuenesse 2007: 49). The engineers' developmental aspirations seemed to come true, and some of them even perceived a continuity from the scientific and infrastructural achievements in the glorious age of Islam to the modern role of doctors and engineers in the postcolonial Arab world (Longuenesse 2007: 52).

But as cracks in the modernization projects widened from the 1970s onward, engineers began to show up in Islamist movements—notably in the early Egyptian militant groups studied by Ibrahim but also among the peaceful Islamist opposition in Egypt (Wickham 2002: 116, 184; Moore 1994: 208). The militant "Fighting Vanguard" group that led the mass insurrection in the Syrian city of Hama in 1982 was led by a civil engineer, Adnan Uqla (who had succeeded a dentist in leading the organization). Among a sample of 1,384 Islamist activists who fell into the hands of the Syrian regime between 1976 and May 1981, "27.7 percent were students, 7.9 percent schoolteachers, and 13.3 percent members of the professions, including 79 engineers, 57 physicians, 25 lawyers, and 10 pharmacists" (Batatu 1982). Engineers, it seems, were rapidly catching up with teachers in their participation in Islamist movements.

Among 73 members of the Islamic Mujahedeen killed in Iran between 1963 and 1977, 14 (or 19 percent) were engineers (Abrahamian 1980: 5). Students with technical backgrounds were strongly represented among the members of the Islamist resistance in 1970s and 1980s Afghanistan (Rubin 1992: 92).[15] In our own sample, engineers also appear in significant numbers only in the cohorts born after the late 1940s, who then became militants in the 1970s and after. Seventeen of 30 extremists with higher education born between 1947 and 1959 are engineers. The share of engineers remains high among subsequent cohorts.

---

14 Sources include Hunter 1988; Wright 2006; and Thomas Pierret, personal communication with the authors, March 2011.
15 None of the cases mentioned here overlaps with our main sample in chapter 1.

It seems hardly a coincidence that previously apolitical engineers appeared on the political scene precisely when development in the Islamic world started to wane and when the status of new cohorts of graduates, who were perceived to be their nations' technical vanguard, was progressively undermined. The Islamic world's development failure that began in the 1970s affected primarily the fields of modernization—technology, infrastructure, and public services—in whose implementation engineers were expected to play the leading role. With the easy phase of consumer-driven economic expansion over, the poorer countries of the MENA region in particular entered a period of chronic indebtedness and technological backwardness, increasingly beleaguered by international competition (Richards and Waterbury 1996; Moore 1994).

The debasement of degrees through mass university enrollment policies from the 1970s onward hit graduates of technical faculties all the harder (Richards and Waterbury 1996: 133–42). Despite the surfeit of engineers and the scarcity of technicians (Wickham 2002: 25–27; Moore 1994: 6–7), the number of graduates in engineering grew at an above-average rate in the 1970s (Longuenesse 1990: 372, 408; Longuenesse 2000: 15), while engineers' labor market opportunities in all Arab republics shrank drastically (Akkache 1990; Hanafi 1990; Cornand 1990; Gobe 2001).[16] Longuenesse, the preeminent social and economic historian of Arab engineers, has written: "In less than half a century, the [Arab] engineer went from the status of a senior civil servant to that of a rank and file technical or bureaucratic employee, becoming a hindrance to administration and public enterprises" (2007: 81).[17] Unlike in the West, where mass higher education has historically been accompanied by continuous increases in economic productivity and private employment opportunities, engineers in the Middle East became underemployed appendices of bloated public administrations. They were increasingly used for manual or simple technical tasks. Their training was abstract and undifferentiated, making it largely irrelevant to a labor market whose absorptive capacity was limited in any case (Longuenesse 2007: 80, 86; Moore 1994: 78). "Few countries have educated higher proportions of

16 Some scholars would consider Iran to be a countercase (e.g., Kurzman 2003). It was growing rather rapidly in the 1970s and had not yet experienced the glut of degree holders that other Middle Eastern states witnessed. Many young Iranian engineers might have had bright labor market chances. Iran did, however, experience strong imbalances in economic development and several sudden setbacks in the years prior to the 1979 revolution, which, according to Keddie (1983), can be plausibly explained by the "frustrated expectations" hypothesis (see also Foran 2005: 79–80; Milani 1994: 96ff.; and Hoffman 1995: 209).

17 "En moins d'un demi-siècle, l'ingénieur passe du statut de grand commis de l'État, a celui de pietaille technico-bureaucratique encombrant administrations et entreprises publiques."

their populations for such little industrialization [than Egypt]" (Moore 1994: 3). A technological vanguard in theory, engineers were underemployed laborers in practice. "The illusion of the role of [technical] knowledge in the process of development [was] increasingly disconnected from a reality of marginalisation and powerlessness, sources of withdrawal and frustration."[18] Regimes' technocratic rhetoric sounded increasingly like a hollow taunt as the "mystified and promethean conception" of the "promotion of science and technology" was progressively removed from dreary administrative reality (Longuenesse 2007: 82, 86).

The employment situation for those in the engineering field in the 1970s worsened palpably, but it still compared favorably to that of other disciplines, not least due to heightened labor demand from the Gulf. A further dramatic deterioration came with the collapse of the price of oil after 1982. Economic contraction combined with further expansion of mass education almost completely halted social mobility (Longuenesse 2007: 80). Real wages started dropping dramatically from the mid-1980s on (Karshenas 1994: figure E1, table M2; Owen and Pamuk 1998: 156, 191, 197). Economic liberalization further undermined the role of the state as the employer of last resort and as the driver of development. Engineers watched businessmen and accountants become the new social elites of an expanding, and increasingly unequal, private economy (Longuenesse 2007: 193, 16).[19]

It appears that beginning in the 1970s, engineers found themselves perfectly and painfully placed at a high-voltage intersection in which high ambitions and high frustration collided. They felt deceived by the development rhetoric of their regimes and thought they deserved more than they were able to get. While this was felt more by people with higher education than by the rest of the population and could thus explain the

---

18 "l'illusion du role du savoir dans le processus de developpement est de plus en plus en décalage avec la realité d'une marginalisation et d'une impuissance, source de désengagement et de frustration."

19 Unlike the engineers from the Mashreq countries discussed in Longuenesse, engineers in Algeria seem to have held onto their elite status for a longer period of time. In line with this, the university departments that were first taken over by Islamists were those of the lower-status subjects that were "Arabized" in the 1970s, notably literature, law, and sociology (Rouadjia 1990: 24, 114, 163). At the time, engineers in the public sector were still doing well, and total enrollment in Algerian higher education was still comparatively low, reaching 4.9 percent in 1980, when it was 17.6 percent in Egypt and 17.8 percent in Syria (Longuenesse 1990: 329). From the 1980s on, however, the presence of technically educated men among Islamists has increased (Michael Willis, personal communication with the authors, April 2006). This seems to have happened at the same time that the public sector witnessed a development crisis induced by a collapse in oil prices and the liberalization measures ushered in during the late 1980s (Merani 2005). Again, relative deprivation seems to best account for variation over time.

general overrepresentation of the highly educated among Islamist radicals, the high achievers in the most demanding subjects felt it even more strongly.[20]

Longuenesse (2007: 134–35) points out the paradox that the most elite and oldest professions, namely engineering and medicine, are today the most Islamized (see also Moore 1994: 214). This is, she surmises, because they experienced the economic and status decline the most acutely, which the evidence seems to demonstrate incontrovertibly.

Individual and Collective Frustrations

Given their vaunted status as their nations' pioneers, Muslim engineers were likely frustrated both individually and collectively, not only because of their personal labor market failures but also because of the technological and developmental failures of their societies.[21] They felt unable to discharge a collective responsibility in modernizing Islamic countries, to live up professionally to the role of the "vanguards" of society (Wickham 2002: 32; Apter 1965: 219–20). It is plausible that many engineers suffered from "group relative deprivation" fed by collective failure as much as from individual economic disappointment.

Engineering curricula anywhere are a gigantic showcase of Western technological achievements, and in the MENA region they throw the economic backwardness of local societies into sharp relief (Moore 1994: 12–13; Hanafi 1997). Unlike those who pursue humanities or law degrees, engineers find it harder to ignore their thriving counterparts in the outside world (Hoffman 1995: 210). In contrast with the humanities field, in the field of technology the West appears "monolithic and properly hegemonic" (Waltz 1986: 666), and students of these disciplines cannot as easily segregate themselves from the developed world. The contrast between Western achievements and MENA countries' failures engendered a sense of collective frustration (Longuenesse 2007: 82), particularly in those with elite degrees.

Moreover, Muslim engineers who studied in the West, itself a sign of an even greater ambition and willingness to make sacrifices, should have felt more deprived, both individually and collectively. At least 27 of the 93 engineers in our sample studied abroad, a ratio that suggests that they are vastly overrepresented among radical engineers. Muslim engineers'

20 The delayed Islamist mobilization in the agricultural syndicate in Egypt—agriculture is a subject that seems similar to engineering—could be the outcome of particularly tight state control over the agricultural sector (Wickham 2002: 185ff.). In line with our account, it could, however, also result from agriculture's much lower status as a discipline (cf. Moore 1994: 46).

21 On relative deprivation and collective grievances, see Kruglanski et al. 2009.

direct exposure to an alien cultural environment probably made their cognitive dissonance worse, as they were at once attracted by Western achievements but disadvantaged in both their home and Western countries' labor markets.

Those who studied in the West are more likely to have experienced not only envy and resentment, emotions derived from unfavorable comparisons even if experienced remotely, but also anger and hatred, emotions aroused by cultural displacement and humiliating interactions.[22] These emotions are more likely to trigger action-responses (Elster 1999: 64–68)—a desire to destroy the object of hatred, the West and its impure social mores, and a passionate embrace of traditional religious values. Mohamed Atta often bemoaned Western influence in Arab cities (Holmes 2005): According to Dittmar Machule, his thesis supervisor at the Technical University of Hamburg-Harburg in Germany, Atta hated skyscrapers because in the Syrian city of Aleppo, on which he wrote his doctoral dissertation, tall buildings stole the privacy of the traditional Arab homes in whose courtyards women were once able to remove their veils unseen by strangers (Rose 2004).

Even the engineers who did not go abroad for their education had reason to resent Western technological dominance at home: Foreign firms often had a commanding position in local markets, especially in public construction projects funded by MENA states and international aid organizations. In Egypt in 1993 there were 60,000 foreign experts, 12,000 of whom were Americans, whose income typically was many times greater than that of local engineers (Longuenesse 2007: 198). This engendered a great deal of bitterness toward not only foreigners but also the state, which was viewed as privileging foreign over local expertise (Moore 1994: 86, 98; Hanafi 1997: 212). Locals were often given no responsibility and only menial tasks (Longuenesse 2007: 87). The collective deprivation they felt must have been as much about material disadvantage as it was about their subordinate or even superfluous role in their local societies.

Further Tests of Relative Deprivation

There is strong evidence that a whole generation of engineers had their hopes first raised then brutally dashed. But if being an engineer indicates that one is hard-working and ambitious, and if these traits lead to particularly deep frustration when development stalls in one's home country, then we should expect the less well equipped and ambitious to be much

---

22 Wright (2006: 304) describes how future Al-Qaida members studying in the West experienced cultural alienation and a lack of belonging, enjoying "little standing in the host societies where they lived" despite their educational accomplishments.

less represented among militant movements. This is exactly what the data presented in chapter 1 seem to show: courses of study that are associated with less prestige in the Islamic world—the arts, humanities, education—which also typically have less stringent admission requirements, are strongly underrepresented in the sample.[23] Different disciplines' ranking of over- and underrepresentation almost directly mirrors their status ranking in Islamic countries.

Frustrated expectations also seem to explain why teachers played a much larger role in all forms of militancy in the early years of political Islam. Before the age of mass higher education, when many towns and villages were proud to send even one young student to university, a degree in education carried some prestige and was a vehicle for upward mobility. At the same time, however, teachers were poorly paid and their task was to cater to the needs of those in the "backward" social strata, which their educated contemporaries saw as unenviable. Longuenesse explains that teachers' frustrations led to their early political mobilization, again reinforcing the relative deprivation argument without actually invoking the concept (2007: 53). By the 1970s, with university education available to many more families, lower-status degrees were losing their allure. Obtaining a degree in education, the arts, or the humanities today is often a sign of poor academic achievement and limited aspirations.[24] Graduates from these programs now seem too marginal to even aspire to rebellion—with the exception of teachers from wealthier Saudi Arabia and, possibly, Libya (see chapter 1).

The story for lawyers—hardly present in our sample at just 1.8 percent—matches that of teachers: in early twentieth-century Egypt a law degree was considered very prestigious (Longuenesse 2007: 56), but later it became one of the least regarded degrees (Moore 1994: 46). Lawyers were among the leaders in the early nationalist struggle (Longuenesse 2007: 57). In the 1950s, the lawyers' syndicate still led the opposition to Nasser, playing a more active political role than either the doctors' or engineers' syndicate up to the 1970s (Springborg 1978: 281; Reid 1974: 46).[25] Among today's Islamist militants, whose ideology has emerged as the default vehicle for broad-based oppositionist politics after the 1970s, they are much less present.

23 On the low status of teachers in postwar Egypt, see Springborg 1978: 288. On the Arab world in general, see Zewail 2010 and Watkins 2011. The lower prestige of arts and humanities also was emphasized in all exchanges we had with regional experts, including faculty at Middle East universities.
24 Zewail 2010; Watkins 2011.
25 Lawyers also played a leading role in Syria's nationalist struggle in the 1920s (Longuenesse 2007: 57).

Mapping the representation of elite degrees of Islamist activists across countries and time helps us distinguish relative deprivation from economic explanations of radicalization that point to rationality rather than psychology. Benmelech, Berrebi, and Klor (2010) and Lee (2011) explain the presence of highly educated militants in stagnant economies in terms of opportunity costs:[26] As economic opportunities dwindle, highly skilled individuals incur smaller relative costs by becoming militant. This explanation would lead us to expect an increase in the general education levels of militants—and insofar as this has occurred, the theory appears plausible. Among university graduates, however, the theory does not predict an overrepresentation of engineers and doctors, as these types of graduates typically continue to enjoy *relatively better* opportunities compared to graduates of second-tier faculties. It is, instead, the tension between subjective expectations and objective opportunities that best explains the distribution of disciplines among extremists over time.[27]

The Saudi Exception Again

There is one major exception to the engineers' overrepresentation: Saudi Arabia, a country with only 1 engineer among 10 graduates in our main sample, no engineer among 14 graduates in the Sinjar sample, and only 1 engineer among 11 graduates in Thomas Hegghammer's sample men-

---

26 Lee's (2011) work on anticolonial activists in pre-independence Bengal is unique in that it compares a large number of violent and peaceful activists pursuing similar political objectives. He shows that the violent activists were more educated and wealthier than the general population but less educated and poorer than the peaceful activists. He explains this by way of opportunity costs, but the data he presents might also be compatible with the relative deprivation hypothesis given that his measures of education appear to differ less between the two types of activists than the variables capturing material status.

27 Benmelech, Berrebi, and Klor (2010) argue that unfavorable economic conditions allow organizations to select from a larger pool of operatives, including highly skilled ones. We cannot rule out that this explains some of the overrepresentation of doctors and engineers. This interpretation does, however, presume very selective recruitment of not only university graduates in general but also those with specific elite degrees—and assumes that this selection effect outweighs any countervailing effect stemming from the relatively better labor market opportunities that doctors and engineers possess compared to other graduates, which according to the authors' theory should make elite students less willing to engage in political violence. As we will see, their model fails to explain why peaceful and "moderate" Islamist groups, which should be as keen on selecting on qualifications, have fewer engineers, as is shown in chapter 3. In chapter 3 we will also show that at least among Western-based jihadis, "self-recruited" militants have as high a share of engineers as cells recruited by larger organizations. Neither of these facts, however, is easily explained by relative deprivation either.

tioned in chapter 1. This is true even though the proportion of engineers in the Saudi population is comparable to that of other Arab states.[28]

What is special about Saudi engineers? Most obviously, they have had much better labor market chances than their peers in any of the non-Gulf MENA states: the Saudi market has been able to absorb virtually all university graduates with prestigious technical degrees. The Saudi private sector has time and again petitioned the government to produce more graduates with technical education,[29] and development plans have repeatedly pointed to the need for more technically educated nationals (Saudi Arabian Ministry of Planning 1999, 2004).

Job market chances for the technically educated have further improved in recent years as the government has been exerting pressure on companies to hire nationals instead of foreigners.[30] Although state employment still plays a large role in the distribution of Saudi oil rents, the Saudi private sector is among the most dynamic in the region and has been recruiting skilled personnel. As the human resources manager of a large Saudi bank told one of us, unlike in other countries where business graduates are the most sought after, their first recruitment targets are engineers.[31] There have been signs of scarcity of engineers during the recent oil boom (*Saudi Gazette*, 21 May 2006, 3 December 2006; *Bahrain Tribune*, 21 April 2006; *Arab News*, 12 April 2007; *Khaleej Times*, 21 June 2007). With such favorable labor market conditions it almost seems surprising that there still are two engineers in our sample.

Compared to the other Arab cases, the Saudi contingent in our Muslim world sample appears quite unaccomplished, with lower education levels and less prestigious courses of study among those who attended university. Thomas Hegghammer has documented that members in "Al-Qaeda on the Arabian Peninsula" have less education than the general Saudi average (Hegghammer 2013); this is a stark contrast to the situation in Palestine and Egypt, where militants are highly educated. According to official sources, the main threat in Saudi domestic militancy comes from individuals who have dropped out of education, not elites (*Saudi Gazette*, 4 January 2011). The latter as yet have little reason to be frustrated.

Still, while the proportion of engineers among graduate extremists is much lower among Saudis than among other nationalities, the proportion of graduates among the Saudi extremists in our sample is only slightly

28 This figure is 10.6 percent among males in the mid-1980s (Longuenesse 1990: 329), compared to 11.6 percent in our general sample. Figures for the 1990s and early 2000s are similar: Kingdom of Saudi Arabia, *Statistical Yearbook*, various issues.
29 Interviews with private sector representatives, Riyadh, 2003 to 2005.
30 Hertog 2010: chapter 6.
31 Norlida Azmi, assistant general manager, SAMBA Financial Group, interview with the authors, December 2005, Riyadh.

lower than the sample's general average—42.4 percent versus 46.5 per-cent.[32] The fact is that the rosy situation of the engineers' labor market has been an exception: graduates from less prestigious disciplines with much lower admission requirements are often unable to compete for mid--skilled jobs with the low-wage foreign workers who dominate the Saudi labor market. There is a large unemployment problem for secondary school graduates and for graduates with degrees in the humanities and Islamic studies (Diwan and Girgis 2002; UNDP 2003b: 10–11, 68, 109; Bahgat 1999), which are strongly represented in our Saudi subsample. The stratification of degrees and labor market chances in Saudi Arabia seems directly reflected in our data: there are 3 students of Islamic law and 2 teachers among the 10 Saudis with known higher education in the main sample; among the 14 Saudis in the Sinjar database, 8 are teachers (see figure 1.5). The only other country with any teachers among the Sin-jar cases is Libya, another oil-rich country in which engineers had favor-able labor market chances until 2011 but where teaching is a dead-end job. Extremist teachers appeared exactly when they were the relatively highest-status group that was still vulnerable to collective frustration—as was the case in early nationalist and Islamist movements in other parts of the Arab world.[33]

CONCLUSIONS, AND FACTS THAT DO NOT FIT

The relative deprivation hypothesis accounts for several facts that have emerged from our investigation of both the level and type of education among secular and Islamist opposition movements from the 1920s on-ward. Let us summarize them:

- the emergence of widespread graduate-led radicalism in important parts of the Islamic world from the 1970s on, as corroborated by the substantial ethnographic and historical work of other researchers;
- the weaker presence of graduates among extremists from countries with better labor market opportunities (see also chapter 3);

32 General male tertiary enrollment levels in Saudi Arabia among the relevant age cohorts were somewhat higher than they were on average in the other countries in the sample (15 percent in 1985, compared to the 1987 weighted average for all countries in the sample of 11.7 percent), so the overrepresentation of graduates among Saudi extremists in our sample is a good deal lower than among other nationalities.

33 A potential complementary explanation is that individuals with Islamist inclinations might become teachers in Saudi Arabia because in the kingdom's religiously dominated education system they have historically been able to use their job as a platform for proselytism in a way that teachers in "secular" Arab republics cannot. But this fails to explain teachers' overrepresentation in Gaddafi's more secular Libya.

- the prominent role of engineers in Islamist radicalism from the 1970s on in countries undergoing economic crises, and their absence among opposition movements in earlier decades;
- the absence from Islamist movements of engineers in Saudi Arabia, a country where they retain excellent labor market chances; and
- the waxing and waning of the role played by other professions, such as teachers and lawyers, in opposition movements in Islamic countries over nearly a century.

Although relative deprivation goes a long way in explaining our puzzle, it does not, however, account for all the types of individuals that mobilized under the flag of radical Islam. A contingent of disenfranchised and less educated were also recruited and joined the highly educated, in different proportions but, as we shall see in the next chapter, everywhere. At the same time, some secondary school students have also joined the movement before experiencing any labor market difficulty (Waltz 1986: 662; Hanafi 1997: 148). Thus the breadth of the movement's appeal suggests that radical Islam cannot be reduced to the effects of high labor market expectations combined with failed economic development. And there are facts that do not fit into the relative deprivation explanation even if we consider only the educated militants: among the extremists we find some graduates who should not be there and do not find some other graduates who should be there.

As for graduates who, according to the relative deprivation hypothesis, should be there and are not, consider the doctors who, compared to engineers, are significantly less overrepresented,[34] even though they were subject to similar mobility closure: the admission requirements for medical school are as rigorous as those for engineering programs, and, like engineers, doctors have enjoyed high status and a social vanguard role (Longuenesse 2007: 95).[35] In proportional terms, medical faculties expanded almost as dramatically as those of engineers,[36] leading to a surplus

---

34 To reach the same odds ratio of overrepresentation among militant graduates as the engineers (see table 1.3), there would need to be 52 doctors in our sample, while in fact there are only 21. The difference between this actual and hypothetical overrepresentation is highly significant in a chi-square test.

35 In Syria, mechanical, chemical, electrical, and electronic engineering programs have high admission requirements, but they are not quite as rigorous as those of medicine, dentistry, pharmaceutics, civil engineering, and architecture (Cornand 1990: 192). In Jordan, prestigious university programs such as pharmacology and medicine require the highest secondary school grade average, 80 percent (Cunningham and Sarayrah 1993: 120).

36 In Egypt, the membership of both engineers' and doctors' syndicates grew about tenfold from 1963 to 1991 (Wickham 2002: 182). In Syria, the number of engineers has

of doctors and, consequently, unmet expectations (Longuenesse 2007: 67). So why, among elite graduates, was it the engineers who, more than any other group, took mobilization to extremes?

There are two ways in which relative deprivation could explain this anomaly. First, engineers' greater dependence on the state could have made them more vulnerable to budget cuts and to the downward mobility of bureaucrats from the 1970s on. It is arguably easier for doctors to practice even in a struggling economy than it is for engineers who rely on large projects or firms to employ them (Longuenesse 2007: 96). Second, if engineering students came from lower social backgrounds than those in medicine did, they would have incurred greater relative costs for their education and entertained expectations of higher social advancement.[37]

The former conjecture is plausible but we have found no evidence to support it. On the latter the evidence cuts both ways. Many of the early Islamist activists had a provincial background (Waltz 1986: 655; Hoffman 1995; Kepel 1993: 73, 163–64; Sonbol 1988: 27), including the original Egyptian militants (Ibrahim 1980: 438–39).[38] Abrahamian argues that engineers were prominent among the Iranian Mojahedin e-Khalk because engineering was the hardest subject that attracted the most ambitious individuals from traditional lower-middle-class families (1989: 229–30). However, Moore shows that Egyptian engineering students in the 1970s had relatively privileged backgrounds;[39] and Longuenesse (2007: 83) also mentions engineers' more urban and privileged background relative to agronomists—which she claims explains the latter's *lesser* role in the political opposition of the 1980s. So, while it is clear that the professional middle class underwent a profound crisis in much of the Islamic world, measuring gradations of failure according to different elite degrees is difficult without detailed demographic and labor market data. But, as we will see in chapter 6, there might be reasons for doctors' weaker presence among Islamist militants that have nothing to do with class or labor markets.

As for graduates who, if relative deprivation were the only explanation, should not be in our sample but are, there are two varieties. First,

grown more rapidly: more than 100 times from 1960 to 2000, compared to more than twenty times for doctors (Longuenesse 2007: 72).

37 Longuenesse (2007: 69) mentions an increasing ruralization of professionals under the Ba'ath regime in Syria and Nasser's Egyptian regime, but she does not distinguish by subject.

38 Students in the radicalized Iranian University of Science and Technology also mostly came from the provinces. Goudarz Eghtedari, personal communication with the authors, July 2006.

39 In Egypt, engineering students in the 1970s came from a higher class background than did students of law, although that may not mean much because law is the least prestigious subject (Moore 1994: 112, 217).

contrary to the case of Saudi Arabia, engineers are strongly overrepresented in three Asian countries that did not experience economic failure or a surfeit of graduates: in our sample, six of eight Malaysian graduates are engineers, four out of five Singaporeans, and seven out of nine Indians. All three countries have experienced rapid growth; while the share of graduates varies among the three cases, engineers are consistently overrepresented among them. Asian engineering graduates probably enjoy less of an economic advantage over other graduates than do Saudi engineers, but this fails to explain their strong *over*representation.

Second, many individuals in our sample do not fit the narrative of blocked social mobility. Among extremist leaders we find both individuals who came from wealthy families and individuals who abandoned a potential or actual promising career. For instance, Abbud Al-Zumur, who was involved in the assassination of Egyptian president Sadat, was born into one of the wealthiest and most prominent families in the Giza Governorate and was a one-time colonel in the military intelligence.[40] Osama bin Laden, who graduated with a degree in business, was a scion of one of Saudi Arabia's richest families. Ayman Al-Zawahiri, bin Laden's successor, comes from an academic, upper-middle-class household (Wright 2002).[41] Sami Al-Arian, who pleaded guilty in a U.S. court in 2006 to having provided support to Palestinian Islamic Jihad, was a tenured professor of computer engineering at the University of South Florida.[42] Azhari Husin, an engineer and the master bomb-maker of Jemaah Islamiyah in Southeast Asia, held a PhD from the University of Reading and worked as a lecturer at the Technological University of Malaysia.[43] He graduated at the top of his class in Malaysia's best school.[44] Assem Hammoud, a Lebanese suspect in the 2006 plot to blow up New York train tunnels, taught economics at the Lebanese International University.[45]

In the new generation of Western-based jihadis (more on these in the next chapter), we also find individuals who are both privileged *and* engineers: Anwar al-Awlaki, a U.S. citizen of Yemeni descent who became a preacher of jihad and was killed in Yemen in October 2011 by a U.S. drone, received a BS in civil engineering from Colorado State University in 1994; he was the son of Nasser al-Awlaki—agriculture minister, president

40 http://en.wikipedia.org/wiki/Abbud_al-Zumar.

41 www.jihadica.com/the-forgotten-recantation/.

42 *New York Times*, 15 April 2006, http://query.nytimes.com/gst/fullpage.html?res=9A0DE5D9163FF936A25757C0A9609C8B63&scp=2&sq=sami%20al%20arian&st=cse.

43 Bloomberg, 10 November 2005, www.bloomberg.com/apps/news?pid=newsarchive&sid=aHdTZ3lDVWps&refer=asia.

44 According to a blogger who was his classmate: http://inspigoblog.wordpress.com/2010/01/13/azhari-hussin-nordin-mat-top-umar-farouk-abdulmutallab/.

45 MSNBC, 10 July 2006, www.msnbc.msn.com/id/13749418.

of Sana'a University, and a relative of Yemen's former prime minister, Ali Mohammed Mujur. Al-Awlaki is believed by the CIA to have played a part in the attacks of underpants bomber Umar Farouk Abdulmutallab and to have inspired Times Square bomber Faisal Shahzad.[46] He could have had access to exactly the kinds of networks of privilege downwardly mobile graduates from lower-class families so strongly resent. But instead of becoming a business magnate or regime crony in Yemen, Al-Awlaki became a jihadi mentor (Scahill 2013).

The background of his supposed disciple Abdulmutallab is in fact almost a carbon copy of his own. The son of a rich and well-connected Nigerian banker who also held political positions, he came to the UK to pursue a BS in mechanical engineering from University College London.[47] While he was at the university he lived in a flat worth $4 million.[48] Al-Awlaki's other famous follower, Faisal Shahzad, who holds a BS in computer science and engineering, is the son of a high-ranking Pakistani air force officer; though not as rich as his underpants-bombing colleague, he is still a child of privilege.[49] Samar Alami and Jawad Botmeh, mentioned in chapter 1 as the two engineers responsible for the 1994 bombing of the Israeli embassy in London, are a banker's daughter and businessman, respectively—neither of whom likely experienced material deprivation.

Individual cases aside, we calculated that in our sample at least 27 individuals originated from or themselves attained an upper-middle-class (16) or upper-class (11) background. Out of those 27, 13 were leaders of extremist groups, representing 6.5 percent of the total number of leaders (200). In his sample of 172 global salafi-jihadis, Sageman reports that "of the 102 people on whom I was able to gather data, 18 were upper class, 56 were middle class, and 28 were lower class" (2004: 73). Group relative deprivation—a theory that remains difficult to operationalize precisely— might leave some of the lucky few frustrated with the broader lot of their professions and societies. But the mechanism appears more plausible for members of the professional middle class than for the (numerically small) upper classes, who especially in the developing world are more often than not socially segregated from the rest of society and its development issues.

---

46 *New York Times*, 8 May 2010, www.nytimes.com/2010/05/09/world/09awlaki.html ?pagewanted=all.
47 *New York Times*, 26 December 2009, www.nytimes.com/2009/12/27/us/27terror.html ?ref=africa.
48 *New York Daily News*, 27 December 2009, http://articles.nydailynews.com/2009-12 -27/news/17942464_1_umar-farouk-abdulmutallab-british-international-school-trafalgar -square; *Guardian*, 27 December 2009, www.guardian.co.uk/uk/2009/dec/27/gilded-life -of-plane-bomber.
49 CNN, 5 May 2010, http://edition.cnn.com/2010/CRIME/05/04/new.york.car.bomb/ index.html?.

The genealogy of global jihadism contains a core of wealth and privilege, as well as a surfeit of engineers—facts that do not sit comfortably with the theory of relative deprivation, making us suspect that it alone cannot explain our puzzle. We cannot go any further within the confines of the information we have in our sample or by using information from other sources on the Islamic world, both of which we have exhausted. In the next chapter we try a different route by focusing on a more recent generation of jihadis who grew up in Western countries—both to probe the reach of the relative deprivation hypothesis and to seek further explanations.

Relative Deprivation Probed

WESTERN COUNTRIES HAVE NOT EXPERIENCED THE DEVELOPMENT FAIL-ures of Islamic countries. If social and economic conditions were to explain the overrepresentation of both graduates and engineers among Islamist radicals, we should find fewer university graduates among the jihadis who radicalized in Western countries: if mobility closure has any effect on radicalization in the West, this should be confined to individuals with lower levels of education and the socially marginalized—and, as in Saudi Arabia, we should not find an overrepresentation of engineers because their professional opportunities in the West would have been so much better than those of their brethren in Muslim countries. If one or both of these scenarios are not borne out, something else is likely at work.

Furthermore, the relative deprivation hypothesis makes only predictions about who is likely to embrace opposition politics, but it cannot predict who will choose which form of opposition: who will opt for violent rather than peaceful means, who will choose to fight under a religious banner and who under a secular one, and who will make it a long-lasting endeavor and who will drop out. In this chapter we will investigate the extent to which engineers differ from other university graduates in these regards. If they do, this is further evidence that more is going on than just relative deprivation.

WESTERN-BASED JIHADIS

To test these expectations we assembled a new sample of 344 Islamist extremists who were born or grew up in Western countries, 338 of whom were male.[1] We include only individuals whose responsibility for acts of

---

1 Just being resident of a Western country at the time of the attack is not a sufficient condition to be in this sample; several individuals in this position have been included in the Muslim world sample we presented in chapter 1, including those who attacked Western targets. Among the 6 women, 4 were spouses or otherwise related to male militants and played a subordinate role. Only 2 women militants showed strong signs of initiative, albeit more of the "lone wolf" kind: Colleen LaRose—a U.S. high school dropout known as "Jihad Jane"—plotted the murder of Swedish artist Lars Vilks, while Roshonara Choudhry, a British college dropout, attacked UK member of parliament Stephen Timms with a knife in 2010.

violent extremism is well established, either because of a court sentence or death in action, or when there is some other clear evidence, including claims by extremists themselves (video, written).[2] The sample includes individuals who targeted or planned to target a Western country and were involved, in a greater or lesser role, in a total of 72 plots: successful attacks, foiled attacks, or planned attacks.[3] On average, plots involved 4 individuals, the minimum being 1 and the maximum 33.[4]

The sample includes a significant share of the Western-based violent Islamist extremists who emerged in the public eye up until September 2010, when our data collection stops. Out of 344 individuals, 341 are citizens of 12 Western countries in which Muslims are a minority (see figure 3.1).[5] Recently there have been many more Islamist radicals who, though born or socialized in the West, have gone to the Middle East, to Iraq and Syria especially, to fight or perpetrate a suicide attack. This large, and still growing, phenomenon is not our main focus but is discussed in the book's conclusion.

The individuals in our Western sample became active mostly after 9/11, more recently than the jihadis included in our Muslim world sample. The median age at the time of arrest or death was twenty-eight; the median year of birth was 1978, ten years younger than the median birth year of the individuals in our Muslim world sample.[6]

2 See Hegghammer 2013: 2ff. for an overview of problems involved in sampling Western-based jihadists.

3 In our sample, 237 individuals are from Bakker (2006), who assembled a list of European jihadists (59ff.), to which we added more recent cases as well as U.S. ones on the basis of press reports, press archival searches, and other secondary literature on Islamist extremists in the West. Bakker's original list contains 242 names, but we removed 5 people who were either acquitted in the meantime or already in our Muslim world sample (as they were born and raised in their country of origin). Bakker collected basic biographical information about his cases (age, country of residence, custody status, criminal records, etc.) but does not mention any information on our key variable, the type of education, which we added individually. We searched for further biographical information on all cases in Lexis Nexis and Factiva news databases and on Google. We also searched many other news media in various languages and a series of online databases, such as Global Jihad and Global Security. All websites were consulted between September 2009 and January 2011.

4 Among them are the Moroccan Spanish individuals responsible for the Madrid bombings in 2004, the Hofstad group in the Netherlands, the Lackawanna Six in the United States, and the German-Jordanian-Palestinian Al-Tawhid movement. However, we do not know how many Islamist groups the sample covers (e.g., two acts in the Netherlands are linked to the same group), and for some plots or acts there is no information on whether the cell belonged to a larger group. A few of these acts involved one person, such as Theo van Gogh's murder. The rest involved clusters of connected individuals.

5 The remaining three are residents of Bosnia but were caught because of their involvement with a Western-based plot to attack British and American warships in the Strait of Gibraltar.

6 We were able to establish the age of 297 individuals, i.e., almost the whole sample.

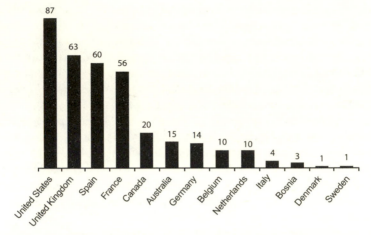

Figure 3.1: Country of birth and/or citizenship of individuals in the Western sample.
Source: Western sample.

Level of Education

Despite the fact that most of these individuals were caught, tried, or died in the West under intense media scrutiny, we found information on the education of only 122 of them and information on the occupation of 42 additional ones.[7] Among the cases with educational information, 9 had less than secondary education, 30 had secondary education only, while 83 had some university exposure or a university degree. Compared to the proportion of people with university exposure in the Muslim world sample of jihadists (46.5 percent), in the Western sample the proportion is much lower at 25.2 percent.[8]

We cannot be certain about this education level estimate, however, as there are 222 people in the Western sample on whom we have no educational information. The number of people with secondary schooling is almost certainly higher than 30 because a high school diploma is not a newsworthy item, and certainly less so than a university degree. For this reason, the number of university graduates or students we found is likely to be closer to the actual number. Furthermore, the fact that the 83 individuals with known university education are not bunched in a few networks but are evenly spread over 45 out of 72 plots is encouraging as it

---

7 These do not overlap with the ones with known education. Among those with known education we found the occupation of 39 individuals.
8 In calculating this share, we exclude 15 individuals in our sample who had not reached college age when they were arrested or died.

suggests fairly comprehensive reporting of university exposure across our sample. In the 27 plots with no known cases of university education this biographical item might on occasion be present but go unreported. In the 45 plots with known cases of university education, however, sources are unlikely to report it for one member of a group but not for another. This supports our surmise that the reason we found no educational information for so many people is that there were no significant accomplishments beyond high school to report. If we calculate the proportion of graduates involved in the 45 plots that include at least one graduate or university student (rather than all plots), we obtain 39.2 percent (83/212), which is still 7.3 points lower than in the Muslim world sample (46.5 percent).[9] In sum, we can be reasonably confident that the proportion of university graduates in the Western sample is lower than that of the Muslim world sample.

But even if this were not the case, the difference in the proportion of graduates in the two samples becomes undeniable and large once we make the comparison more accurate by taking into account that the number of people with university exposure in Western countries is much higher than it is in Islamic countries: in 1999, the male enrollment rate in tertiary education in the countries from which the Western sample is drawn, weighted by the number of cases per country, was 43 percent (UNESCO data). This means that in the Western sample individuals with university exposure among the extremists are not over but *under*represented, and strongly so: the odds of having university exposure are less than half of what we would expect given the enrollment rates. Contrast these with the corresponding odds in the Muslim world sample, which are at least six times *higher* than they are in the relevant population, and the result is striking. To appreciate further how large the difference is, consider that to be on a par with the proportion of educated individuals present in the Western sample, the frequency of educated extremists in the Muslim world sample should decrease to around 6 percent, while, as we know, it is 46.5 percent.

It is clear that our cases are less educated than the general Western average. But are they also less educated than Muslims living in the West? To find out we can use the large, multiyear European Social Survey (ESS), which covers the European countries whence our individuals originate and records both education level and religious affiliation of all those

9 In his study of Al-Qaida networks, Sageman also shows that in the Maghreb Arab cluster, which largely consists of Western-based individuals, only 19 percent of individuals hold a degree, while 51.6 percent do so in his other clusters that are based in the Islamic world (2004: 75, table 3). While his sample overlaps with ours, he and we assembled our educational data independently of each other.

interviewed.[10] This allows us to calculate the proportion of individuals with a university degree as reported by respondents, rather than the enrollment rates. Among male non-Muslims in the relevant age group, 34.4 percent have a degree, while among Muslims it is only 17 percent. The share of militants with a degree (rather than just university exposure) in our Western sample is comparable: 19.1 percent of the relevant age segment.[11] This means that education levels in our Western sample broadly reflect the Muslim sub-populations they stem from—but these sub-populations in turn are quite educationally disadvantaged compared to the broader societies in which they live.[12]

Several other fragments of information show that the new generation of Islamist extremists in Western countries has not only lower levels of education but also lower and more marginal occupational qualifications than do its counterparts in Islamic countries. First, 41 individuals in the Western sample are converts to Islam, most of them drifters or former inmates who converted in jail. Second, among the 42 individuals in the Western sample whose occupation we found (non-overlapping with the university-exposed group), only two had a professional occupation: one a pharmacist, the other a computer programmer.[13] Finally, Bakker found that a quarter of those in his sample of 242 cases, most of whose members are also in ours, had a criminal record, unrelated to terrorist activities (2006: 42). According to Spanish authorities, 20 percent of those imprisoned for jihadist terrorist offenses between 2005 and 2011 in Spain had

10 From the ESS1-3 Cumulative File 2002, 2004, 2006, we selected Western countries in our sample (except the United States and Canada, which are not in the ESS), and then we included only males aged 26 to 40 reporting a degree. There are a mere 40 male Muslim cases with a degree in the ESS data, so our estimate of education levels is rough.

11 We assume that individuals younger than age 26 in both our sample and the ESS would not have had the chance to complete a degree. This leaves 183 cases in our sample, 35 of whom have a degree. There are 7 younger cases in the sample who have a completed degree but whom we left out as in the younger age segment most other individuals with university exposure are students who cannot be compared to the ESS sample, which only records completed education (among older members of the sample, there are at least 6 college dropouts, so the fact that an individual begins university studies does not allow us to predict graduation).

12 The comparison is not perfect as ESS data do not include the United States and Canada. This, however, creates a conservative bias: the sample's education level might in fact be even lower than that of the general Muslim background population, as these two countries have particularly high rates of tertiary education.

13 Thirteen had unskilled manual or clerical jobs, 9 owned shops or were employed in retail activities, 6 had a skilled manual occupation, 5 a technical one, 3 had a military background, and 2 were clerics (plus 1 electrician, 1 X-ray technologist, 1 medical assistant, and 1 apprentice electrician). We also gathered information on the occupation of 6 university students and 2 graduates in the sample: 1 was a trainee probation officer, 1 hotel worker (type of work not specified), 1 chartered surveyor, 2 counselors—at a local community center and at a job center—and 1 worked at a debt collection agency.

previously been in prison for other crimes.[14] In Australia, police fear growing links between biker gangs and networks of radical Islamists— not the types of links one would expect in the professional middle class.[15]

Some of the most notorious cases of Western jihad involved petty criminals who reinvented themselves as Islamic warriors. Cherif Kouachi, for example, the younger of the two brothers whose attack on the *Charlie Hebdo* offices in Paris claimed twelve victims in January 2015, was a one-time would-be rapper with a record of petty crime.[16] Amedy Coulibaly, an accomplice who killed a policewoman and four hostages in a kosher supermarket in Paris during the manhunt for the Kouachis, had been convicted five times for armed robbery.[17] A study of 117 U.S.- and UK-based Islamist extremists, partially overlapping with our cases, found that "Terrorists in this study were less frequently married, of a less privileged socio-economic upbringing, and had both a weaker educational background and weaker professional prospects than previous studies suggest is typical of the global terrorist movement as a whole" (Gartenstein-Ross and Grossman 2009: 14). Almost all Australians known to have left for jihad in Syria or Iraq by early 2015 were reported to have been receiving welfare payments.[18] And Sageman (2004: 74, table 1) reports the class background of jihadis broken down by the clusters in his sample: the proportion of individuals with lower-class origins is much higher in the Maghreb Arab cluster, which largely consists of Western-based individuals, than in the other clusters which are based in the Islamic world: 48 versus 22 percent.[19]

Our Muslim world sample is taken from a much larger, unknown population of activists, which might bias our estimates of education levels among Muslim world radicals upward. The Western sample is more exhaustive and hence might be more effective at capturing less qualified, lower-tier, and less salient individuals. But this logic should not apply if

14 *Europa Press*, 10 October 2014, www.europapress.es/nacional/noticia-gobierno
-autoriza-creacion-centro-inteligencia-contra-terrorismo-crimen-organizado-fusiona-cnca
-cico-20141010160638.html.
15 *Daily Star* (Lebanon), 22 November 2014, http://dailystar.com.lb/News/Middle-East/
2014/Nov-22/278504-australia-fears-islamists-joining-biker-gangs.ashx#axzz3JqYZ8rDI.
16 *The Guardian*, 12 January 2015, www.theguardian.com/world/2015/jan/12/-sp-charlie
-hebdo-attackers-kids-france-radicalised-paris.
17 *Wall Street Journal*, 14 January 2015, www.wsj.com/articles/paris-attackers-path-to
-terror-1421204761.
18 *Daily Telegraph* (Australia), 21 February 2015, www.dailytelegraph.com.au/news/nsw/
aussie-jihadists-were-on-the-dole/story-fni0cx12-1227233046278.
19 A study by Altunbas and Thornton (2011) purports to contradict these results; using a sample of 77 extremists in the UK, the authors claim that their level of education is higher than that of a representative sample of the Muslim population in the UK. However, levels of education among the missing cases are imputed based on averages among the known cases, ignoring the likely selection biases we refer to in this chapter.

we restrict ourselves to movement leaders, who should be similarly visible across samples. Among 88 clearly identified leaders in the Western sample, however, only 12 have university exposure; 4 are known to have finished only high school. Only 13.6 percent hence are known to have undertaken university studies, a figure that is considerably lower than that for the total sample. In the Muslim world sample, by contrast, 94 out of 169 leaders are known to have some form of higher education: 55.6 percent. Not only the foot soldiers but also the leaders of jihad in the West are of lower caliber in terms of education.

Assuming that graduates have better prospects and more to lose in the West than they do in poorer Islamic countries, the relative deprivation hypothesis leads us to expect fewer of them among militants. This is borne out by the data. Relative to the levels of education in the general populations, the level of education attained by Western-based Islamist extremists is drastically lower than that of extremists based in Muslim countries.

Type of Degree

What of our second prediction, that among Western extremists we should not find an overrepresentation of engineers and doctors, as their professional opportunities in the West were much better than they were for their counterparts in Muslim countries?

We found information on the type of degree pursued by 71 of the 83 with university exposure (figure 3.2). The result is unexpected: 78.9 percent pursued "elite" degrees—engineering, medicine, science, and business—which is an even higher proportion than the 64.7 percent share in the Muslim world sample. Engineers alone represent 45.1 percent, practically the same proportion that we found in the main sample (44.9 percent).

As in chapter 1, we would not expect the observed distribution to be biased compared to the "true" population of militants, as there is no reason why some types of degrees would be reported more than others. In addition, the 83 individuals with university exposure are not concentrated in a few plots; we know they were involved in 45 of the 72 plots in the sample. This makes a bias based on the type of degree particularly unlikely, as skewed reporting of degrees would have had to occur across a large number of plots. Considering the 32 engineers in particular, we find that they were involved in 22 plots, with no group containing more than 4 engineers. This confirms that in this sample, too, the frequency of engineers is not an effect of local social networks but follows an independent dynamic, as it does in our Muslim world sample.

A hefty 45.1 percent share of engineers among Western Islamists with university exposure is not the result we anticipated on the basis of the

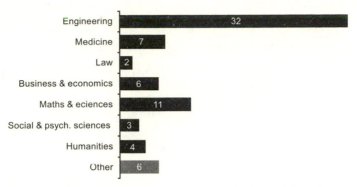

Figure 3.2: Islamist extremists in Western countries by discipline of study (71 individuals).
Source: Western sample.

relative deprivation hypothesis. But how strongly overrepresented are they? According to the UNESCO data, the weighted share of engineering students in the total male student body in 1999 in all the countries present in our sample is 16.2 percent (table 3.1).

This means that the odds of being an engineer among the extremists are more than four times what one would expect if the militants in our sample were randomly drawn from the student population—almost as large as the overrepresentation of engineers we found in the Muslim world sample. A chi-square test shows this bias to be highly statistically significant. It does not appear to be an artifact of Western-based Muslims predominantly studying for engineering degrees: in ESS data we find that the frequency of individuals working as engineers in the relevant European countries is the same for Muslims and non-Muslims.[20] Doctors, by contrast, are not overrepresented in the sample as their odds of being in the sample are close to those of being in the background population.

And there is more. One might suspect that this distribution did not reflect a greater enthusiasm among engineers for joining a radical group but was driven by the selection methods or preferences of the recruiters, biased in favor of engineers. We devised a test for this: we divided the 72 cells/plots in our sample into those that are part of larger groups or networks and those that were self-started independent cells. The results are striking (table 3.2): while the rate of those with higher education is stable across different types of groups, the proportion of engineers is *higher* in

20 This is based on small numbers, as in the ESS sample there are only 40 Muslim males with a degree; the likelihood that this subsample underreports the share of engineers by a multiple is very low, however.

TABLE 3.1
Islamist extremists, in Muslim and in Western samples, with exposure to engineering and medicine compared with corresponding enrollment rates in Western countries

Education	Muslim countries (%)	Western countries (%)	Male population in Western countries, 1999, weighted*; UNESCO (%)
Exposure to university degree	45.0	25.2	43.3
Of those with exposure to degree: engineering	44.9	45.1	16.2
Of those with exposure to degree: medicine	10.1	9.9	6.7

* Weighting done in line with representation of different nationalities in the Western sample.
Source: Muslim world sample and Western sample.

the independent groups (50 percent) than it is among the cells or plots that depend on larger organizations (38 percent). This means that in units in which members are selected by recruiters, engineers are less frequent than in groups in which members are *self-recruited,* a good indication that the overrepresentation of engineers is not due to a recruitment bias but is supply driven. Either their skills give them greater opportunities to start new jihadi groups or they have a greater willingness to do so, or both.

Anecdotally, we know that some engineers have persevered in their jihadi efforts even when they failed in their attempts to join larger groups. Syed Haris Ahmed is a Pakistani American who migrated to the United States with his parents in 1997 at the age of twelve and lived in an upscale neighborhood in Atlanta. While his father was a computer science professor at North Georgia College, Syed began pursuing a mechanical engineering degree at the Georgia Institute of Technology in autumn 2004.[21] As a student, he embarked on an Internet-based "spiritual journey" to find out more about Islam and, frequenting jihadi websites, grew

21 *Frontline,* "Canada: The Cell Next Door" (transcript of PBS radio broadcast aired 30 January 2007), see www.pbs.org/frontlineworld/about/episodes/602_transcript.html; *New York Times,* 21 April 2006, www.nytimes.com/2006/04/21/us/21georgia.html?_r=1&oref

TABLE 3.2
Level and type of education by type of Western-based group

Type of groups	Groups	Members	With Higher Education		With known discipline	Engineers	
			N	%		N	%
Independent	15	72	18	25%	16	8	50%
Cells of larger groups	41	215	50	23%	40	15	38%
Unknown	16	57	15	26%	15	9	60%
Total	72	344	83	24%	71	32	45%

Source: Western sample.

increasingly radicalized.[22] Ahmed engaged in paramilitary training with a local friend named Ehsanul Islam Sadequee, who had unsuccessfully tried to join the Taliban while living in Bangladesh in 2001.[23] In spring 2005, the two took sixty-two "amateurish" casing videos of Washington, D.C., landmarks like the World Bank and the Capitol.[24] In summer 2005 Ahmed traveled to Pakistan, apparently to study Islam in a local madrasa and to join a local militant group, Lashkar-e-Taiba. Having gained admission to neither madrasa nor Lashkar, he returned to Atlanta, doing further research on "explosive charges and methods to defeat surveillance by government authorities"[25]—the latter to no avail, as he was arrested in March 2006 and sentenced to thirteen years in prison in 2009.

In sum, the evidence indicates that compared to our Muslim world cases, there are far fewer graduates among the Western-based jihadists and many more from a lower-middle or lower-class background, with

=slogin; *National Review*, 29 September 2006, www.nationalreview.com/articles/218862/terrorists-dixie/john-mccormack.

22 *Atlanta Journal-Constitution*, 10 June 2009, www.ajc.com/services/content/metro/stories/2009/06/10/terrorism_trial_tech.html.

23 U.S. Department of Justice, "Terrorism Defendants Sentenced in Atlanta," 14 December 2009, www.justice.gov/opa/pr/2009/December/09-nsd-1338.html.

24 *Atlanta Journal-Constitution*, 10 June 2009, www.ajc.com/services/content/metro/stories/2009/06/10/terrorism_trial_tech.html.

25 Anthony Lake, "Syed Haris Ahmed Trial: Allegations," *Federal Criminal Defense Blog*, 2 June 2009, www.federalcriminaldefenseblog.com/2009/06/articles/terrorism-1/syed-haris-ahmed-trial-allegations/.

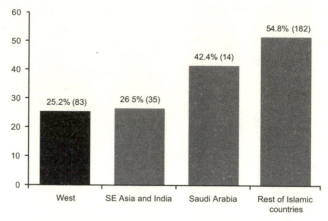

Figure 3.3: Individuals with exposure to higher education by area (% and number).
Source: Western sample and Muslim world sample.

even a substantial criminal component. Yet, strikingly, despite the marginal social status of Islamist extremists in the West, we still find among them an overrepresentation of engineers, comparable to that which we found in the Muslim world sample. The number of graduates is tiny in absolute terms, but nearly half of them are engineers.

What can we conclude? Frustration with the personal and collective consequences of failed economic development seems to be the catalyst that led graduates to radicalize across the Islamic world. Figure 3.3 illustrates how levels of education among militants in different regions represented in our samples appear to be inversely correlated with the economic opportunities open to graduates in these regions.[26] Graduates radicalize disproportionately when they are most deprived of opportunities.

We have argued that engineers have been at the sharp end of relative deprivation that has driven university graduates in the Muslim world into high-risk militancy. The ill-fated history of the engineering profession in the Middle East and the shifting composition of Islamist movements in the course of the twentieth century make this reading highly plausible. There is ample evidence that the relative deprivation hypothesis explains different levels and types of education among militants around the world. Our data confirm the (hitherto untested) prediction of Lee (2011) that in societies with better economic opportunities, those who participate in po-

26 We subdivide our Muslim world sample from chapter 1 into the three columns on the right of the graph.

litical violence have lower social status. Lee argues that this would be due to (a) the higher levels of political awareness among the deprived in richer societies and (b) the higher opportunity costs of violence among higher-status individuals. While both are likely to play a role, both narrative case histories and the presence of Islamic world militants with elite degrees indicate that subjective relative deprivation is as critical a factor.

But the degree distribution in our Western sample presents patterns that challenge both Lee's account and the broader theory of relative deprivation. As figure 3.4 shows, unlike doctors, radical engineers have a strong presence not just in Muslim countries but also among Western-based extremists who have a degree, although these should not have suffered from relative deprivation. As we saw in chapter 2, moreover, they are strongly represented among Southeast Asian and Indian militants, although developmental failures in these regions have been far less pronounced than in the Middle East. In addition, a significant share of militants, including many engineers, comes from privileged backgrounds. Even if relative deprivation is at the core of the phenomenon, *we cannot reduce the puzzle of militant Islamist engineers to just that cause.*

Furthermore, relative deprivation predicts only dissatisfaction with the status quo and a greater willingness to engage in opposition politics. It does not predict the *type* of action that will be taken, whether violent or peaceful, religious or secular, enduring or ephemeral. If engineers had features that set them apart from other graduates, their peculiarity should

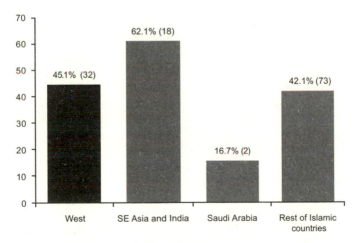

● Western sample ● Muslim world main sample

Figure 3.4: Engineers among those with known discipline of higher education (%, number of individuals in parentheses).
Source: Western sample and Muslim world sample.

carry over in these regards. This is what we will be trying to test in the next sections.

Violent vs. Nonviolent Opposition

The individuals in both our samples include only members of violent groups, but what about members of *nonviolent* Islamist opposition movements and their education? Does their education differ from that of violent militants in interesting ways? In our account of the Islamic revival in chapter 2, we implicitly conflated peaceful and violent activism in the Muslim world and explained the emergence of highly educated elites in both since the 1970s with relative deprivation. But are the elites in the two strands of activism really the same in terms of education?

Nonviolent Islamist parties and movements contain, as do their violent counterparts, a fair share of highly educated individuals. In a sample of 738 Syrian Muslim Brothers active in the 1980s, 25.8 percent were doctors, lawyers, or engineers, and another 32 percent were university or secondary school students (Lobmeyer 1995: 394). Even in Nigeria, a country in which only a third of children attend secondary school, the leadership of the (largely peaceful) Muslim Brotherhood is "highly educated" and "the typical leader is a university graduate" (Best 1999). Islamists' high level of education is well-documented across the whole Muslim world.[27]

With respect to subjects of study among those with higher education, there are both similarities and differences between our Muslim world sample and the nonviolent Islamist parties and movements. The main commonality is that elite degrees, engineering included, are strongly represented in both types of groups. In Egypt, for instance, nonviolent Islamists scored their initial electoral victories in the professional associations of doctors, pharmacists, and engineers in the mid-1980s, while gains in the journalists' and lawyers' syndicates were more modest and were barely noticeable in commerce, agriculture, and education. It took Islamists until 1992 to gain control of the lawyers' association, which remained one of the last liberal-leftist bastions (Wickham 2002: 178, 185; Longuenesse 2007: 58; Fahmy 1998: 553). Islamists have also played a dominant role in the student politics of elite faculties at Egyptian universities since the late 1970s. In the 1990–91 elections to the Cairo University student union, Islamists won 47 of the 48 seats in the science faculty student board, all 72 in the medical faculty, and all 60 in engineering. Liberals and leftists

27 Best 1999; Hoffman 1995; Lobmeyer 1995; Moore 1994; Munson 1986; Munson 2001; Wickham 2002.

continued to have a strong presence in economics and political science, where Islamists won only 13 out of 49 seats (Wickham 2002: 117–18).

Engineers are also strongly represented among nonviolent Islamist movements in other MENA countries. We already mentioned the role they played in the Iranian Revolution, in which student activists in Islamic associations tended to be from science and engineering faculties rather than from the social sciences.[28] The Jordanian syndicate of engineers, an important forum of oppositional mobilization, is dominated by Islamists, and Laith Shubailat, former head of the syndicate, was also a leader of the Islamist opposition for a long time.[29] In Turkey, engineers are strongly represented among Islamist parties, although these are not all politically radical (Göle 1990). Islamist sympathies were particularly strong in the engineers' syndicate in 1970s Syria (Moore and Salloukh 2007: 66), into which the Muslim Brothers made inroads earlier than they did into the leftist-dominated lawyers' association (Longuenesse 2007: 93). Engineers have also been prominent among North African Islamists.[30] Conversely, administration, politics, and other nontechnical faculties have often been latecomers to Islamist mobilization.[31]

But what about the percentage of engineering degrees versus that of other elite degrees such as medicine, pharmacology, and science, often mentioned in the literature as similarly "Islamicized"? To answer this question, we collected data on a variety of nonviolent groups in eight of the Islamic countries in our sample (see table 3.3).[32] The data show a

28 According to Iran expert Hossein Partovi, the "exceptionally active role of science and engineering students and faculty in the Iranian political experience of the last half century is undeniable" (personal communication with the authors, July 2006). Another researcher has commented that "in my research on student activism in Iran, I have found more science and engineering students in Islamic Associations than those from social sciences" (Akbar Mahdi, personal communication with the authors, July 2006).

29 www.highbeam.com/doc/1P1:2389549/Leading+opponent+of+King+Hussein +is+jailed .html?refid=SEO; www.voanews.com/english/archive/2005-02/2005-02-04-voa17.cfm ?CFID=3684699&CFTOKEN=41778570.

30 Michael Willis, personal communication with the authors, November 2006.

31 For Jordan, see Longuenesse 2000: 34ff. In Kuwait, administrative sciences remains a bastion of liberals; Kuwait Times, 3 September 2006.

32 Sources include a variety of secondary literature with biographical information, published membership data from movements and parliaments as well as data shared by other researchers. The sample is opportunistic in that it simply focuses on all cases in which we found larger sets of biographical data. It is more systematic than our samples of violent groups, however, in the sense that particular categories of actors (e.g., MPs, members of party committees) are exhaustively sampled within several of the cases. In any case, it is unlikely that any selection biases would affect the reporting of type rather than level of degree. The sources used are: Azam 1997: 92–98; Stephane Lacroix, personal communication with the authors, April 2007, April 2012; Hizb ut-Tahrir 2002; Mohamad Mahdi Akif, "Speech to Introduce the Muslim Brother MPs," Intercontinental Hotel, Madinat Nasr, Cairo, 11 December 2005, as reported by Joshua Stacher, personal communication

TABLE 3.3
Degree distribution among members of nonviolent Islamist groups by country

Country	Groups	Engineers	Other elite degrees*	Of which doctors	Total members**
Egypt	Muslim Brotherhood MPs	18	12	6	88
Jordan	Islamic Action Front founders	10	25	18	200
Syria	Hizb ut-Tahrir prisoners	10	17	7	59
Saudi Arabia	Islamist dissidents	5	6	1	129
Morocco	Justice and Development Party MPs	3	10	7	42
India	Jamaat-e-Islami Hind	3	4	0	20
Malaysia	Pan-Malaysian Islamic Party	2	3	2	22
Kuwait	Islamist MPs	1	3	2	21
Malaysia	ABIM	0	2	1	11
Total		52	82	44	592

* This includes medicine, veterinary medicine, pharmacology, and sciences.

** The total includes nongraduate members. The count of other elite degrees does not include 57 university professors or lecturers whose subject either was non-elite (literature, commerce, Islamic studies, etc.) or could not be established (11 Egyptians, 14 Jordanians, 11 Moroccans, and 21 Saudis). Their presence further highlights the high level of education of the Islamist opposition.

Sources: See note 33.

with the authors, April 2007; www.ikhwanweb.com/Home.asp?zPage=Systems&System =PressR&Press=Show&Lang=E&ID=4990; www.parlement.ma/sitefr/partis/dep09-04 -2007/total09-04-2007.shtml; web research of South East Asian and Kuwaiti movements; www.jamaateislamihind.org/. In the case of Egypt, Jordan, Morocco, and Syria, degrees are inferred based on individuals' reported profession; for the other cases, there is direct evidence of the subject of study.

striking difference from our samples of violent groups: in nonviolent Islamist groups, engineers, although present, do not appear to be dominant: only 38.8 percent of the total elite degrees are in the field of engineering while among violent extremists they are 69.4 percent. In the nonviolent groups, engineers are joined by a stronger contingent of graduates with other elite degrees. For example, in Egypt, in the (generally nonviolent) Muslim Brotherhood engineers share both leadership positions and middle ranks with geologists, doctors, pharmacologists, and others with comparable educational backgrounds, and the doctors' association in particular has been a bastion of Islamists (Wickham 2002: 185).

What stands out in the data on nonviolent Islamists is not the engineers' dominance but the strong presence of a broader swathe of elite degrees: if we consider that together other elite degrees make up only around 10 percent of the total number of degrees earned by the male students in Egypt and Jordan (a figure equal to or less than that for engineers), they appear to be clearly overrepresented among nonviolent groups and at least as strongly so as engineering degrees.[33] The total number of doctors (44) stands out in particular; this is almost as high as the number of engineers (52), despite the smaller number of doctors in the background population. By contrast, in our Muslim world sample there are only 21 doctors, compared to 93 engineers.

In line with our account of frustrated elites and mobility closure in chapter 2, Islamist mobilization seems to appeal to both engineers and other elite students.[34] But engineers seem more likely to be drawn to violent groups (figure 3.5).[35]

Perhaps it should come as no surprise that peaceful mass movements attract a somewhat different membership than do smaller militant groups.

33 By contrast, the larger and less selective faculties, such as humanities, commerce, administration, and education, appear generally underrepresented in three of the four cases where we could obtain detailed information (Egypt, Syria, and Morocco; Kuwait is the exception). They are also underrepresented among the Islamic Action Front's 17 parliamentarians in Jordan; www.jabha.net/NOWAB.ASP.

34 As far as we know, the only violent group in which the share of scientists has been high is Japanese Aum Shinrikyo, a sect rather than a politically motivated group, which reportedly attracted economically successful high achievers who, according to Reader (2000), suffered from spiritual malaise in modern Japanese society.

35 When told in generic terms about our research, Holger Albrecht, an expert on Egypt, commented—without being primed by us—that although several types of professionals are represented among nonviolent Egyptian Islamists, *within the latter group* the engineers seem to entertain the most radical views (personal communication with the authors, March 2006). Engineers also seem to have been more strongly represented among the more radical parties in Turkey (Demiralp 2006: 21).

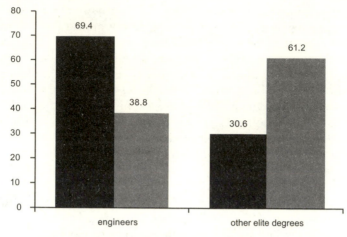

Figure 3.5: Engineering degrees and other elite degrees as a percentage of the total elite degrees among members of violent and nonviolent groups. *Source:* Muslim world sample and Muslim world nonviolent sample.

Research on Pakistani survey data by Shapiro and Fair (2009) does indeed show that support for the political goals of legal Islamist parties is at best loosely linked to support for militant organizations. Interview-based research on Western-based Islamists further indicates that it might be militancy rather than group size or degree of ideological rigidity that drives the distinction between disciplines: peaceful Islamist "radicals" who espouse a drastically conservative social model and segregation from society are more likely to have been educated in the humanities and social sciences, while militants are more likely to be engineers (Bartlett, Birdwell, and King 2010: 24). Bartlett and colleagues' research relied on a small sample, however, and the interviewees were not randomly sampled, so their findings are at best preliminary. Whatever we make of it, our data, which are drawn from a much larger and diverse pool of peaceful Islamists, further highlight the puzzle of what is special about engineers.

RELIGIOUS VS. SECULAR MILITANTS

When they have a choice, are engineers who decide to rebel also more likely to join *religious* extremist groups rather than secular groups? We have found two pieces of evidence that can help answer this question, one from Iran before the ayatollah's revolution and the other from Palestine.

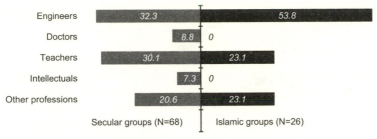

Figure 3.6: Distribution of professions of Iranian militants killed in the struggle against the Shah, 1971–77, by group.

Note: Two hundred forty individuals in secular groups, of whom 68 had higher education; 101 in Islamic groups, of whom 26 had higher education.

Source: Abrahamian 1980.

A number of Iranian opposition groups fought a small-scale guerrilla war against the Shah's regime in the 1970s. They included both religious groups such as the Islamic Mujahedeen and secular ones such as the Marxist Fedayi. According to Abrahamian (1980), from 1971 till October 1977,

> when the Islamic revolution began to unfold in the streets of Teheran, the regime, notably its secret police SAVAK, killed 341 members of guerrilla organisations and political parties advocating armed struggle. 177 died in gun battles; 91 were executed—some without trial, others after secret military tribunals; 42 were tortured to death; 15 disappeared; seven committed suicide to avoid capture; and nine were shot "trying to escape." (3)

Abrahamian was able to determine the professions of 306 of the 341 dead militants (1980: 5). The proportion of those with a degree in the secular group and the proportion of those with a degree in the Islamist group are nearly the same, just over a quarter of the total membership in each group: 28 percent and 26 percent, respectively.[36] However, the shares of engineers as a proportion of those with university training differ markedly between the two groups (and significantly, with $p < .1$ in a chi-square test): they make up less than a third of the secular groups and more than half of the Islamist groups. All six doctors, by contrast, are in the secular groups. Although we have no data on engineers in particular, evidence from Afghanistan in the 1970s seems in line with the Iranian pattern: students of "science and technology" were strongly present among the

---

36 We infer whether subjects had a degree from their profession, as categorized by Abrahamian.

four Islamist militant groups on which there are data, but only in one of two Marxist groups.[37] Doctors, again, were more strongly represented among leftist groups (Rubin 1992: table 4, p. 92).

After 1977, during the Iranian Revolution, the same pattern is discernible: although engineering students played a strong role in Iranian politics during the last half century and did not limit themselves to one ideology—for example, the students of the Polytechnic University had radical leftist leanings (Farideh Farhi, personal communication with the authors, July 2006)—engineering students were present in proportionally larger numbers among radical Islamists, and the Islamist wing of the national movement had many more engineers than did the secular one (Chehabi 1990: 89–90, 113, 120–21). Engineers also featured prominently among the Mojahedin E-Khalk, a violent Islamo-Marxist hybrid, while purely Marxist guerrilla groups included more students of humanities and social sciences than they did engineers (Abrahamian 1989: 229–30; Hoffman 1995: 206).

Our second test case is Palestine, where prospective militants can choose between a secular and a religious organization to fight for their cause. The two main groups, the secular Fatah and the Islamist Hamas, have been vying for supremacy in the struggle against Israel. We estimate that among the militants of Hamas 38 percent are engineers; we calculated this ratio using our main sample, which contains 94 individuals from this organization.

In order to discover the degree distribution of the Palestinian militants who belong to secular groups, mostly Fatah, we used the biographies collected by Glen Rangwala.[38] We selected 64 individuals who clearly started out as militants rather than as technocrats or diplomats. Among them, engineers constitute only 11.7 percent, less than a third of the share of the engineers in Hamas (see figure 3.7).[39]

---

37 The shares of "science and technology" graduates are 12 percent for the Parcham Marxist group and 39 percent for the Khalq group, while they lie between 20 and 50 percent for the four Islamist groups. Some of the overrepresentation of technical graduates among the Islamist groups and the Khalq group might be due to their provincial background (Rubin 1992: 88), as provincial families and students might see engineering programs as their preferred vehicle of social mobility. If sharia graduates are excluded, however, the share of science and technology students among the Islamist groups rises dramatically to almost two-thirds of the remaining secular degrees, while they constitute only about 40 percent of the secular-trained cadres in the provincial leftist group (Khalq). Because of the small numbers, the difference is not statistically significant.

38 www.al-bab.com/arab/countries/palestine/biogAB.htm.

39 Members of the Fatah sample are on average considerably older than in the Hamas sample: average known dates of birth are 1939 and 1971, respectively. This does not appear to be driving the difference, however, as the range of birth years in the samples

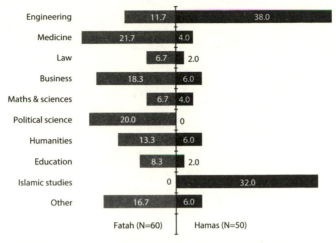

Figure 3.7: Distribution of disciplines of study of Palestinian militants by group (%)

Note: In the case of Fatah, where 14 individuals studied more than one subject, the counts are those of disciplines rather than individuals (resulting in a total of 74 counts for 60 individuals). This does not materially affect the results, which would look very similar even if combined subjects were counted as half units.

Source: Muslim world sample, and biographies collected by Glen Rangwala (www.al-bab.com/arab/countries/palestine/biogAB.htm).

In both the Iranian and Palestinian cases, engineers who embrace radical politics seem to be more inclined to do so in religious than in secular groups, while doctors in both cases veer in the opposite direction—in line with what we know about their presence among early nationalist movements (Longuenesse 2007: 60, 120). As figure 3.8 illustrates, there is a neat segregation between Hamas and Fatah in terms of the type of degree their members attained: Hamas is dominated by engineering and Islamic studies students while those pursuing all other degrees, above all medicine, are relatively more frequent in the secular Fatah. Statistically significant biases are highlighted with a filled black circle.[40] The 45-degree line emanating from the origin represents the null hypothesis: this is where disciplines would lie if they were similarly frequent among both groups.

overlap (1911–61, 1938–85), and in both of them younger members are *less* frequently engineers.

40 The significance relies on Fisher's exact test, comparing the actual counts of degrees on left and right with the distribution one would expect if the frequency of degrees was independent of ideology; $p < .01$ for all significant cases.

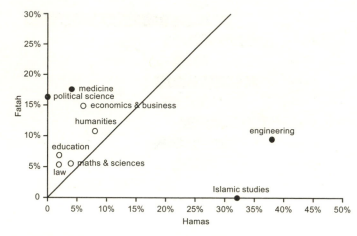

Figure 3.8: Share of disciplines of study of members of Hamas and Fatah compared.
    Source: See figure 3.7.

Die-hard Militants vs. Defectors

Radical engineers in the Islamic world appear to be much more frequent among religious rather than secular groups. What about the intensity and duration of their commitment to violent jihad? We have already seen that radical Islamist engineers in the West seem to more often be self-starters rather than recruited by a larger organization—one possible indicator of strong internal motivation. To assess whether commitment to violent jihad is evenly distributed across degrees we assembled a database of 81 defectors, individuals who were once part of a violent Islamist group and chose to leave.[41] Their median date of birth was 1957, about ten years older than the median birthdate in the Muslim world sample.[42] Most of

41 We searched for names and biographical details of defectors in newspaper archives as well as in a wide range academic reports, articles, and books about disengagement and deradicalization. Our main sources include Bjorgo and Horgan 2009; Ashour 2009; Horgan 2009; and Jacobson 2010.
42 To make sure we were comparing samples from the same era we checked the proportion of engineers among the subsample of radicals of the Muslim world with a median date of birth of 1957 (taking the oldest cohort and adding increasingly younger members until the median reached 1957). The share of engineers in this subsample (99 individuals, 76 with a known discipline of study) is 43.9 percent, nearly identical to that of the whole sample.

these individuals are from Muslim countries, and many of them were members of groups included in our main sample.[43]

The defections we have in the database occurred for any number of reasons, but repression is prominent among them. Kamal El-Said Habib, for instance, who was born into a lower-middle-class family in a large village in the Nile Delta in the same generation as Ayman Al-Zawahiri, graduated from Cairo University in 1979 at the top of his class with a degree in political science (Gerges 2006: 20–21). Devout before matriculation, he later became a member of Al-Jihad, and had some part in the Sadat assassination plot in 1981. After being jailed and tortured he recanted:

> We were naive, arrogant and immature, fired up by the spirit of youth.… We had big dreams but few resources, and there was a pronounced gap between the means at our disposal and our ambitions. Gradually, we lost sight of the balance between ends and means and fell into the trap of armed escalation with the government. We were no match for its powers … we had no vision or an intellectual framework of what a state is or how it functions and how it should be administered, except that it should express and approximate the Islamic idea … we had little awareness of the challenges that needed to be overcome. We were terribly naive and didn't appreciate the complexity of society and the requirements of social and political change. (Gerges 2006: 54–56)

But repression can also have the opposite effect and harden the radicalization of some of its victims: "Some left the prisons and the country [Egypt] determined to exact revenge on their tormenters and torturers. The authorities' brutal methods nourished fanaticism and sowed the seeds for more violence and bloodshed" (Gerges 2006: 58). One of the newly fanaticized prisoners was Al-Zawahiri, who talks about the torture that took place in the

> "dirty Egyptian jails … where we suffered the severest inhuman treatment. There they kicked us, they beat us, they whipped us with electric cables, they shocked us with electricity! They shocked us with electricity! And they used the wild dogs! And they used the wild dogs! And they hung us over the edges of the doors"—here he bends over to demonstrate—"with our hands tied at the back! They arrested the wives, the mothers, the fathers, the sisters, and the sons!" (qtd. in Wright 2002)

---

43 Twenty-five of the defectors are also included in our other databases: 19 in the Muslim world sample and 6 in the Western world sample.

As a result, "Egypt's prisons," according to Wright, "became a factory for producing militants whose need for retribution—they called it 'justice'—was all-consuming" (2002).

Are the "Kamal response" and the "Ayman response" found in the same proportions across individuals with different degrees?

We found that 36 of the 81 dropouts in our sample (44.4 percent) had some form of higher education, which is roughly the same ratio as in our Muslim world sample; thus the level of education does not seem to have had any effect on the likelihood of defecting.

We also were able to determine the types of degrees 30 of the 36 individuals pursued (figure 3.9). Engineers are, proportionally, far *less* likely to defect relative to individuals with other degrees, and the key differences are dramatic: the odds of an engineer defecting are only 40 percent of what one would expect given their share among the radicals in our main sample, and the difference in the engineers' share among the main sample and defectors is statistically significant at $p < .01$. The odds of humanities students defecting are, by contrast, 14 times greater than what one would expect. That implies that, relative to engineers, the odds that humanities students defect are almost 40 times higher. The overrepresentation among defectors of humanities students as well as social science students is also statistically significant at $p < .01$.

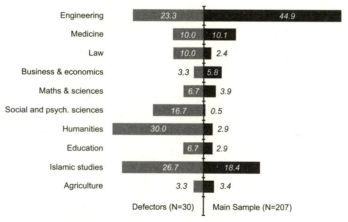

Figure 3.9: Discipline of study of defectors from Islamist violent groups.
    Note: Several of the defectors studied more than one subject; the counts are those of disciplines rather than individuals (resulting in a total of 41 counts for 30 individuals). Seven of these cases involve humanities, and in 3 of these 7 the second subject is a social science. But even if combined subjects are counted as half units, the outliers in figure 3.10 remain significant.
    Source: Authors' calculations.

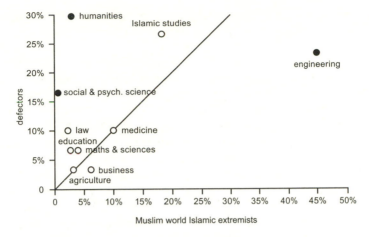

Difference between groups: ● significant ○ not significant

Figure 3.10: Discipline of study of defectors compared with the discipline of study of extremists in the Muslim sample.
Source: See footnote 41.

The engineers' behavior is a striking outlier—it resembles Ayman's response while everyone else's is much closer to Kamal's. Engineers seem to stay the course with greater determination than do those with other degrees, especially those in the humanities and social sciences.

Conclusions

Although taken in isolation each of the data sets we used in the preceding sections may be too limited to draw firm inferences, taken together they offer a striking confirmation that engineers who join radical political groups do so with a special intensity and devotion, and with a particular bias toward religious extremism. The affinity between radical Islamism and engineering seems to be both stronger and more robust to multiple ways of slicing the data—by militancy, religiosity, and tenacity—than the relative deprivation hypothesis by itself can account for. The latter explains the uniquely large share of engineers among the total pool of radicals in the Islamic world. However, it cannot make sense of their disproportionate presence among the (much smaller) stratum of radical university graduates in the West.

The peculiarity of engineers stands out even more when we consider doctors, whom we have encountered intermittently but not yet compared systematically with the engineers. While they are the only other group with a secular degree that is overrepresented in our Muslim world sample, the data pertaining to them differ from those of the engineers in several ways: doctors are less overrepresented in the Muslim world sample and not overrepresented at all in the Western sample (see figure 3.2); they are better represented than engineers among nonviolent Islamists; and, unlike engineers, when they have a choice, they prefer secular groups (see figures 3.6 and 3.7). They also defect in proportion to their presence from violent groups, rather than underproportionally, as do the engineers (figure 3.9). So even a group that appears socioeconomically similar to engineers differs systematically in its militant behavior.

While the relative deprivation hypothesis suffices to account for doctors' political mobilization in the Islamic world, it does not suffice to account for the levels, manners, and distribution of the engineers' radicalization. In order to establish which further factors might be involved we need to cast our net beyond Islamism.

The Ideology of Islamist Extremism Compared

ENGINEERS PREVAIL AMONG RADICAL ISLAMISTS IN VERY DIFFERENT CON-
texts and economic conditions, and display systematic tendencies toward
a draconian, devout, and determined kind of extremism. It is hard to
imagine how social circumstances alone could account for such peculiar-
ities. We suspect that either there are aspects of the education engineers
receive that shape them into suitable and eager recruits or that there is a
type of person who is susceptible to the lure of radical politics, a kind of
person found more frequently among engineers. In the former case the
effect would be caused by pursuing an engineering degree and would affect only those who do so. In the latter the effect would result from self-
selection: whatever the trait (or traits) that makes a certain type of person
more likely to choose engineering would also make that person more
likely to become an extremist. That trait would then not be limited to
people educated as engineers, and being an engineer would merely indicate a greater likelihood of its presence.

In addition to the source of these traits, their nature itself is an open
question, in the following sense: it could be a *generic* feature, that is,
engineers (or the traits they are more likely to carry) could be more
amenable to extremism per se regardless of which ideological makeup is
involved, or they could be attracted to only one specific ideological
package and not to another. Are they ready to jump on whatever extremist wagon hurtles by or are they choosy? If engineers were rudderless
hotheads, (1) we should find them overrepresented among extremists of
all stripes. If instead attraction was *conditional* on ideology, (2) their
presence should vary across the radical ideological spectrum—consistent
with the evidence we presented in the previous chapter indicating that
engineers, unlike doctors, are more inclined to join religious rather than
secular movements. This would be in line with a core assumption of political psychology, namely "that different psychological motives and tendencies underlie ideological differences" (Jost et al. 2003: 339).

If ideology does matter, is it just the *Islamist* radical variety that offers
a felicitous match for the engineers, or does any ideology sufficiently akin
to that of radical Islam provide the same appeal? In the former case (2a)
we should find no overrepresentation of engineers in any other extremist
group, while in the latter (2b) we should find engineers overrepresented

only at whichever end of the political spectrum offers a greater match with the ideological makeup of Islamist extremism, and not in any other.

In order to discover which of these predictions outlined above obtains we will investigate the type of education pursued by the members of violent extremist groups on both the right and the left sides of the political spectrum, in different countries and at different times. We will do this in the next chapter. Here, first of all, we want to establish in theory which of the last two predictions is more plausible, whether, that is, the ideology of radical Islam is sui generis or whether it is more akin to that of the extremists on the right or on the left. This is a worthwhile exercise in its own right, which as we shall see yields some surprising results.

HISTORICAL LINKS

The European far left initially supported the Iranian Revolution of 1979 as a popular uprising against the rule of the Shah, "a servant of the United States," to whom it had been vocally opposed for several years. Those on the far left soon changed their minds, however, as the reactionary nature of the new regime became clear when women's rights were revoked and homosexuals executed—which happened almost immediately. Only the French philosopher Michel Foucault persisted, describing the Ayatollah Khomeini as reflecting "the perfectly unified collective will" of the Iranian people and the revolution as "perhaps the first great insurrection against global systems, the form of revolt that is the most modern and most insane" (Afari and Anderson 2005: 179ff.). Some sections of the European left are sympathetic to peaceful Islamist opposition movements and broader, anti-Israeli nationalist movements such as Hamas and Hezbollah. But there are no signs of sympathy for the smaller violent networks that attack their own regimes or the West, which are the main focus of this book. Perhaps more important, there are no signs of cooperation between leftist militants in the West and Islamists.

The Western left has manifested sympathy for fundamentalists in Iran and Palestine more because of perceived Western-supported oppression than because of ideological affinity. Far from ephemeral were instead the links of the radical left in the West with *secular* militant movements in the Islamic world: the German RAF had close ties to the PFLP in Palestine, while the Red Brigades enjoyed support from the PLO.[1] The PLO also organized joint bomb attacks with the IRA and provided both arms and

1 *New York Times*, 17 March 1982, www.nytimes.com/1982/03/17/world/around-the-world-red-brigades-leader-tells-of-ties-to-plo.html.

training for IRA and the socialist INLA in Ireland[2] while maintaining close links to various Latin American leftist groups (Oppenheimer 2009; Heritage Foundation 1983). Several left-wing militant and separatist groups in the United States, Europe, and Latin America, moreover, received support from the unbalanced but secular and socialist-leaning Libyan dictator Muammar Qadhafi during the 1980s (Smith and Morgan 1994: 45–46).

While the militant left has kept its distance from radical Islam, there is, conversely, considerable historical evidence showing connections between the far right and Islamist movements and extremists. The Islamophobic sentiments found in some far-right groups today—such as the English Defence League—are a recent phenomenon, emerging from the anti-immigration movements that have been growing everywhere in Europe over the last quarter century. During the 1930s and 1940s, important sections of political movements in the Islamic world found points of convergence with fascism and Nazism.

The history of their links, while now known only to specialists, is rich and complex, as can be gauged from the account of Fabei (2003), a historian who researched this topic in depth. Amin al-Husseini, for instance, grand mufti of Jerusalem from 1921 to 1937, entertained close links with the dictatorial regimes in Italy and in Germany. Hitler, with whom Amin met, promised him the leadership of the Arab world after the British defeat. Leading Nazis professed sympathy for the Islamic religion; both Hitler and Himmler declared that they preferred its manly and "soldierly" virtues over those of soft Christianity (Motadel 2015). It is not very well-known that both the German and the Italian armies formed military units with Muslim volunteers who fought alongside the Axis troops in World War II (Fabei 2003, chapters 21–24). The Egyptian Muslim Brothers also set up "a paramilitary organization whose slogan 'action, obedience, silence' echoed the 'believe, obey, fight' motto of the Italian Fascists" (Boroumand and Boroumand 2002: 7). Wright (2006: 39) similarly claims that the "germ" of fascism was transmitted to the Middle East via ascending radical Islamism in Egypt toward the end of World War II.

To some extent cooperation between Islamic movements and European fascists was driven by shared antagonism to Zionism and the colonial powers of France and Britain (in fact, this cooperation went beyond Islamism and extended to nationalist leaders from Syria, Iraq, and Egypt). Yet the rapport between the far right and Islamist extremists goes deeper than the pursuits of shared interest. It reaches beyond World War II and rests also on common values, beliefs, and even, oddly enough, literary and iconographic tastes.

2 *Jerusalem Post*, 7 April 2009, www.jpost.com/Opinion/Op-Ed-Contributors/IRA-PLO -cooperation-A-long-cozy-relationship.

Shared Values

Julius Evola (b. 1898, d. 1974), an at once esoteric and reactionary Italian thinker who condemned the materialism of modern civilization, and whose work has been inspiring European far-right politics since World War II, expressed admiration in his writings for the values of self-sacrifice and heroism that are part of the concept of jihad (Weinberg 2003: 286). In the early 1990s Evola's writings, already translated into several languages, even started to feed back on their source of inspiration and became known in the Islamic world.[3]

There are also a few individuals who entertained far-right convictions and converted to Islam without shedding their right-wing ideas. First and foremost is Johann von Leers (b. 1902, d. 1965), an early member of the Nazi party and honorary Sturmbannführer in the Waffen SS who was a leading Nazi ideologue and anti-Semitic propagandist (Rees 1990: 227). After the war, he went first to Argentina and then to Egypt where he was welcomed by Amin al-Husseini, the former grand mufti we already encountered. There he continued his anti-Jewish propaganda in his support of Nasser's regime and eventually converted to Islam, changing his name to Omar Amin. Next there is Aribert Ferdinand Heim (b. 1914, d. 1992), who, as revealed by the *New York Times* in February 2009, was "a member of Hitler's Waffen-SS and a medical doctor at the Buchenwald, Sachsenhausen and Mauthausen concentration camps"; he also ended up in Egypt in 1962 after being identified by Nazi hunters, converted to Islam, and took the name Tarek Hussein Farid. Like many Nazi war criminals, Heim lived safely in Egypt for perhaps as long as three decades. Both he and Omar Amin seem to have converted out of conviction as much as convenience, as both are described as having become very devout.[4] There were at least 120 known Nazi fugitives in the Middle East, many of whom converted.[5]

Also worth mentioning, finally, is Ahmed Huber (b. 1927, d. 2008), a Swiss German who converted to Islam, once again under the influence of Amin al-Husseini, whom he met in 1965, as well as of Johann von Leers. At meetings of far-right groups around the world, Huber stressed the points of convergence between National Socialism and Islamist principles—such

---

3 Claudio Mutti, a sympathizer of and an autodidact writing about Evola, provides details of the two-way relations between the philosopher and Islam in an essay called "Islam in the Eyes of Julius Evola," www.claudiomutti.com/index.php?url=6&imag=1 &id_news=130.

4 *New York Times*, 4 February 2009, www.nytimes.com/2009/02/05/world/africa/05nazi .html?pagewanted=all.

5 http://mobile.nytimes.com/2015/01/11/sunday-review/old-nazis-never-die.html?referrer =&_r=0.

as opposing usury, homosexuality, and degenerate art— and viewed both National Socialism and Islam as antimodern forces.[6]

> [H]e attended a private assembly [in Chicago, in the 1990s] that brought together, in Huber's words, "the authentic Right and the fighters for Islam." Huber told journalist Richard Labeviere that "major decisions were taken [in Chicago].... [T]he reunification is under way." Huber acknowledges meeting al-Qaeda operatives on several occasions at Muslim conferences in Beirut, Brussels and London. (Lee 2002)

This "empathy" with Islamists is not limited to "old Nazis." In recent times, thanks to their shared hatred of Israel and the United States, radical Islamist and neo-Nazi groups have had frequent contacts in Germany.[7] Western neo-Nazi movements have come out in support of the Islamic revolution in Iran and Ayatollah Khomeini's fatwa against British novelist Salman Rushdie (Lee 2002). More recently, numerous Western right-wing extremists and Holocaust deniers have been hosted and supported by the Ahmedinejad government in Iran (Maegerle 2006). Founded in the late 1980s, the Stockholm-based extremist radio channel and later website Radio Islam has been promoting "contact between Islamists, neo-Nazis and Holocaust deniers, and publishes standard anti-Jewish works" (Whine 1999: 131).

On many and diverse occasions right-wing extremists have appeared in the company of Islamist ones. In Germany, for example, Horst Mahler— a lawyer and member of the Baader-Meinhof Gang who later recanted terrorism only to join the National Democratic Party, a neo-Nazi party— attended a convention of the Islamist movement Hizb ut-Tahrir in Berlin in 2002 (Eschenhagen 2004). Hizb ut-Tahrir was banned from Germany in 2003: "The organization supports the use of violence as a means to realize political interests," the German interior minister Otto Schily said. He added, "The organization is still more dangerous in that it has also sought contact with the far-right.... It must be quite clear that such organizations have no business in Germany."[8]

In the United States, Louis Farrakhan, head of the Nation of Islam, a black supremacist group, also entertained relations with local neo-Nazis:

---

6 http://en.wikipedia.org/wiki/Johann_von_Leers; http://en.wikipedia.org/wiki/Aribert _Heim; http://en.wikipedia.org/wiki/Ahmed_Huber. For a similar more recent case of conversion from Nazi to devout Muslim in the UK, see http://en.wikipedia.org/wiki/ David_Myatt. George Michael's book (2006) offers ample evidence about Huber and Myatt, whom he interviewed.
7 *Washington Post*, 16 January 2003, http://news.google.com/newspapers?nid=2482 &dat=20030116&id=S5FJAAAAIBAJ&sjid=NwwNAAAAIBAJ&pg=2480,33981.
8 Ibid.

Former Klan and White Aryan Resistance leader Tom Metzger was so impressed with Farrakhan's anti-Semitic bombast that he donated $100 to NOI after attending a Farrakhan rally in Los Angeles in September 1985. Given that white supremacists share NOI's belief in separation of the races, a month later, Metzger and 200 other white supremacists from the United States and Canada gathered on a farm about 50 miles west of Detroit, where they pledged their support for the Nation of Islam. (Lee 2002)[9]

In a related move, August Kreis, head of the Aryan Nations, a white supremacist U.S. movement, said of the 9/11 attackers, "I don't believe that they were the ones that attacked us. And even if they did, even if you say they did, I don't care!" Kreis says that the Aryan Nations and Al-Qaida share the same enemies: Jews and the American government.[10] He was not alone in making these statements.

Admiration for the culture of self-sacrifice manifested in Evola's writings resurfaced after 9/11: "An official of America's premier neo-Nazi group, the National Alliance, said he wished his own members had 'half as much testicular fortitude'" as those who carried out the attacks. "The Philadelphia-based American Front thinks highly of Osama bin Laden, too, describing him as 'one of ZOG [Zionist Occupation Government, the name many extremists give to the U.S. federal government, which they believe is run by Jews] and the New World Order's biggest enemies'" (Lee 2002).

Again, admiration for Al Qaida was not just a U.S. phenomenon. Celebrations of 9/11 were held at the headquarters of the French Front National. In Germany "neo-Nazis, some wearing chequered Palestinian headscarves, rejoiced at street demonstrations while burning an American flag. Jan Kopal, head of the Czech National Social Bloc, declared at a rally in Prague that bin Laden was 'an example for our children.' Horst Mahler ... proclaimed his solidarity with the terrorists and said 'America had gotten what it deserved'" (Lee 2002).

SHARED TASTES AND BELIEFS

In searching for ideological links between far-right and Islamist extremists, we discovered unexpected similarities of a different kind: a shared

9 As early as the 1960s, the Nation of Islam, in a surreal twist, entertained relations with members of the Ku Klux Klan and even invited the American Nazi Party chief George Lincoln Rockwell to address a Nation of Islam convention in Chicago (Lee 2002).
10 CNN, 29 March 2005, http://articles.cnn.com/2005-03-29/us/schuster.column_1 _aryan-nation-qaeda-white-supremacists?_s=PM:US; Michael 2006: 140–42.

Figure 4.1: "Islamicised" images from the film *The Fellowship of the Ring*.
Source: http://occident.blogspot.com/2009/12/cyber-jihadis-lord-of-rings-obsession
.html.

backward-looking aesthetic of chivalry and of medieval (Islamic and European) myths. Jihadi publications and websites are cluttered with pictures of knights, swords, horses, and medieval figures such as Salah al-Din (Combatting Terrorism Center 2006). Extreme rightists similarly are obsessed with medieval imagery and ancient, often Norse, myths. *Braveheart* and *Gladiator* are among the favorite movies of U.S. neo-Nazis.[11]

Most rightists and at least some radical Islamists are also fans of Tolkien's trilogy *The Lord of the Rings*. In the 1970s, the Italian neo-fascists named a paramilitary camp Campo Hobbit, after one of the characters in Tolkien's book, which they interpreted as a fascist fantasy. As can be evinced from several websites, fascists read the books as an anti-immigration story and long for a lost mythical past that is woven throughout Tolkien's work. This passion for grandiloquent literature, which imposes no realistic constraints on the self-righteous delirium omnipotentiae of its heroes, is seen in the writings of Gianluca Casseri, a neo-fascist author and self-styled intellectual, who in December 2011 shot two Senegalese immigrants in Florence before taking his own life.[12] A sizable portion of Casseri's texts were devoted to Tolkien and kindred writers. As remarked by Stephen Shapiro, professor of English literature at Warwick University, "[Tolkien's] books came out in the 1950s coinciding with the start of immigration into Britain and neo-Nazis are interpreting them in that way.... Tolkien wrote *The Lord of the Rings* because he believed England's original culture and mythology was destroyed by the Norman invasion, and thought his story-cycle would recreate the world of pre-invasion Britain."[13]

11 Thomas Hegghammer, personal communications with the authors, 2015. A good example of medieval imagery is Anders Breivik's video manifesto: http://crooksandliars
.com/david-neiwert/norway-terrorist-anders-breivik-leav.
12 *The Guardian*, 13 December 2011, www.guardian.co.uk/world/2011/dec/13/florence
-gunman-shoots-street-vendors.
13 *Birmingham Post*, 18 December 2002, http://icbirmingham.icnetwork.co.uk/0800
whatson/tolkien/news/page.cfm?objectid=12463394&method=full&siteid=50002.

Odder still is that jihadi radicals have also used the imagery of *The Lord of the Rings* films on some of their websites and have superimposed their messages over the film images. According to Christopher Anzalone, an American scholar at the Institute of Islamic Studies at McGill University, "In my research on Islamist artwork and visual media, I have surprisingly discovered that some cyber *jihadi* dorks are just as obsessed with J.R.R. Tolkien's classic series *The Lord of the Rings* as some non-*jihadi* dorks. They view themselves, with one exception, not as the forces of the dark lord Sauron and his wizard ally Saruman, but as the Fellowship and its allies in Gondor, Rohan, and the Elven kingdoms."[14]

While the *Lord of the Rings* link is limited to a few jihadi websites, it reflects a broader shared taste for chivalry and millenarian mythology.[15] We can speculate as to which particular ingredients of the *Lord of the Rings* narrative strike a chord with both militant right-wingers and Islamists: a Manichean world divided into camps of good and evil, a backward-looking quest to restore a mythical lost order, and a leading role for a small vanguard of heroes struggling against betrayal and conspiracy. Even when jihadis do not refer to Tolkien explicitly, their bombastic and baroque rhetoric can resemble his style: according to a 2007 *New Yorker* profile, now-deceased American Al-Qaida spokesperson Adam Gadahn on occasion "sounds like a character from 'The Lord of the Rings'" (Khatchadourian 2007).

As a further sign that jihadists and right-wingers represent a particularly dangerous brand of "geekiness," many of them also appear to be into computer gaming: Norwegian far-right mass murderer Anders Behring Breivik locked himself up for about a year in his mother's flat in Oslo to play the online role-playing game "World of Warcraft" reportedly for sixteen hours a day.[16] Western right-wing groups are known to disseminate racist, violent computer games.[17] Similarly, ISIS has used modified "first-person shooter" computer games as a recruitment tool.[18] Online jihadi communities as well as at least one U.S. white supremacist online forum have been "gamified," allowing members to collect points and badges for

14 Anzalone gives many more details about the iconographic tastes of radical Islamists on his website, from which the quote is taken: http://occident.blogspot.com/2009/12/cyber-jihadis-lord-of-rings-obsession.html.

15 Thomas Hegghammer, personal communications with the authors, 2015.

16 www.telegraph.co.uk/news/worldnews/europe/norway/9207691/Anders-Behring-Breivik-spent-a-year-playing-World-of-Warcraft-role-playing-game-online.html.

17 www.adl.org/combating-hate/domestic-extremism-terrorism/c/racist-groups-use-computer.html.

18 english.alarabiya.net/en/variety/2014/09/20/Grand-Theft-Auto-ISIS-Militants-reveal-video-game.html.

their posting activities.[19] We have not found evidence of similar activities on the left.

The magical, prescientific setting of *The Lord of the Rings* might be a further attraction. In our review of ideologies, we discovered that Islamists and right-wingers also share a multipronged range of beliefs about how the world works that include superstition, mythology, and esotericism, all of which are rarely held by left-wing extremists.

While left-wing radicalism is rooted in the Enlightenment and in a belief in scientific progress (however oddly framed by dialectical materialism), right-wing and Islamist extremists share an antiscientific worldview. Nazis denounced "Jewish science" and abhorred the Enlightenment. Several leading Nazis such as Himmler and Rosenberg (incidentally also an engineer) held esoteric beliefs, and occultist groups like the Thule Society had strong links to the Nazi movement.[20] Many modern right-wing movements remain fascinated by heathen cults and by Norse and Germanic mythology; Ferracuti and Bruno (1981) list superstition and a belief in magic as core traits among post–World War II Italian right-wing terrorists. Contemporary ideologues like German Jan Udo Holey mix right-wing extremism, conspiracy theories, antiscientism, and esotericism into a reactionary ideological cocktail.[21] Radical Islam, too, while austere, has its pageant of spirits, jinns, witchcraft, and so forth that occupy the minds of salafi radicals in particular, as these phenomena have a literal basis in the scripture and hadiths.[22] As Thomas Hegghammer wrote to us:

> Radical Islamists are open to a whole range of explanations for why things happen the way they do, explanations that we would dismiss as belonging to the realm of superstition. Dreams and visions, for example, are extremely important to them and form the basis for many important decisions (joining, leaving, volunteering for operations, launching campaigns, etc.). They also firmly believe in the possibility of divine intervention, notably in battle. They talk extensively about how corpses of martyrs emit beams of light, speak after death and don't decompose, despite the fact that many will have observed the grim realities of death in the battlefield. I think this belief that the world does not function completely according to Western laws of physics is a very important part of their mindset. (Personal communication with the authors, January 2012)

19 foreignpolicy.com/2011/04/13/the-world-of-holy-warcraft/.
20 On "brown esotericism," see www.esowatch.com/ge/index.php?title=Braune_Esoterik.
21 http://en.wikipedia.org/wiki/Jan_Udo_Holey.
22 See Roy 1990 for the superficial and mechanical understanding of "science" among modern Islamist intellectuals more broadly.

Among ISIS members in Iraq and Syria, the belief in ancient prophecies is widespread. Beliefs in conspiracy theories and tales of betrayal are also common among neo-Nazis and radical Islamists. While the radical left is prone to a conspiratorial worldview too, right-wingers and Islamists sometimes share the very *same* conspiracies: consider their shared belief in the veracity of *The Protocols of the Elders of Zion*, a text dating to the late nineteenth century, most likely a forgery by the tsarist secret police, which describes a meeting of prominent Jews conspiring to achieve world domination.[23]

RADICAL IDEOLOGIES COMPARED

The greater similarity of values and beliefs between Islamist and right-wing extremists rather than left-wing extremists rests on evidence that, while anecdotal, is quite strong. But we need to take a more systematic step: we need to establish the extent to which the core ideological traits of Islamist ideology are sui generis or shared by other extremists. To this end, we compiled a list of ideological tenets of radical Islam and, after a review of the literature on Islamist ideology and consultation with experts on radical Islamism, identified fifteen key ones (table 4.1) that all radical Islamist groups manifest to some degree.[24] We then determined which of these tenets are also present in the extreme right or the extreme left and found that thirteen of these features are clearly shared with the extreme right while two are partially shared. This overlap is marked with ✓ and (✓), respectively. By contrast, only five elements are shared with the extreme left, and only one of these is shared more perhaps with the left than the right, the rejection of Western cultural imperialism. There is not a single trait that radical Islam shares *only* with the left.[25]

Social conservatism and a focus on (real or invented) traditions is perhaps the most obvious trait that Islamism and right-wing radicalism have in common. The two movements also share a corporatist, mechanistic, and hierarchical view of the ideal society.[26] Extremist Islamist literature

23 Hamas even mentions the "Protocols" in its 1988 founding charter; http://avalon.law
.yale.edu/20th_century/hamas.asp.
24 We exclude nationalism, which can be present or absent in all kinds of Islamist groups.
We also exclude the beliefs in mystical and magical events as these are found mostly
among jihadi salafis and less so in other Islamist groups.
25 For further arguments about the similarity of Islamism and fascism, see Arjomand
1986 and Rodinson 1978.
26 The founding father of Egyptian militant Islam, Sayyid Qutb, explicitly compares
Islamic society to a "body" because it is a community of believers (Loboda 2004: 29).
Oswald Mosley of the British Union of Fascists, describing fascist corporatism, said
that "it means a nation organized as the human body, with each organ performing its

TABLE 4.1
Features of Islamist ideology compared with right-wing and left-wing extremist ideology

	Right	Left
Traditionalism (including women's subordination)	✓	×
Corporatist/organic view of society	✓	×
Hierarchical view of social order	✓	×
Acceptance of social inequality	✓	×
Authoritarian vision of order, rejection of popular sovereignty	✓	×
Anti-Semitism	✓	×
Restoration of a lost order, nostalgia of a mythical past	✓	×
View of society as polluted and corrupt, in need of purification	✓	×
Membership of militants in rigidly defined in-group	✓	×
Rejection of pluralism and political competition	✓	✓
Monocausal view of origin and solution of social problems	✓	✓
Rigid division of the world into opposing camps	✓	✓
Violence as a legitimate means of political action	✓	✓
Rejection of Western cultural "imperialism"	(✓)	✓
A lifestyle highly regulated by routines (especially among salafis)	(✓)	×

Sources: Based on Hegghammer 2009a, 2009b; ICG 2005; Shepard 1987; Wagemakers 2008; Wiktorowicz 2005, 2006; personal exchanges with experts on radical Islam.

rejects Western pluralism and democracy and argues for a unified, ordered society ruled by a strong and just Islamic leader according to clear laws, in which an unassailable division of labor is created between men and women, Muslims and non-Muslims, leaders and their flock. Even if the components differ, right-wing movements pursue similarly hierarchical

---

individual function but working in harmony with the whole" (Eccleshall et al. 1994: 208, cited in http://en.wikipedia.org/wiki/Corporatism). Schulze has detected a "cybernetic view of society" in modern Islamism (1990: 22), which aims at preserving integrity in the social order. On corporatism in Islam, see Cantori 1997 and Ayubi 1993.

and authoritarian social models implying the promotion or at least toleration of social inequality.[27]

The fear of chaos undermining the established social order is also a leitmotif of Islamist thought (Hoffman 1995: 218–19) that echoes loudly among right-wing thinking. Unlike left-wing extremism, which aims at sharing power and privilege more widely and equally, right-wing extremism aims to restore a lost, often mythical order of privileges and authority, and emerges as a backlash against displacement or status deprivation in a period of sharp social change (Lipset and Raab 1971; Ferracuti and Bruno 1981). The resemblance to radical Islamist ideology is undeniable: the theme of returning to the order of the prophet's early community is omnipresent in most jihadist texts, especially those of salafis, and radical Islam more broadly strives to rehabilitate the glorious past of the Islamic "ummah" (Shepard 1987).

This glorious past has given way to an ignominious present because society has become polluted and corrupt, and is in need of purification. Radical right-wing movements aim for ethnic and cultural purification, Islamists aim for religious purification, and both aim for a purity of social mores.[28] Liberal decadence needs to be fought, violently if necessary. God's law needs to be rigorously implemented to bring about social order (Shepard 1987: 314–15; Rodinson 1979). Militant salafis in particular—the variant of radicals that have come to dominate violent Islamism during the last two decades or so—are obsessed with cleansing Muslim creed and society of deviant elements, with disassociating themselves from nonbelievers and "bad" Muslims, and with separating "halal" (permitted) from "haram" (forbidden).[29] (Non-salafi) Sayyid Qutb was obsessed with the dangers of sexual seduction and homosexuality (Wright 2006: 14–15; Loboda 2004: 14); the latter at least has been a bugbear of right-wingers around the world, too.

27 While some proponents of radical Islam such as Muslim Brother Sayyid Qutb believe in the socioeconomic equality of believers in the ideal Muslim society (Loboda 2004), all envisage broader inequalities such as the subordination of non-Muslim communities and women. For radical salafis, who are strongly represented in our sample, "economic inequality usually comes after wars against Muslims, secular legislation, and police repression in their list of grievances" (Thomas Hegghammer, email correspondence with the authors, April 2015). While there have been socialist elements in fascism and Nazism, in practice these movements have cared little about distributional issues. Post–World War II U.S. right-wing terrorists in particular are known for their "opposition to affirmative action, welfare, and educational programs for the economically disadvantaged that exclude nonminorities … terrorists of the right have little sympathy for the wayward and dispossessed" (Smith and Morgan 1994: 46).

28 Rodinson (1979: 8) points to the dominant image of "Islam as guardian, guarantor, surety, and protector of traditional morals."

29 For an analysis of salafis' obsession with drawing boundaries between themselves and unbelievers and improper Muslims, see Wagemakers 2008.

For both Islamists and right-wingers, the distinction between the in-group to which they belong and the out-group that they fight is an essential and immutable feature of their identity, while on the left such distinctions are more circumstantial: one has to be a Muslim to fight for the ummah, and one needs to be a white American to belong to the Aryan Nation, but one does not need to be a worker to fight for the working class; as we will see in chapter 5, most leading leftist radicals around the world have fought on behalf of classes they themselves are not part of. Drawing identity boundaries and defining one's own belonging are core preoccupations on the right and among Islamists.

Even the last two features of Islamist ideology listed in table 4.1—rejection of Western cultural imperialism and highly regulated lifestyles—are shared by some right-wing groups or ideologues. The rejection of cultural Westernization as a debased form of modernity is prominent among ideologues such as the above-mentioned Julius Evola. His *Revolt against the Modern World*, which first appeared in 1934, was published in Turkish in 2006. Both right-wing and Islamist groups purport to fight foreign cultural influences that threaten to corrupt their societies—a claim that is often laced with anti-Semitic rhetoric. As Lee (2002) points out,

> The peculiar bond between white nationalist groups and certain Muslim extremists derives in part from a shared set of enemies—Jews, the United States, race-mixing, ethnic diversity. It is also very much a function of the shared belief that they must shield their own peoples from the corrupting influence of foreign cultures and the homogenizing juggernaut of globalization. Both sets of groups also have a penchant for far-flung conspiracy theories that caricature Jewish power.

Many right-wing and Islamist groups also share a belief in a highly regulated lifestyle with fixed routines,[30] although in the latter group the routines consist of religious rituals (particularly among salafis) and in the former they are militaristic. Hitler himself admired the structure that Islam provides in daily life: "The precepts ordering people to wash, to avoid certain drinks, to fast at appointed dates, to take exercise, to rise with the sun, to climb to the top of the minaret—all these were obligations invented by intelligent people," he remarked in October 1941 (Motadel 2015).

So, if we abstract from the transcendental beliefs that by definition concern religiously inspired groups such as the Islamists, there is a near complete coincidence between the ideological cocktail of Islamist extremism and that of right-wing extremism. Not even religiosity is a watertight

---

30 Islam more broadly has been characterized as a religion of law and rules, like Judaism but unlike Christianity (Goldziher 1981; Schacht 1982).

divide as several far-right groups, especially white supremacists in the United States, are manifestly religious and adorn their insignia with religious symbolism, albeit Christian rather than Muslim. The traits that radical Islamism shares with both left and right, by contrast, are more generic, to the extent that they arguably form part of the definition of political extremism: rejection of pluralism, a simplified view of the causes and remedies for social problems, a polarized worldview, and a belief in the legitimacy of political violence.

Many Islamist militants have limited interest in details of doctrine, and the Islamic society they are fighting for remains a long-term, fuzzy, and contested concept. Most are motivated by concrete social and political frustrations, on which militant Islamist movements give them opportunities to act. Yet, as Stern has shown (2003) through a wide range of first-person interviews, even the foot soldiers of radical Islamism usually fight for the reestablishment of a strong social order, want to reassert their cultural and religious identity in the face of perceived humiliation, share a hatred for the West and other out-groups, are socially conservative, and aim to purify society in some fashion.[31] Many of these traits are pre-ideological and are manifested in concrete action as much as in abstract political pamphlets and debates. At least on the margin, they will influence individuals' decisions to join or not to join a movement. Incidentally, Stern has interviewed not only Islamist militants but also right-wing fundamentalists in the United States and Israel, who in her account share the same outlook on the world.

The world of radical Islam is complex and ideologies are not identical across groups. One might argue, for example, that salafist radical groups come closest to ticking all the boxes in table 4.1, while larger and better-established Islamist movements like Hamas are less doctrinaire on moral and ritual issues, have accepted elements of democracy, and have added secular objectives such as socioeconomic equality to their agenda. But there is little doubt that they remain closer to the ideal type we have constructed than do leftist movements.

Conclusions

The cultural context and philosophies that inspire the ideological tenets of radical Islamism and right-wing extremism differ. Although it is remarkable that they should generate so many similarities of sentiment and

---

31 Khosrokhavar's interview-based research on Islamist extremists around the world uncovers similar themes of perceived humiliation coupled with anti-Westernism and a desire for order and moral and cultural purification (Khosrokhavar 2005).

belief, it is hardly surprising that they also produce differences. These would include, of course, religiosity, as not all right-wing movements are religious, and some are in fact antireligious. This carries further differences downstream; for instance, among right-wingers the quest for purity does not necessarily imply a puritan sexual morality. Recall the propaganda pictures of naked Nazis frolicking in the woods to promote health and parade Aryan beauty. On the other hand, right-wingers conceive of purity in racial terms, while Islamists do not. Moreover, Islamists may accept social inequality, but they do so passively rather than promoting it in the name of some "Darwinian" philosophy. In a related area, order for Islamists is the result of social conformity to a religious law, while for right-wingers order is due either to a strong central power organizing the national community or to the spontaneous working of some "law of the jungle," in some cases through unbridled market forces. Finally, while some right-wingers reject cultural modernity and invoke traditional values, others embody a muscular version of Western cultural imperialism. Islamists, by contrast, are more like the former and focus exclusively on defending their culture.

Yet, the overlap of weltanschauung between radical Islamism and right-wing extremism and the near complete lack of overlap with left-wing extreme ideology are striking. It suggests that if "engineers" are attracted to extremism other than that of the Islamist kind, it would be to right-wing extremism and not left-wing.

The Education of Other Extremists

IF THE MATCH BETWEEN ENGINEERS AND ISLAMIST EXTREMISM WERE DUE to some unknown factor unique to this type of movement, engineers should not be overrepresented in any other violent group, whether on the left or the right. If, by contrast, engineers were "hotheads" and had some personality trait that made them more prone than other graduates to take radical action of whatever kind, we should find a significant presence of engineers in other violent groups regardless of the type of group. Finally, if, as we conjecture in chapter 4, ideology did matter in sorting different individuals into different types of groups, we should find engineers significantly present only on the right because its ideological makeup strongly overlaps with that of Islamist extremism.

Armed with these conjectures, we assembled data on the education of an assortment of extremists, members of either left- or right-wing groups, both before and after World War II, who adhere to ideologies that support the use of violence as a means for pursuing their political goals. We created several data sets from a wide range of primary sources, supplementing them with information drawn from academic literature. Although of course the information we gathered did not encompass all violent extremist groups, it embraces an array that is rich enough and diverse enough to reveal any of the potential patterns mentioned in the opening to this chapter.

In gathering and analyzing all of these data we achieve something else. As we will see in chapter 6, political psychologists have provided strong evidence that left- and right-wing attitudes are linked to different cognitive traits (Jost et al. 2003). Still, some authors claim that the traits linked to extremism in particular are the same for those on both left and right (e.g., Greenberg and Jonas 2003). We can contribute to this debate from a new, powerful angle: the psychological tests in this literature are usually based on self-reported attitudes ascertained through questionnaires. Our empirical analysis in this chapter will, by contrast, show whether ideologies have different *behavioral* correlates by determining whether they systematically attract different people from different disciplines into *militant action*—a very costly step to take.

Focusing on such costly behavior is likely to reflect deep-seated preferences and personality traits more accurately than the anonymous and cost-free choice of placing oneself on left-right or psychometric scales in a questionnaire. Should the educational profile of militants vary systematically across ideological camps, this would be strong evidence that different extremist ideologies do indeed attract different "types." What we assume at this point is simply that the discipline of choice is a reflection of certain traits that discriminate among extremist ideologies, even though we do not know what these traits are.

LEFT-WING EXTREMISTS

To establish the educational profile of left-wing extremists, we collected primary data on militants in post–World War II Germany and Italy and surveyed the academic literature on left-wing militants in the United States, Latin America, and Asia.

The Rote Armee Fraktion (RAF)—a.k.a. Baader-Meinhof Gang—was a violent left-wing group that had its roots in the 1960s student movement and was active in what was then West Germany. During a quarter of a century of activity, the RAF killed thirty-eight individuals, among them judges, industrialists, and American military personnel. By the standards of political violence, their lethality was miniscule. But judging by the political and institutional storm the RAF unleashed, which shook the establishment and brought tanks to the streets of West Germany, it proved supremely cost-effective. The tiny size of RAF's membership—eighty-nine are known to the police—makes their efficacy all the more striking.

The founders—Andreas Baader, Gudrun Ensslin, Ulrike Meinhof, and Jan-Carle Raspe—died in jail. Meinhof apparently hung herself in 1976 (this is still seriously disputed). The others, facing the prospect of spending their lives in prison, killed themselves a year later in an apparent suicide pact intended to make the state appear responsible for their deaths (this version, too, is contested). Over the years most of the other members were caught and sentenced to jail; a few were killed in violent clashes with police. In 1998 the few still at large sent a letter to the press announcing their decision to disband.

Those who have now been released from jail live quiet lives, seldom coming to media attention. Not Horst Mahler, though, whom we mentioned in the last chapter and whose claim to infamy has taken a surreal turn. A lawyer and member of the original Baader-Meinhof Gang, he later recanted terrorism and was released from jail early, in 1980. He went on to join the NDP, a neo-Nazi party. In February 2009—exactly sixty years after his father, "a fanatical Nazi and anti-Semite [dentist], shot himself"—Mahler, who is now nearly eighty, was sentenced to six years in jail for posting videos on the Internet denying the Holocaust and distributing CDs promoting anti-Semitic hatred.[1]

---

1 The information on the RAF is derived from Aust 2008 and Gambetta 2010.

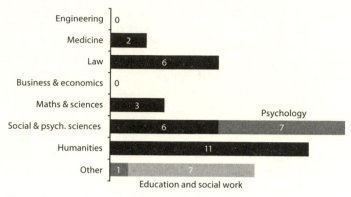

Figure 5.1: Disciplines of study of members of the Rote Armee Fraktion (33 individuals, 43 disciplines).
Sources: Aust 2008; Jäger et al. 1981; von Bayer-Katte et al. 1983; Wikipedia; www.rafinfo.de; web and newspaper archive survey.

We collected educational data on the RAF's entire membership, 89 males and females. Like other left-wing groups, RAF members had a high level of education: at least 35 (39 percent) attended university. For 33 of these we know the discipline(s) they studied; because several individuals studied more than one discipline, the total count of subjects is 43.[2] The humanities and social and psychological sciences were the most frequently studied disciplines (see figure 5.1).[3] Law constitutes a sizable contingent, but a far less dominant one, as we shall see, than among neo-Nazis. We found three scientists who had been active in the RAF but no engineers.[4] One of the scientists, Ulrich Scholze, a physics student, now reportedly works as a professor of engineering at a polytechnic institute in southern Germany. His case might be the closest any engineer ever came to this movement.[5] He decided to drop out of the group after only a few

2 As far as the tables in this chapter report subjects of study directly, university education is recorded even if it is incomplete. When the number of subjects is higher than the number of individuals with university exposure in all of the tables, this is due to the fact that some individuals studied more than one subject.
3 The figure includes 19 women. Taking them out changes the distribution of the most frequent degrees (law becomes the most prominent subject with 5 counts out of a total of 20, while psychology drops from 7 cases to 1 and education and social work from 7 to 2), but the fairly weak presence of sciences and the absence of engineering remain unchanged.
4 The dominance of social sciences and humanities degrees is also described in the detailed case study literature on the RAF; Jäger, Schmidtchen, and Süllwold 1981; Von Baeyer-Katte et al. 1983.
5 www.enotes.com/topic/Members_of_the_Red_Army_Faction; www.theweek.co.uk/25423/baader-meinhof-gang; http://maps.thefullwiki.org/Members_of_the_Red_Army_Faction.

months underground and moved back in with his mother to continue his studies.[6]

The absence of engineers did not prevent the RAF from deploying violence in an organized and highly effective fashion. At the same time, its political strategy was based on the dubious belief that the German state's oppressive retaliation to terror attacks would unleash a popular uprising. This shows that the radical left's strategies can be as quixotic and their theories of society as deluded as those of any extremist group.

The Italian Red Brigades, active during the same period as the RAF, were equally violent and operated underground, but they had more members and were better organized. Unlike their brethren in the RAF they were driven less by romantic empathy for the oppressed than by cool revolutionary zeal. They saw themselves as a Leninist vanguard sowing the seeds of a proletarian revolution. Like the RAF, they thought that by provoking the state into unleashing repression they would trigger a mass uprising. Unlike the RAF, the group was rooted in factories and counted working-class individuals and low-level technicians among its ranks. By 1982, when they began to fragment, the Red Brigades had killed at least 56 individuals and kneecapped or otherwise wounded 75 more—among them politicians, journalists, trade unionists, judges and law enforcement agents.[7] In 1982 the Italian government introduced legislation designed to provide incentives for left-wing militants to turn state's evidence, which very much helped the state crush the movement. (Interestingly, these incentives were later used by prosecutors for a purpose that was far from the legislators' original intentions: to fight the Sicilian mafia.) While phantom groups still surface sporadically claiming to be part of the Red Brigades, the group was effectively defeated by the Italian state and most of its key members jailed.

The educational profile of 120 members of the Red Brigades, about a quarter of the total membership, looks similar to that of the RAF: 47 (39 percent) have university exposure (23 of whom finished their degrees); of these we know the discipline for 39 cases (figure 5.2). Again, humanities and social sciences constitute the lion's share (22). Unlike the RAF, however, there is only 1 law student, while there are 8 scientists and 4 engineers.

In his memoirs Alberto Franceschini, one of the three founders of the group and one of the four engineers, writes that the only reason he enrolled in engineering was because of his father's pressure to do so. He adds that he was able to persuade his father to agree that, among the menu of

6 www.thefirstpost.co.uk/45715,features,briefing-the-baader-meinhof-gang.
7 Valeria Pizzini Gambetta's elaboration on data from Galleni 1981: 328–72 and Moss 1989: 67.

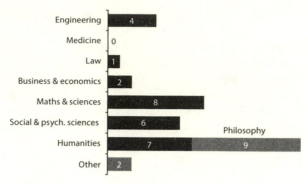

Figure 5.2: Members of the Red Brigades by discipline of study (39 individuals).
Source: Database collected by Valeria Pizzini Gambetta.

engineering subfields, he could pick mining—a specialization that he could use in support of Cuba because "Castro needed engineers who could explore for oil." Even so, halfway through the course Franceschini dropped out because "I hated the engineers, tied to an absurd profession made of schemes and numbers. I was imagining my life as a prison. Marriage, wife, children, everything laid out and organized" (Franceschini 1988: 15). How alien the engineering mentality appeared to some members of the group is brought home by Enrico Fenzi, a former member of the Red Brigades, who spent ten years in jail and is now a scholar of Dante: "among the brigatisti I met in Genoa there was a tinge of frustrated engineer-like positivism, which made them absolutely different from the other militants of the group and made them serious and pedantic" (2006: 54).[8]

One is tempted to think that being a radical leftist engineer is an unstable state that individuals cannot but leave—by quitting either one's left-wing group (as Scholze did) or engineering (as Franceschini did). The experience of Pasquale Pasquino, an Italian political scientist, reveals that the engineers he met in a smaller Italian extreme left-wing group either were extreme among extremists or dropped out:

> I belonged to Sinistra Universitaria, an extremist left-wing Neapolitan group active in 1967–70. I was a student of physics—only later I switched to philosophy. The leaders were professors at the institute of theoretical physics. In the group there were a few engineering students. They were amongst the most radical and toughest. Two of them I will not name saved themselves and dropped out at the last moment [be-

8 The Genoese branch of the Red Brigades had a higher concentration of skilled workers and technicians.

fore embarking on violent actions] and are now academics. A third one, the late Piero Losardo, joined a particularly vicious group, Il Collettivo di via dei Volsci, in Rome. Unlike myself, he did not revert back to a normal life, and I remember him as someone particularly aggressive and ferocious. I think he looked at me with suspicion because I was for the theory and he for the practice. (Personal communication with the authors, 2009)

Although we did not collect primary evidence on the educational profile of other post–World War II leftist radical groups from around the world, both the literature and specialists we consulted confirm the patterns we found in the German and Italian cases. Among leftists the level of education is high: in the United States "over one half of the leftists indicted during the 1980s for terrorist activities were college or university graduates" (Smith and Morgan 1994: 53; Handler 1990 reports similarly high levels of education); and as far as disciplines are concerned:

Violent leftist groups in our sample [of U.S. radicals] were more likely to have members who were physicians, attorneys, teachers, and even government workers. For example, the 18 members of the Macheteros indicted in 1986 for the 1983 robbery of the Wells Fargo Depot in West Hartford, Connecticut [were] all attorneys. Most of the remaining indictees in this case hold university degrees in political science, sociology, and anthropology and are employed as teachers, occupational therapists, and independent artisans. (Smith and Morgan 1994: 54)

In Latin America, left-wing radicals in the late 1960s were mostly urban-based graduates in the humanities, law, and medicine (Russell and Hildner 1971). Members of the Japanese Red Army were mostly university students or graduates, from liberal arts fields; only a few were medical doctors or students and one was a physicist (Patricia Steinhoff, personal communication with the authors, July 2006).[9] Engineers appear to be scarce in the radical left in India as well.[10]

9 Higher education patterns have proven harder to establish among another type of militant political groups, which are often left-leaning: separatists. The main reason is that graduates seem to constitute a tiny minority among them. Among a sample of 1,117 ETA members presented by Iribarren, only 1.8 percent were university graduates and 2 percent were university students (Iribarren 1998: 47, cited in Smith et al. 2003). Most members of Colombian FARC were poorly educated and of rural background (Hudson 1999: 106). IRA members similarly were mostly working class. Those among them who decided to pursue a degree in prison took mostly humanities courses (Heather Hamill, James Spencer, personal communications with the author, July 2006).

10 "My own sense of Indian higher education as well as Indian internal security (I am working on both areas) is that in the Indian case of the major extremist movements within the country (Kashmir, North East, SIMI, Hindu extremist groups, Maoists), there are actually very few engineers not just in the rank and file but also in the leadership. SIMI

RIGHT-WING EXTREMISTS

To construct comparison groups on the extreme right we collected information on neo-Nazis in Germany and Austria, in Russia, and in the
United States.

Neo-Nazis in Germany and Austria have often been as violent as the
radical left in Germany and Italy but typically have been less well and
centrally organized—an ironic finding given the European right's craving
for order. Rather than members of the political elite, their targets typically have been individuals on the social margins like immigrants or
sometimes the homeless, members of the radical left, or random pass-
ersby (killed or maimed by bombs planted in public places). From German unification in 1990 until 2013, according to one count right-wing
extremists killed 152 people in the country.[11] None of the radical right-
wing groups seems to have developed a strategic vision on the scale of the
RAF's—possibly because much of the radical right has been recruited
from the social periphery, a far cry from the intellectual elites of the RAF.
The violent right, it seems, consists of the weak looking for even weaker
targets.

Among 287 right-wing extremists and neo-Nazis in Germany and
Austria involved in 33 groups, we found only 32 individuals with higher
education and were able to establish the disciplines studied for 29
(among whom 4 studied more than one subject). The fact that we found
hardly any educational data on the remaining 258 cases probably reflects
lower levels of education on the extreme right, an assumption supported
by several sources.[12] Among radical right-wingers, the dominant degrees
are law (41 percent) and engineering (21 percent).[13] While law degrees
also have some presence on the left, this is not the case for engineering.

We collected information on 110 members of nine *Russian neo-Nazi
and extreme right-wing groups* as well as several networks of skinheads
identified in publications by Russian research institutes. Active since the
1990s, all these groups are strongly nationalistic and racist, and some of

---

(an Islamic student radical group) might be an exception" (Devesh Kapur, personal
communication with the authors, May 2011). SIMI is reported to be linked to the Indian
Mujahedeen (Fair 2010), which are represented in our Muslim world sample and do
indeed have a high share of engineers, 6 of 8 individuals with known higher education.
11 www.dw.de/germany-may-underestimate-right-wing-victims/a-17059028.
12 For the United States, see Smith and Morgan 1994: 53 and Handler 1990: 205. For
France and Germany, see Hudson 1999: 50ff. and Kolinksy 1988.
13 Twelve of the 258 cases are women, and 2 of them have pursued higher education; the
subject in both cases is education. Taking these two out would shrink the "other" bar in
figure 5.3 and change nothing else.

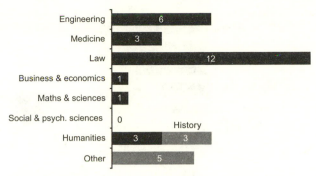

Figure 5.3: Discipline of study of Austrian and German neo-Nazis (29 individuals, 34 disciplines).
Note: "Other" includes education, journalism, agriculture, and modern languages.
Source: Antifaschistisches Autorenkollektiv; survey of German-language newspapers and journals; websites of movements; web and newspaper archive survey.

them have a marked religious component.[14] Their diffuse ideologies tend to combine racism and a mythological appreciation of the Russian race's struggle against the Mongols, the Ottomans and other "impure" peoples; Soviet imperialism (but not communism); and, in some cases, a rather improbable veneration of Nazism. Even by the standards of the militant right, Russian extremists appear to be particularly brutal and engaged in a variety of hate crimes. "Between January 2004 and May 2010, about 450 race murders were committed on Russian territory and more than 2,500 people were injured as a result of racist attacks" (Laryš and Mareš 2011: 137). In some cases, right-wing vigilantes record and post online "snuff videos" in which they kill immigrant victims (Laryš and Mareš 2011). Among major extremist groups, perhaps only the Islamic State (ISIS) in Iraq and Syria matches this level of brutality: even Al-Qaida has repeatedly rejected the practice of posting execution videos online because it revolts fellow Muslims.

Among the 110 members, 58 attended university.[15] This high proportion of individuals who went to college is not, however, indicative of the educational profile of the much larger membership of these groups, as we

14 The groups include the National Bolshevik Party, the National Socialist Society, Narodnyi Sobor, Narodnyi Soyuz, Spas, the Party for the Protection of the Russian Constitution ("Rus"), the Party of Freedom, the Russian Movement Against Illegal Immigration, Russian Truth, and various smaller and less formal skinhead groups.
15 Four of the 110 individuals are females, of whom only one is known to have attended university, studying pedagogy.

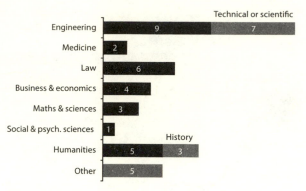

Figure 5.4: Russian neo-Nazis and extreme nationalists by discipline of study (45 individuals).
Sources: Vyacheslav Lichachov, "Fascism in Russia" (published in the series Ekstremizm, Panorama Center, Moscow 2002); Aleksander Verhovskij and Galina Kozhevnikova, eds., *Radical Russian Nationalism: Organisations, Ideas and People* (Moscow: Informational and Analytical Center Sova, 2009); www.labyrinth.ru/; www.anticompromat.org/ and other Russian websites.

were able to sample only the leadership echelons. There is evidence that the first wave of post-Soviet right-wing extremism emerged from poor housing estates but has since spread to students from lower-middle-class families, which often suffered severe social dislocation in the wake of the Soviet collapse (Laryš and Mareš 2011). Like militant Islamism in the Muslim world, Russian right-wing militancy seems to originate from relative deprivation.

As for other partially sampled groups, however, there is no reason to believe there are strong reporting biases regarding the *type* of degree obtained. For 45 of the 58 extremists, we found the type of degree pursued or at least the faculty they attended (see figure 5.4). Nine of the 45 (20 percent) are clearly engineers, and we know that another seven (15 percent) studied in technical and scientific departments in which they could have pursued engineering degrees. The next largest group is, again, the lawyers.[16]

A curious sign of the prominence of engineers among Russian fringe nationalists is worthy of an aside. It comes from a strand of successful popular "neo-Stalinist" literature. These semifictional books are devoted to rewriting Russian history of the last century on shaky bases: They

---

16 Taking out the one female with higher education, who has studied pedagogy, would reduce the "other" category in figure 5.4 to four cases.

TABLE 5.1
Type of higher education of the top ten best-selling authors of neo-Stalinist literature in Russia

Author	Number of books	Copies sold	Higher education
Yuri Mukhin	117	871	Engineering
Nikolay Starikov	74	361	Engineering
Arsen Martirosyan	36	230	Military (?)
Sergey Kremlev	41	204	Engineering
Vladimir Bushin	49	167	Literature
Elena Prudnikova	33	162	Journalism
Igor Pyhalov	33	140	Engineering
Yuri Zhukov	17	75	History
Alexander Djukov	18	71	History

Source: Chapkovski 2012 (measured from Ozon.ru, the biggest Russian online bookstore, in March 2012).

uphold anti-Western values, are nationalist in nature, conspiratorial, and anti-Semitic, express nostalgia for a mythical past, support a strong authoritarian order, and, above all, while denying Stalin's crimes, unfailingly defend his achievements. Chapkovski, who compiled a list of the ten most successful writers of this type of literature, who together had sold 2.3 million copies by 2012, discovered that among them there are four engineers, three of them in the top four authors (whether ranked by number of copies sold or by number of books written).

We identified 25 *U.S.-based neo-Nazi and white supremacist groups* from the Anti-Defamation League (ADL) census of such networks, most of which were active at the time of writing. Some of the names of these groups are revealing: Aryan Nations, Michigan Militia, The Order, The Covenant, the Sword, and the Arm of the Lord, the League of American Patriots, and National Socialist Movement. All of them are white supremacist and have employed or supported violence, most of them are anti-Semitic or antigovernment or both, and six of them have a strong religious connotation with some Christian sect. They generally have a more pronounced antigovernment orientation than do European right-wingers, who typically venerate a strong state. Estimates of the harm these groups have inflicted on ethnic and sexual minorities are few and far between, but according to data from the New American Foundation, between September 2001 and the end of 2012, there were 29 murders committed by right-wingers.[17] The most lethal right-wing attack committed in the United States was the Oklahoma City government building bombing that killed 168 people in 1995.

Our search in the ADL database as well as in other sources yielded 71 names of members of these groups, all males; the list includes only the prominent members, many of them founders or leaders, and a few others who simply gained notoriety through their deeds. This is but a small fraction of the overall membership, whose number no one is able to establish, but a good representation of their elites.

We found educational information on 44 individuals out of 71. Out of the 44, 15 never attended college while 29 had either a degree or exposure to higher education. The high proportion of individuals who went to college is the result of the fact that we were only able to get detailed information on the top tier of those groups (general education levels of the broader membership are known to be low).[18] For 29 out of 30 militants we found information on their degrees.[19]

The results, illustrated in figure 5.5, show that, just as among the Russian neo-Nazis, engineering is the dominant degree (9 cases, 31 percent) followed by law (7 cases, 24 percent). As a point of reference, consider that out of all bachelor degrees awarded to males in the United States in 1966, engineering constituted only 11.8 percent.[20] Thus, even if our numbers are small, relative to the male graduate population with an engineering degree, engineers among U.S. right-wing groups seem strongly overrepresented.[21]

Another indicator reveals that engineers have had an even larger impact on their groups than have those who pursued other degrees: seven out of nine engineers were either founders or leaders of their group, while only four out of seven lawyers were. At least two of these engineers worked in the aeronautics and defense industry: Dick Butler, the founder

17 www.motherjones.com/politics/2013/04/charts-domestic-terrorism-jihadist-boston-tsarnaev.

18 Both Smith and Morgan (1994) and Handler (1990) report low levels of education below the leadership stratum of extreme right-wing groups in the United States, considerably lower than those of left-wing extremists in nonleadership positions. Of 75 right-wing cases in Smith and Morgan's sample, only 12 percent had a degree.

19 For 28 of these the information was direct while for one it was inferred from his occupation.

20 www.nsf.gov/statistics/nsf11316/pdf/nsf11316.pdf. The members of the supremacist groups in our sample with a degree went to university sometime between the 1940s and late 1960s, and 1966 is the first year in which we found data on the discipline composition of degrees in the United States.

21 The difference between actual and expected is significant at $p < .1$ according to Fisher's exact test.

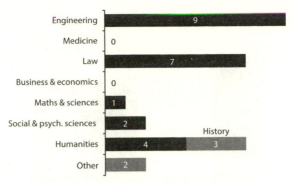

Figure 5.5: Neo-Nazis and white supremacists in the United States by discipline of study (29 individuals).
Sources: Anti-Defamation League; Handler 1990; Smith and Morgan 1994; websites of groups; newspaper articles; web and newspaper archive survey.

of Aryan Nations, was an aeronautical engineer with Lockheed, and Wilhelm Schmitt, leader of the Sheriff's Posse Comitatus, a militant antigovernment group with an antitax agenda and extremist Christian views, was also an engineer with Lockheed, where he was honored for his part in developing the Polaris nuclear missiles before being sentenced to twenty-six years in prison in 1985 for a conspiracy to injure an IRS agent (Smith and Morgan 1994: 54).

The picture becomes more remarkable still once we single out the six groups with an overtly religious component. Among these the engineering dominance becomes overwhelming: five engineers out of nine belong to religious right-wing groups while only one of the lawyers does;[22] lawyers are more frequent in the non-overtly religious groups (see figure 5.6).[23]

In conclusion, our data leave little doubt that engineers are more prominent among the right than among the left. This is independent of the general levels of education, which are lower among right-wingers. It is not surprising, then, that even Julius Evola, the Islamophile philosophical muse of the post–World War II European extreme right whom we met in chapter 4, was a quasi-engineer: He "broke off his engineering studies before the last exam, in spite of his excellent record (so that he

22 Due to small numbers, the bias is not statistically significant.
23 There is also some evidence of engineers' considerable presence among nonviolent right-wing groups: among 19 members of the rabidly anti-Communist John Birch Society in the United States whose degrees we could establish, 4 were engineers; the only larger group was that of business graduates (7). Among the technocrats surrounding Pinochet, engineers also featured prominently, even among the "Chicago Boys" who are usually believed to have been only economists (Huneeus 2000).

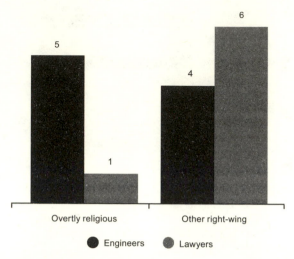

Figure 5.6: Presence of engineers and lawyers by religiousness of U.S. right-wing groups.
Source: Authors' calculations.

wouldn't be, as he writes, a 'Doctor' or a 'Professor' like the others)"
(Hansen 2002: 4).

The strong presence of engineers in the extreme right appears robust
to country variations; this implies that it also survives variations in ideology between the more state-oriented, secular right-wing extremism in
Europe and the more libertarian, religious-oriented movements in the
United States. But how strong is this bias, and are there any other degrees
that have a systematic tendency to show up on one side or the other?
Figure 5.7 combines the data on the two left-wing groups discussed earlier and the three right-wing samples in this section into a scatterplot that
compares the frequencies of specific degrees on the left and the right in
total.[24]

In fact, no other major subject group seems to behave the way engineering does. Instead, there are three degrees common on the left and rare
on the right: social and psychological sciences, natural sciences, and humanities (all biases are statistically significant).[25] The humanities, however,

24 Frequencies are derived by summing up all counts of a specific subject across all
left-wing (or right-wing) groups and dividing the result by the total counts of all subjects
across all left-wing (or right-wing) groups. The results are hence weighted by the size of
individual samples. The graph would look very similar if groups were equally weighted.
25 The significance is derived using Fisher's exact test, comparing the actual counts of
degrees on the left and on the right with the distribution one would expect if the

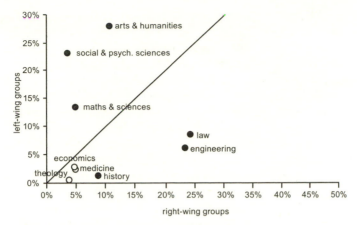

Figure 5.7: Frequency of degrees among graduates in post–World War II extremists groups: left vs. right.
Source: Authors' calculations.

are so because we retained only languages, literature, and philosophy and excluded history and theology, subjects more frequent among the right. Apart from history and engineering, law also is seldom seen on the left and frequent on the right—but less markedly so than engineering (all biases here, too, are significant). While numbers in many cases become too small to be statistically significant when individual country samples or groups are compared, *all* of the six major biases are reproduced in *all* six possible pairings of samples. The systematic nature of these biases alleviates the concern that we are comparing apples and oranges as the countries involved on the left and the right overlap only partially.

Are the Dividing Lines Robust?

How robust are the observed patterns if we change historical periods? While geographically varied, our comparison is limited to post–World War II settings, the period in which the violent Islamists emerged, and one might suspect an era-specific effect. Pre–World War II biographical data are harder to collect, but to test for variation over time we can rely on a handful of well-documented cases.

---

frequency of degrees was independent of ideology. For history, $p < .05$, for all other significant cases, $p < .01$.

The earliest, on the left, is the Spartakusbund (Spartacus League), named after the famed slave who led a rebellion against Rome. It was a Marxist revolutionary movement active in Germany during and soon after World War I. Among its founders were Karl Liebknecht and Rosa Luxemburg. The movement's activity peaked in January 1919, with an uprising in Berlin. The German government under social democrat Friedrich Ebert used both the army and right-wing militias, the infamous Freikorps, to quell the rebellion. Later that month, Liebknecht and Luxemburg were abducted by Freikorps thugs (while the government allegedly turned a blind eye), tortured, and summarily executed.

Of the 22 founding members or leaders of the Spartacus League, 12 were highly educated, which is all the more striking given that during that period the tertiary enrollment rate in Germany was minuscule: in 1914 it was 1 percent and in 1920 around 2 percent.[26] In many cases, graduates held degrees in more than one subject, for a total of 24 subjects.[27] The most frequent degrees are in the humanities (especially philosophy), followed by economics and social sciences (figure 5.8). At that time economics, especially in Germany and Austria, was an integral part of the other social sciences, much more sociological and less technical, and a far broader church ideologically than it is today, in which labor supporters were as likely to be found as were the supporters of capitalism. Even Max Weber was perceived as much a political economist as a sociologist. Both engineering and natural sciences are absent.[28]

Our main case on the right is that of German Nazis, whose history and ideology are well-documented and need little introduction. There is also accurate and plentiful information about their membership and a considerable literature on the role of students and graduates in the Nazi movement. A study of members' professions reports that in the early 1930s "young and technical professionals especially succumbed to the Nazi lure" (Jarausch 1986: 110), arguably due to overcrowding of universities and a surfeit of graduates on a job market hit by the Great Depression (ibid., 109). The pattern is reminiscent of what we found for Middle Eastern societies from the 1970s on.

---

26 Windolf 1990.
27 Two of the 12 individuals with degrees are women. Excluding the subjects they studied (which included one count each of history, philosophy, math, social science, and economics) does not materially change the results.
28 While we were not able to collect sufficient biographical data on pre–World War II leftist movements in other countries, secondary sources indicate that Russian Bolshevists also included few engineers. Table 7 in Evans Clements (1997) shows occupations of male and female Bolshevists. The group comprising agronomist, attorney, engineer, journalist, librarian, and student is only 2.5 percent for women and 9.4 percent for men.

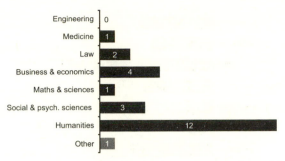

Figure 5.8: Disciplines of study of prominent members of the Spartakusbund (12 individuals, 24 disciplines).
Sources: Wikipedia; web survey; Munzinger biographical archive.

German engineers in the Nazi era are the subject of a thorough study by Herf, who reports their presence in the Nazi party from the very beginning (1984: 197–98). Quoting Joseph Goebbels, Herf writes that "German victories were possible only because German engineers and scientists approached their work with the 'same fanaticism and wild determination' as did German soldiers, workers and peasants" (1984: 197). He further reports, however, that "the reception of Nazism among German engineers also appears to have been enthusiastic, but less so than that of the legal and medical professions, as indicated by the results of student elections in German technical universities"—41 percent voted for the Nazis in student elections compared to 48 percent of the students in nontechnical universities. "After 1933, the number of engineers in the Nazi party doubled but the increase in the other middle-class professions was even greater (about 230 percent). Only 13.1 percent of the leadership positions in the mid-1930s were held by engineers, compared to 56 percent for lawyers and 15.5 percent for doctors" (Herf 1984: 198).

To establish more precisely how many engineers appeared among the Nazi movement and when, we collected a sample of 434 leading Nazi activists and found educational information on 320 of them. Nazi elites were well educated: 219 enjoyed higher education, and of the 101 individuals with no university education, only 19 had less than secondary school education. Eighty-six individuals had professional military training, 63 of whom are in the group without higher education.[29]

Figure 5.9 shows that among those with a university education, as Herf argues, the appeal of the Nazis extends to all disciplines, including a fairly

29 Three of the 434 individuals were female, one a doctor, one a teacher, and one with only primary education.

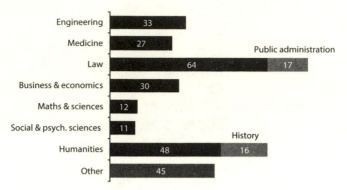

Figure 5.9: Disciplines of study of leading Nazis (219 individuals, 278 disciplines).

Note: "Other" includes training in military colleges, education, agriculture, and various smaller disciplines.

Sources: German and English Wikipedia; web survey; Munzinger biographical archives.

strong presence in the humanities—among them literature and philosophy, which are absent among the Islamists and which in the post–World War II context are associated more with left-wing than with right-wing extremism. In their fully developed form, which our sample represents, National Socialism became a broad church mobilizing individuals from all sectors of German society.

Engineers do not seem to stand out. A closer look, however, shows that this is to some degree an artifact of the strong representation of law graduates (29.2 percent, 37 percent if individuals who studied public administration are added), who dominated the Nazis then as much as engineers dominate Muslim militants now. If we disaggregate humanities into individual disciplines, the engineers are the second largest group after the lawyers and constitute 15.1 percent of all individuals with higher education (just slightly above the share documented by Herf).[30] In fact, the three most frequent subjects after law are the same as in our Muslim world sample: engineering, economics and business, and medicine.[31]

30 In line with the typical division of faculties, seven architects are counted as engineers. One of the architects, Alfred Rosenberg, also studied engineering and is hence counted only once.

31 The figure represents the number of times engineering was studied over the number of individuals with known higher education. The number of times individual subjects are mentioned over the total number of subject mentions (rather than individuals) in the sample is lower for all subjects, as many individuals studied more than one subject: 219 individuals with known higher education as compared to 278 subject mentions recorded.

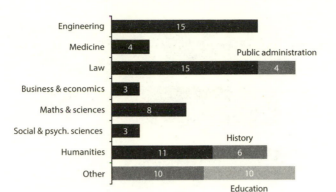

Figure 5.10: Disciplines of study of early Nazi militants (73 individuals, 89 disciplines).
Sources: German and English Wikipedia; web survey; Munzinger biographical archives.

But above all, once we take into account the distribution of disciplines among German graduates, we discover that in the 1910s and 1920s only 1–4.3 percent of students were enrolled in technical faculties, while 20–30 percent were enrolled in law faculties (Flora 1983: 589). This indicates that engineers among Nazis were *more* strongly overrepresented relative to the total student population than the lawyers, even if there were more of the latter in absolute numbers.

We also found evidence that the engineers were ideologically more committed than the lawyers in their decision to join the Nazis, as well as more willing to incur higher risks. For 210 of the individuals with higher education we were able to reconstruct the year in which they joined the movement. That way, we could establish the education of those who joined before 1924, when the Nazi movement was a small militant organization that often violently clashed with both communists and authorities. The Nazis of that period are more comparable with the groups of extremists, both left-wing and Islamist, which we consider in this chapter, than the full-blown, society-wide Nazi movement that followed Hitler's rise to power and is documented in figure 5.9.

Figure 5.10 shows that among early Nazis, there were as many engineers as lawyers *even in absolute numbers*: each group constituted 20.5 percent of the early activists,[32] while all other disciplines trail at some distance.

Engineering students combined their subject with other disciplines about as frequently as non-engineering students.

32 Three of the 15 were architects, including Alfred Rosenberg (see note 30), who also held an engineering degree.

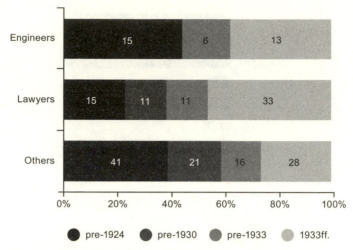

Figure 5.11: Share of engineers, lawyers, and others who joined the Nazis at different stages.
Source: German and English Wikipedia; web survey; Munzinger biographical archives.

From 1923 to 1933, the Nazi movement evolved from a small, militant fringe party into a large organization: joining implied progressively lower risk, weaker commitment, and belief in its ideology. Thus the stronger the early presence of a specific discipline, the more likely its graduates joined out of conviction. If we divide our Nazi sample into different periods during which members joined the movement (figure 5.11), we can see that the share of engineers who joined before 1924 is significantly higher than that of lawyers (44.1 vs. 21.4 percent).[33] The proportion of lawyers grew faster but only in subsequent periods. The larger number of "March violets" (38.2 vs. 47.1 percent), as the Nazis branded those who joined the movement after Hitler's electoral victory in March 1933, could be a sign of greater opportunism among lawyers compared to engineers. In conclusion, the evidence shows that the engineers were both the most committed and, relative to the general population of students, the strongest group among Nazis.

How do the early Nazis compare with the Spartakisten, a similarly small and radical leftist movement in the same country and era? Figure 5.12 shows that economics is predominantly on the left, unlike the post–World War II results—but as mentioned earlier, it is probably the one discipline discussed here whose nature has mutated the most during the twentieth century. As for the rest of the disciplines, with the exception of

---

33 The difference is significant at $p < .05$ in Fisher's exact test.

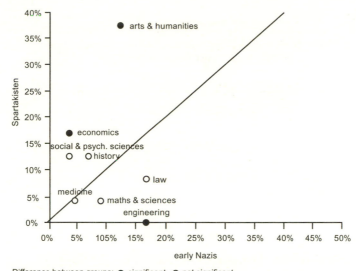

Figure 5.12: Frequency of degrees of Nazis and Spartakisten compared. *Source:* Authors' calculations.

history, their distribution in figure 5.12 looks remarkably similar to the post–World War II comparisons in figure 5.7: humanities graduates are significantly more frequent among the left, as are engineers on the right. Social science degrees also cluster on the left, although the bias of this group just about fails a significance test.[34]

Italian fascists were the first major right-wing movement in interwar Europe that, though less brutal and absolutist in their racism, shared the Nazis' worship of strength and social order, of a powerful state, and of their nation's superiority. We did not find reliable data on their education.[35] However, we can glean some idea of their educational background using Roberto Franzosi's large data set that contains, in codified form, newspaper articles about violent political incidents, including clashes, beatings, and assassinations, which occurred in Italy from 1919 to 1923. Crucially, the database includes events that involved fascists on the one hand and socialists or communists on the other. It hence allows for another comparison across ideologies that controls for country context and

34 Fisher's exact test allows us to reject independence of engineering and humanities from ideology at $p < .05$; for social sciences, $p < .1$.
35 The only immediate biographical data we found were on occupations, from Adrian Lyttelton, who has assembled a sample of 93 "federali," fascist party regional secretaries, who were in power in 1935, and for 29 of whom we know the profession: 15 were lawyers, 5 accountants, 4 "professors," and 4 engineers (Lyttelton 1973: 305–6).

TABLE 5.2
Frequency at which the professions of fascists and socialists/communists are mentioned in direct connection with violent episodes in articles in the fascist and socialist dailies, *Il Popolo d'Italia* and *L'Avanti* (1919–23)

	Popolo d'Italia		L'Avanti	
	Fascists	Socialists	Fascists	Socialists
Lawyers	89.1%	66.7%	50.0%	85.4%
Doctors	2.2%	27.8%	0%	11.8%
Engineers	8.7%	5.6%	50.0%	2.8%
Total	100% (n = 138)	100% (n = 18)	100% (n = 18)	100% (n = 144)

Source: Our calculations on Roberto Franzosi's data set.

potentially increases the external validity of our findings as it involves a different country.

The articles are taken from two dailies, the fascist *Il Popolo d'Italia* and the socialist *L'Avanti*. Franzosi kindly calculated for us the number of times a given profession of either fascists or socialists involved in the violent clashes or "punitive expeditions" is mentioned in the articles.[36] Three main professions emerge: in both fascist and leftist articles, "lawyer" is the profession most frequently mentioned by far; doctors are more frequent among the socialists than among the fascists; and engineers are more frequent among the fascists than among the socialists.[37]

Though the Italian data are circumstantial and refer to professions rather than degrees,[38] they confirm our finding that engineers are predominantly found on the radical right. The data also underline lawyers' high level of politicization, mostly on the right, in the European context.

EXTREMISTS COMPARED: ISLAMISTS, LEFTISTS, AND RIGHTISTS

Here we return to what originally led us into pursuing the left-right comparisons: the hypothesis that the ideological makeup of radical Islamism is closer to that of right-wing extremism than to that of the leftist kind.

36 We counted only those professions that require a degree.
37 Fisher's exact test shows that the difference is significant at $p < .05$.
38 Recording profession rather than degree might understate the overall presence of engineering graduates if we assume that engineers are more likely to end up in non-engineering professions than are law or medical students outside of their respective professions. This should not systematically affect the ratio between the engineers counted on left and right, however.

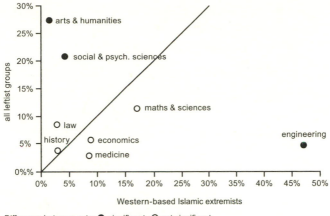

Difference between sets: ● significant ○ not significant

Figure 5.13: Frequency of degrees of leftist groups and Western-based Islamists compared.
Source: Authors' calculations.

To properly assess this hypothesis, we now compare whether the left-right patterns recur in a comparison between the left and Islamists. Figures 5.13 and 5.14 compare the three leftist groups in our sample (RAF, Red Brigades, Spartakisten) with Western-based and Muslim world Islamists, respectively.

The two graphs are quite similar, the main difference being that math and science end up on the left in figure 5.14, although they are not a strong outlier. More important, core patterns with regard to engineering, social sciences, and humanities are identical to those in the previous left-right comparisons (see figures 5.7 and 5.12).[39]

Table 5.3 summarizes the main patterns emerging from the data in chapters 1–5. It shows different disciplines' degree of over- and underrepresentation in paired comparisons of (a) all rightist versus all leftist militants, (b) all Islamist versus all leftist militants, and (c) all Islamist versus all rightist militants. Statistically significant biases are highlighted with a double plus sign if in any one comparison a discipline's share among graduates is more than three times larger in the first than in the second group, and with a double minus sign if it is more than three times smaller. Smaller but significant biases are indicated with one plus or one minus sign, while the absence of statistical significance is denoted as 0.

---

39 As expected, similar scatterplots of right-wing versus Islamist radicals show less pronounced differences regarding subject groups apart from law and humanities, which are much more frequent among the right.

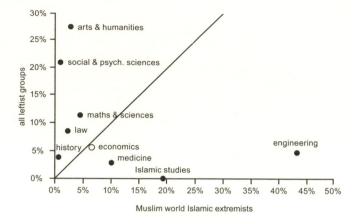

Difference between sets: ● significant ○ not significant

Figure 5.14: Frequency of degrees among leftist groups and Muslim world Islamists compared.
Note: P-levels for engineering, social and psychological sciences, and humanities are < .01, for other disciplines < .05 (only economics does not have a significant bias).
Source: Authors' calculations.

Combining all three comparisons, we see that the disciplines of the *social sciences*, *humanities* (excluding history), and *engineering* show the most extreme and consistent biases. Humanities and social sciences are strong on the left but weak among both the right and the Islamists. Engineering is the exact mirror image: absent among leftists but strongly present among rightists and Islamists. The results for the social sciences and engineering perfectly match those in the Hamas versus Fatah comparison as well as that for defectors from Islamist extremism from chapter 3, giving us further confidence in their robustness.

The patterns for other disciplines are less clear cut: *math and science* exhibit only weak and unsystematic biases and are not strongly present in any group. *Law* and the humanities subfield of *history* are more frequent among the right than the left but almost completely absent among the Islamists. Islamists' aversion to history as an academic subject is unsurprising: it is a culture- and often country-specific subject with a secular orientation—better fodder for nationalists in search of a legitimizing ancestry than for Islamists whose imagined community is global and for whom only a highly stylized and divinely guided history of Islam matters, which is taught in Islamic studies rather than in history departments. A similar logic explains the contrast between the weak but discernible pres-

TABLE 5.3
Presence of different disciplines in different radical groups compared

	Right vs. Left	Islamists vs. Left	Islamists vs. Right
Engineering	++	++	+
Medicine	0	0	0
Law	+	-	--
Economics	0	0	0
Math & science	-	-	0
Social & psycho-logical sciences	--	--	0
Humanities	-	--	--
History	0	-	--

Note: + or - = significant bias; ++ or -- = significant bias with ratio > 3 or < 1/3
Source: Summary of the results in Figures 5.13 and 5.14.

ence of other humanities subjects among right-wingers and their complete absence among Islamists.[40]

The absence of law studies among Islamists—the only other subject
with a rightward bias almost as extreme as that of engineers—is also no
surprise: radical Islamists do not care for secular law. Its equivalent for
Muslims is arguably Islamic studies or, to be more precise, sharia. Students of Islamic studies are strongly present in our Muslim world sample,
and this discipline typically has a strong sharia component. Islam is often
described as a religion of law and of rules-based "orthopraxis" (Ruthven
1997). Students of Islamic studies and secular lawyers might share a preference for "law and order"—which, as we argued in chapter 4, is a shared
element of right-wing ideology and Islamism—that some of them take to
extremes.

The discipline of medicine is weak among both leftists and rightists
(apart from the fully developed Nazi movement in which *all* professions
were present). It is somewhat stronger among Islamists but not as strong

40 Consider the different meaning of such secular cultural subjects in the West: while
in the Muslim world, their methods and themes tend to be seen as a Western import, in
Europe humanities are studies of one's own cultural heritage. They hence can be attractive
also to individuals with a strongly conservative or nationalist orientation. For conservatives interested in defending their social order and cultural heritage, humanities in the
West might in some ways be the equivalent of Islamic studies in the Muslim world.

as engineering by far. This is in line with our conclusions from chapters 2 and 3 that doctors have more contingent and context-driven links to Islamism. The weak presence of doctors among secular movements has one exception, however, which concerns a group whose educational composition we have yet to present: the anarchists.

While perceived as left-leaning, anarchists are a rather special case, for their worldview is distant from both the Marxist-Leninist tradition and the organized labor movements. They are more action-oriented and less interested in grand, long-term schemes yet also quite utopian in their views of how immediate action can bring about social change. A survey of nineteenth- and twentieth-century anarchists we conducted[41] on the one hand confirms our findings for all other radical left-wing groups: among anarchists, too, the presence of engineers is small, representing 5.6 percent of all disciplines studied and 6.4 percent of all individuals with university exposure, and the dominant degrees are in the humanities. On the other hand, the survey yielded some surprises: first, there is a significant presence of lawyers, paradoxically for an ideology antipathetic to order. This accentuates the impression that lawyers tend to be "men for all seasons": while more enthusiastic to join right-wing extremists, they do not shy away completely from the far left. Next, uniquely across all extremist groups we considered, medicine among anarchists is a dominant discipline, preceded only by the humanities and arts combined (figure 5.15). The strong presence of doctors might reflect the tradition of voluntary work in the medical profession: anarchism is a decentralized, community-oriented ideology focused on immediate action, making it po-

41 We searched 834 biographies of anarchists active over a century and a half in 27 nations—most European countries, the United States, and Russia. We found that no fewer than 125 anarchists had studied at university; for quite a few of the rest we found no information at all on their education so there may be more. We identified the disciplines studied by 109 of them (the oldest was born in 1808, the youngest in 1941). (We also know that 57 of them were engaged in violence or actively supported violent groups. For the other 68 we do not know enough to establish their relations with political violence. However, when we looked at the separate distributions of degrees for the certainly violent ones and for the rest, they turned out to be remarkably similar, so we kept them together.) We found the biographies in *L'Ephéméride Anarchiste*, a website run by two French self-described "anarchistes individualistes et naturistes" who mention themselves only by their first names, Eric and Cathy (http://epheman.perso.neuf.fr/). The website compilers state that their sources include "d'ouvrages historiques ou de chroniques extraites de journaux libertaires provenant en grande partie de notre bibliothèque (voir la bibliographie d'ouvrages sur l'histoire générale de l'Anarchie). The data ought to be taken with caution for the galaxy of activists and thinkers known as "anarchists," who appeared in Europe in the first half of the nineteenth century, is very diverse.

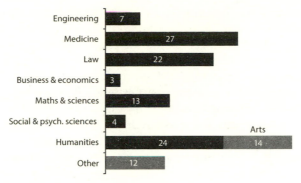

Figure 5.15: Disciplines of study of anarchists (109 individuals).
Source: Our survey of biographies on http://epheman .perso.neuf.fr/.

tentially attractive for individuals possessing skills that are of direct use in community and grassroots work.[42]

Conclusions and Summary So Far

In chapter 4, we argued that militant Islam shares much with radical right-wing ideologies while having much less in common with leftist ones. If similarity of ideologies matters, engineers should hence be found on the right rather than the left. Conversely, degrees underrepresented among Islamists should also be underrepresented on the right and strongly present on the left. We have indeed failed to find engineers among left-wing extremists: apart from a handful in the Italian Red Brigades, there is hardly any trace of them. There are two further groups of disciplines that

---

42 Elisabeth Longuenesse contrasts the practical orientation of the Islamist-dominated doctors' syndicate in Jordan with that of the (similarly Islamist) engineers' syndicate in similar terms: "Le discours des médecins est différent, leur engagement n'est pas de meme nature. Sans doute leur compétence scientifique est-elle une dimension importante de leur légitimité, leur intervention dans la société se place néanmoins à un niveau plus concret, moins idéologique, de définition des politiques de santé publiques. Sur un plan différent, c'est la situation de guerre ou d'occupation qui leur donne une responsabilité particulière en tant que professionnels: la situation en Palestine ou au Liban sous occupation israelienne. En 1981, l'épidémie de choléra dans la région rappelle la mission qui leur incombe. A la différence des ingénieurs qui, eux aussi se mobilisent pour la Palestine ou le Sud-Liban occupés, cette fois en tant que citoyens, c'est comme professionnels, mettant leur compétence au service d'une cause, que les médecins interviennent" (2000: 28–29).

evince the exact opposite patterns observed for engineers: the humanities and social sciences. Almost absent among Islamists, they also have a weak presence among right-wingers (with the exception of history students) but a strong one on the left.

The left-right patterns described appear to cut across geographic and historical contexts. Our set of extremist groups has been selective yet quite varied across geographies and eras. At the same time, it has included within-case comparisons of left and right for Germany (at several points in time) and Italy (in the pre–World War II period), alleviating the concern that differences in degree distributions simply reflect broader differences between the countries in the sample. We have also covered a wide range of right-wing ideologies, showing that their affinity to engineering is robust to doctrinal nuances as long as the core right-wing ideas, as identified in chapter 4, are present. Finally, the major patterns also seem insensitive to variations in the general level of education among right-wing militants.

This consistent link between discipline and ideology, incidentally, drives another nail into the coffin of the "skills hypothesis" and demand-driven explanations more broadly: if radical organizations have a stronger demand for engineers because of their technical skills, or engineers are more easily detected because of their operational role, then this bias should show on the left too, but it does not. The observed pattern must hence be driven by the individual supply behavior of militants, not militant movements' demand or the higher visibility of engineers. Even if radical organizations should have a preference for engineers, the latter are willing to go along with it only on the right.

These results allow us to conclude that there is a deep-seated affinity between students of specific disciplines and specific types of radical politics, even if this affects only a tiny fringe in each discipline. Social causes no doubt explain much about political radicalization, but they are insufficient to explain the peculiar, consistent disciplinary biases that recur across the radical spectrum in different eras and places. It is likely that individuals self-select into different types of radicalism because of individual-level factors that are independent of context and that are in some way correlated with the discipline they choose to study at university.

We can distill the evidence presented thus far into seven main conclusions about engineers and radical politics.

1. Engineers radicalize in the Islamic world partly as a result of acute relative deprivation.
2. However, they disproportionally radicalize even in the absence of frustrated aspirations, as their strong presence among South Asian and Western-based Islamists shows.

3. Engineers are frequent among right-wing extremist movements in the developed world but rarely join left-wing extremist movements.
4. Graduates in the humanities and the social sciences disproportionately join left-wing extremist groups but avoid both right-wing and Islamist radical groups.

Points 3 and 4 indicate, we argue, that certain degrees are a proxy for personality traits. It is likely that different types tend to react differently to frustration and political repression. If specific traits of engineers drive some of them to the radical right, the absence of these traits or opposite ones among humanities and social science students is arguably what causes them to avoid Islamism and right-wing extremism but makes them susceptible to radical politics on the left. The importance of traits, in the case of engineers in particular, is further revealed by three additional findings:

5. Engineers prefer to join violent rather than peaceful Islamist opposition groups.
6. Engineers prefer to join religious rather than secular leftist and nationalist groups, even when they have a choice between the two (e.g., pre-revolutionary Iran, 1970s Afghanistan, and Palestine). Engineers' religious proclivity is also evident among right-wing extremists in the United States.
7. Engineers appear more firmly committed to their cause, as shown by the fact that they are less likely to defect from Islamist groups and by their early commitment to the nascent Nazi movement.

"Type" is not reducible to socioeconomic factors, and precisely which traits constitute it will occupy us in the next chapter.

Mind-sets for Extremists

RESEARCHERS WHO HAVE LOOKED FOR PATHOLOGICAL TRAITS IN THE minds of violent extremists have found none, and generally uncovered little that distinguishes extremists from anyone else—"they are just like you and me!" is a somewhat disquieting comment heard in academic circles. This non-finding is taken as evidence of tabula rasa and, by implication, that only social and economic circumstances determine who becomes an extremist and of what kind (Kruglanski and Fishman 2006; Ruby 2002; Silke 1998). Yet the absence of pathological traits does not imply that extremists are like everyone else with regard to *other traits* or that they are similar to each other irrespective of the brand of extremism they embrace.

The systematic differences in the educational composition of different extremist groups we described in chapter 5 is a strong indication that different *types* of people are attracted to different types of extremism: engineers appear mostly on one side, and social scientists and humanities graduates appear mostly on the other side. In so far as the choice or practice of different disciplines reflects different mind-sets, those differences imply that people with different psychological traits will lean in different political directions. What exactly these traits might be, and whether engineers have some that social scientists and humanities graduates lack, will occupy us in this last chapter.

Let us recapitulate what we know thus far:

1. Right-wing and Islamist extremism share many ideological features, while left-wing extremism differs from both.
2. Engineers are more likely than other graduates to join either Islamist or right-wing radical groups but unlikely to join left-wing extremist groups. The latter are joined by humanities and social sciences graduates who are conversely absent from Islamist and right-wing extremist groups.
3. Islamist engineers are more likely than even other Islamist-leaning graduates to choose religious and violent groups over secular and peaceful ones, and to be more strongly committed to persevere in pursuing their cause.

We ideally need to find out

- which cognitive and emotional traits might be associated with right-wing extremism and which with Islamist extremism;

- whether these traits overlap among members of both types of extremist groups; and
- whether the overlapping traits are more pronounced among engineers than among graduates in other disciplines.

Traits that are found among both right-wing and Islamist extremists are likely to be more important than those found only in one or other type of group; and traits found in both *and* among engineers are the best candidates to explain our original puzzle.

The political psychology literature, which we examine shortly, offers extensive evidence of the traits associated with conservatism and right-wing authoritarianism. We also have solid evidence on the prevalence of certain personality traits among graduates of different disciplines. But evidence from the field of psychology on Islamists is scant, so we have to rely on anecdotal evidence and on the joint force of two inferences. First, the extensive ideological overlaps between the two extremisms we established in chapter 4 could imply that the two serve similar cognitive and emotional needs: what is a "good fit" for right-wingers is a good fit for Islamist radicals too. Second, given the presence of engineers in both camps, if we found that engineers have traits overlapping with those associated with right-wing extremists, then the likelihood that the same bundle of traits is also associated with Islamist extremists increases.

TRAITS FOR TYPES OF EXTREMISTS

Die-hard social scientists still claim that the mind-sets of extremists are irrelevant. But in recent years a large body of research has been amassed showing that individuals with left and right political preferences have sharply distinct profiles. The evidence that political attitudes are linked to personality traits, all the way down to variations in brain structure, is mounting rapidly—whether derived from surveys, experiments, or measurable neural processes—and is just too compelling to dismiss wholesale (Thorisdottir et al. 2007; Amodio et al. 2007; Jost, Federico, and Napier 2009; Hatemi et al. 2014; Kanai et al. 2011).[1]

A thorough review of the literature, which focuses mostly on the personality traits underlying right-wing and conservative attitudes, reveals

---

1 Political attitudes appear to some extent to be inherited, further pointing to the presence of deep-seated traits influencing them (Alford, Funk, and Hibbing 2005). Some recent research even indicates that instead of traits being the cause of attitudes, genes might simultaneously determine political attitudes and personality traits (Verhulst, Eaves, and Hatemi 2012). But even if personality traits do not determine political attitudes and are only correlated to them, traits (or bundles of traits and attitudes) might still produce specific types of extremist behavior.

that three traits stand out as the most relevant: one trait, an emotional one, is the proneness to experience disgust; another trait, the most multi-faceted of the three, involves a strong "need for cognitive closure"; the third, at once cognitive and emotional, is an urge to impose strict distinctions between in-group and out-group members. The evidence that those who score high on these traits are significantly more likely to hold right-wing and conservative views is overwhelming.[2] We review it below.

Disgust

Right-wingers' desire to keep their social environment pure and reject intrusion by alien forces perceived as corrupting seems linked to, or even caused by, a fundamental trait that psychologists have linked to conservatism: a proneness to be easily disgusted. This characteristic appears to underlie conservatism in particular on social issues like abortion or gay rights, both of which relate to notions of morality or purity (Inbar, Pizarro, and Bloom 2008; Inbar et al. 2009; Inbar et al. 2012; Jost and Amodio 2011).[3] Nazis were particularly well-known for their rabid homophobia and obsession with cultural purity. Paul Schultze-Naumburg, an architect and leading proponent of "Aryan" art under the Nazis, organized exhibitions juxtaposing modern art and real-life pictures of deformity and sickness to illustrate the former's decadence.[4] Conversely, disgust is weak among those with leftist inclinations—perhaps explaining why post–World War II left-wing student activists in Europe and the United

2 There is some dispute over whether the traits in the political psychology literature are linked to conservatism or to right-wing authoritarianism (RWA) and extremism—two arguably different phenomena. Some authors link specific cognitive traits directly and only to rightist extremism. For instance, Crowson and colleagues show a stronger link of cognitive rigidity to RWA than to mainstream conservatism; they also claim that RWA "appeared to partially mediate the relationship between cognitive rigidity and mainstream conservatism" (2005: 571). Others argue for a broader link to conservatism (Jost et al. 2007). Even the latter, however, include extreme versions of conservatism in their definition. Jost and Napier (2011) show that uncertainty avoidance (operationalized as high need for order and low openness to new experience) is *negatively* correlated with extremism in general (i.e., one's distance from the middle-of-the-road positions on the ideological spectrum) but positively with conservatism (as measured by the rightward bias on the spectrum). This would suggest that uncertainty avoidance might not push individuals into right-wing extremism per se, but if an extremism is chosen, it will be right-wing, as conservative extremists will still have stronger uncertainty avoidance than left-wing extremists. Whichever of the two schools is right, both imply that there is a link between extreme political attitudes and certain cognitive traits.
3 Inbar, Pizarro, and Bloom (2008) also show that disgust sensitivity is not linked to religious affiliation.
4 http://en.wikipedia.org/wiki/Paul_Schultze-Naumburg.

States tried to shock the conservative establishment with their use of feces in various protest events (including so-called "shit-ins").[5]

What matters for us is that purity is a core concern of radical Islam, specifically in its salafi variety; orderliness and ritual define the routines of salafists' daily lives. Some Islamist groups' concern with "takfir," that is, declaring bad Muslims infidels in order to be entitled to fight and kill them, is also essentially an attempt to purify the community of believers. While there are no hard data on Islamists and proneness to disgust, there are many anecdotes on Islamist extremists' squeamishness, including repugnance at being exposed to women's "pollution." Faisal Shahzad, who planted a bomb in an SUV parked in Times Square in 2010, was very clean and diligent, and left his apartment in immaculate condition: "his landlord, Stanislaw Chomiak, walked through Mr. Shahzad's apartment, pointing out the spot where he had been building a wooden replica of a mosque. He looked around, as if searching for clues. Mr. Shahzad had been nice, pleasant—a perfect kind of tenant. He had even lined the burners of the stove with aluminum so they would not get tarnished."[6] Hosam Maher Husein Smadi, a young Jordanian national whom the FBI "lured [in 2009] into a plot to blow up the Fountain Place tower in downtown Dallas," was described by his friends as "obsessively clean; three times a week, he removed the furniture from his bungalow and cleaned the floors."[7] Most striking of all is Mohamed Atta, the 9/11 attack mastermind, who wrote in a sort of will, "an almost hallucinatory document," instructions on how to treat his body after death: "'I do not want any women to go to my grave at all during my funeral.'" He also asked "the men [who] would be washing his dead body to avoid unshielded contact with his genitals" (Holmes 2005: 138). And while homophobia is a hallmark of mainstream conservative Islam, militant Islamists go to particular lengths to denounce homosexuality—and, where possible, punish it by death.

Need for Closure

The most extensively researched personality trait underlying political attitudes is the "need for cognitive closure" (NFC), which denotes a preference for order, structure, and certainties. It encompasses "intolerance of ambiguity," a notion introduced in connection with authoritarianism by Else

---

5 www.monopol-magazin.de/artikel/20101076/essay-die-schnoede-masse-hat-substanz
.html; https://stronglang.wordpress.com/2014/12/16/remembering-the-shit-in-2/.
6 *New York Times*, 16 May 2010, www.nytimes.com/2010/05/16/nyregion/16suspect
.html?ref=global-home.
7 *New York Times*, 28 September 2009, www.nytimes.com/2009/09/28/us/28texas.html
?ref=us&pagewanted=print.

Frenkel-Brunswik, a psychologist who worked with Theodor Adorno on *The Authoritarian Personality* (1950). The political psychology literature investigates NFC alongside a collection of related traits such as threat perception, (lack of) openness to experience, fear of loss, and death anxiety.[8] This literature does not rely on a standardized conceptual map, so it is hard to gauge which traits in this constellation are fundamental and which derivative, or how independent they are from each other. Regardless, many studies have found that individuals who score high on any of these traits, however measured, are more likely to be right wing and conservative (Jost et al. 2003; Jost, Federico, and Napier 2009; Jost and Napier 2011; Thorisdottir et al. 2007), while the profile of liberals and left-wingers is the very opposite: they are "more open-minded, creative, curious, and novelty seeking" and more likely to tolerate disorder, complexity, and rebellion (Carney et al. 2008: 807–8).

More precisely, surveys and experiments conducted in North America and Europe link high scores of NFC and its sister traits to a range of specific political outcomes: ideological conservatism, right-wing voting, attempts to maintain group norms and traditions, racism, right-wing authoritarianism,[9] and "social dominance orientation," a measure of individuals' preference for social hierarchy and domination over lower-status groups (Kemmelmeier 1997; Kruglanski and Orehek 2011; Roets and Van Hiel 2006; Van Hiel, Pandelaere and Duriez 2004). Kruglanski and Orehek (2011) show a correlation of high NFC and tough anti-terror positions, while Federico and colleagues (2005) link NFC to support for military action against Iraq. Studies conducted in Poland and Flanders show a strong link between NFC and cultural conservatism and, to a lesser extent, political conservatism (Kossowska and Van Hiel 2003). According to a study of Italian students, individuals high on NFC also value religion more highly (Chirumbolo, Areni, and Sensales 2004). All of these positions are generally considered "right wing."

Except for the attitudes related to Western security, once translated into local country context, these traits seem to faithfully reflect those of Islamists. Several of the characteristics that right-wingers share with radical Islamists (table 4.1) correspond to traits identified in the empirical literature: a hierarchical and authoritarian vision of social order as well as acceptance of social inequality are ideological features in table 4.1 that

8 American conservatives also score higher on measures of conscientiousness, including orderliness and rule following, than do American liberals (Carney et al. 2008; Gerber et al. 2010), traits that could be related to NFC (and, in the case of orderliness, to proneness to disgust). These links, however, are not made explicit in the literature.

9 Right-wing authoritarianism is a measure of individuals' willingness to submit to authority, endorse aggression toward those who violate rules, and follow the established traditions of society (Altemeyer 1998).

dovetail with social dominance orientation as a psychological trait. Traditionalism and a yearning to restore a lost order correspond to the maintenance of group norms and traditions and cultural conservatism.

More broadly, most of the features in table 4.1 appear to meet the NFC-based craving for order and rejection of ambiguity. In addition to the traits already mentioned, the corporatist and organicist view of society and the rejection of popular sovereignty all reflect a desire to live in an ordered and controlled society.

The nexus with Islamism works in another direction, too: in a study of NFC and political conservatism, Jost and Napier (2011: 100) used agreement with the statement "consistent routine enables me to enjoy life more" as a proxy for NFC. A statement such as this would resonate deeply with salafists in whose credo daily routines of prayers and cleansing feature centrally.

In-group and Out-group Distinction

A close companion of a high NFC is a proclivity to perceive and to impose a sharp in-group/out-group distinction. This matters because a strong group identity can drastically affect basic psychological patterns of empathy and antipathy, including schadenfreude, the pleasure that comes from seeing out-group members being harmed (Cikara et al. 2014). Individuals high on NFC prefer groups with impermeable boundaries, prefer their in-group more strongly, and reject out-groups more firmly. Individuals with strong NFC also like their in-group particularly fervently if they perceive it as homogeneous (Kruglanski and Orehek 2011). Hinze and colleagues (1997: 297) found that conservative individuals "possess a somewhat restricted range of construct assignment flexibility," that is, an ability to combine negatively and positively connotated terms to describe individuals; these limitations "may lead to viewing others in a categorical manner." A wide range of literature demonstrates general links between right-wing authoritarianism and social dominance orientation on the one hand and intergroup prejudice and negative attitudes to out-groups on the other (Duckitt 2006; Heaven and Bucci 2001; Whitley 1999).

A rigid in-group preference is commonly identified as a core trait of radical Islamist ideology. This trait matters also because it may sustain, in conjunction with NFC, a disposition to take action, a *decisiveness* that pushes people who become extremists beyond armchair theorizing and thrusts them into the fray. We'll never know how many people mull over blowing up this or that or assassinating this or that autocrat to redress humiliations and injustices—what is clear is that few act on such thoughts, which remain daydreams for the vast majority. Federico and colleagues (2005) found that one causal mechanism that linked NFC with support for military action against Iraq was identification with the national in-group, suggesting a connection between NFC, in-group preference, and support for violence. Similarly, in a study of Polish students, Golec de Zavala et al. (2010: 521, 522) found that "among participants who iden-tify themselves as conservative, need for cognitive closure was positively and significantly related to a preference for aggressive actions against the out-group" and that "high need for closure predisposes people to see inter-group relations in a 'black and white' way that encourages compe-tition." McGregor and colleagues (2011), moreover, found that more conservative aspects of religious morality, such as in-group loyalty, purity, and deference to authority, can lead to aggression.

The connection between NFC and in-group preferences might also explain anti-immigrant attitudes and cultural chauvinism among individ-uals with high NFC scores. Italian students with strong NFC have proved to be not only more right-wing and in favor of centralized, authoritarian leadership but also anti-immigrant, less pluralist, and less multicultural than their peers (Chirumbolo 2002; Chirumbolo, Areni, and Sensales 2004; Chirumbolo and Leone 2008). U.S. students with strong NFC also had more negative attitudes toward immigration (Kruglanski and Ore-hek 2011).

Radical Islamists are not anti-immigrant in a traditional sense; they often live in societies with limited immigration or are of migrant back-ground themselves. But they vigorously reject foreign cultural intrusions and defend their religious in-group: keeping it doctrinally or at least cul-turally pure is their declared raison d'être. Salafists in particular are ob-sessed with the stricture of "al-wala' wal-bara'," which commands loyalty toward the community of pure Muslims and rigid rejection of social con-tact and cooperation with everyone else (Wagemakers 2008). Atran et al. (2014) have found that strong identification with in-groups like family, religion, and country among Moroccan respondents is a strong predictor of willingness to fight for the defense of Islamic sharia. It stands to reason that personality traits favoring stark in-group/out-group distinctions, and the active defense of these distinctions, are at work for both right-wing and Islamist militants.

The Three Traits among Graduates

Our task now is to find out how these three traits are distributed among graduates with different degrees, and in particular whether engineers as well as graduates of the humanities and social sciences stand out in this regard. The best source we could find is the European Social Survey (ESS): drawing on cumulative data from four waves (2002, 2004, 2006, and

2008), we assembled a sample of 11,183 *male graduates* from 17 Western European countries, 3,320 of whom are engineers, 690 trained in the social sciences, and 928 in the arts and humanities.[10] The ESS includes numerous questions on social and cultural attitudes that approximate the traits of our concern and, crucially, it allows us to break down the data by the same set of disciplines we have used throughout the book. The ESS has been used by political psychologists, but never with a view to establishing differences between graduates of different disciplines.[11]

ESS subjects were asked attitudinal questions in either of two ways: whether they agreed with a certain statement, or the extent to which a person with the views described by the question could, to some extent or another, be said to be "like me" or "not like me." With regard to the former type of response, the graphs we present report the share of subjects who agreed somewhat or more with the statement; with regard to the latter type of response, we report the frequency with which subjects declared to be at least to some extent like the person described in the question.[12] The dotted vertical line shows the average measured over all disciplines (including smaller ones not reported),[13] while the horizontal "whiskers" of discipline-specific markers indicate a 95 percent confidence interval.

The trait on which the ESS data offer minimal information is the proneness to disgust. The only attitude we can use is aversion to gay freedom, which previous research has linked to disgust. Engineers stand out as those most opposed to gay freedom (figure 6.1); just under a quarter of them are opposed, while graduates in medicine, law, and economics hover around 20 percent (which is also the overall graduate average), and all

10 The seventeen countries are Austria, Belgium, Cyprus, Denmark, Finland, France, Germany, Great Britain, Greece, Ireland, Luxembourg, Netherlands, Poland, Portugal, Spain, Sweden, and Switzerland. We excluded Eastern Europe because the experience of communism and its demise is likely to have heavily colored individuals' preferences on the ideological spectrum; individuals, moreover, often could not choose their discipline of study freely before the transition. Including Eastern European cases does not materially change the results. Unfortunately we could not separate out history as a discipline from the arts and humanities as we were able to do in chapter 5.
11 The ESS's exact categories for disciplines are technical and engineering, transport and telecommunications, medical/health services/nursing, etc., law and legal services, economics/commerce/business administration, science/mathematics/computing, etc., social studies/administration/media/culture, "art, fine/applied," and humanities. We merged technical and engineering with transport and telecommunications into our engineering category and arts and humanities into one category (arts by itself totals only 284 cases).
12 This dichotomization also allowed us to produce cross-tabs with simple chi-square significance tests and run logistic regressions. Regressions using the Likert scale responses as continuous dependent variables result in substantially similar results.
13 The latter are "general/no specific field," agriculture/forestry, teacher training/education, personal care services, and public order and safety.

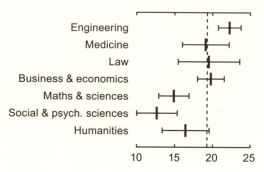

Figure 6.1: Proneness to disgust (percentage who disagree with statement "gays free to live as they wish").

Source: ESS, male graduates, 17 European countries, cumulative data for 2002, 2004, 2006, and 2008.

other subjects, including humanities and social and psychological sciences, seem more tolerant, showing opposition at around 15 percent.

More indicators are available for NFC and in-group bias. In a study of psychological traits associated with right-wing and left-wing attitudes, Thorisdottir et al. (2007) used eight ESS questions to assess five components of NFC: traditionalism (figure 6.2), tolerance of inequality (figure 6.3), preference for order and hierarchy (figure 6.4), threat perception (figure 6.5), and openness to new experiences (figure 6.6). We do the same but also break the results down by discipline of study.

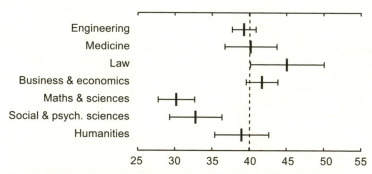

Figure 6.2: NFC, traditionalism (percentage who agree with statement "family/religious traditions are important").

Source: ESS, male graduates, 17 European countries, cumulative data for 2002, 2004, 2006, and 2008.

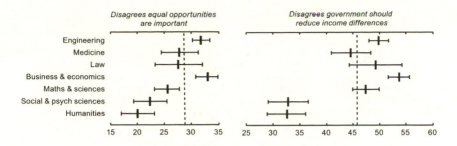

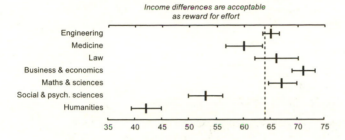

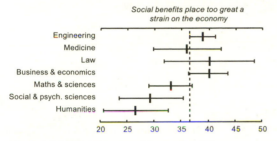

Figure 6.3: NFC, tolerance of inequality (%).
Source: ESS, male graduates, 17 European countries, cumulative data for 2002, 2004, 2006, and 2008.

We find that engineers are not particularly traditional (figure 6.2). They are also somewhat in favor of creativity (figure 6.6), but this indicator is generally the least discriminating among academic disciplines. All other results are in the expected direction, showing graduates in engineering scoring at or near the top. While engineers are often "beaten" to the top position by graduates in economics, they are the most consistent, showing higher scores across all indicators. Results are very systematic not only for engineers: at the other end of the spectrum of attitudes, the social sciences, arts, and humanities consistently show lower scores on all the NFC-related traits.

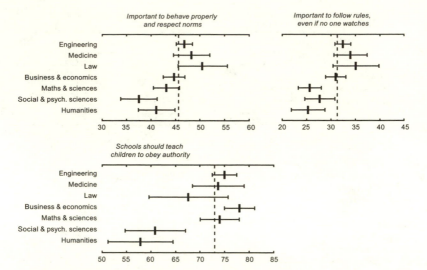

Figure 6.4: NFC, preference for order and hierarchy (%).
Source: ESS, male graduates, 17 European countries, cumulative data for 2002, 2004, 2006, and 2008.

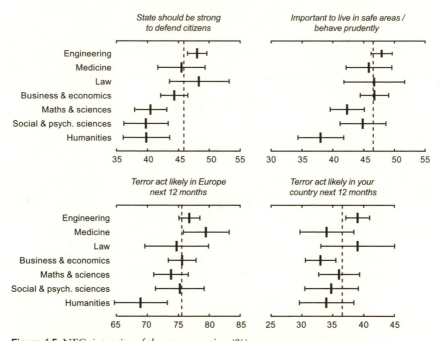

Figure 6.5: NFC, intensity of threat perception (%).
Source: ESS, male graduates, 17 European countries, cumulative data for 2002, 2004, 2006, and 2008.

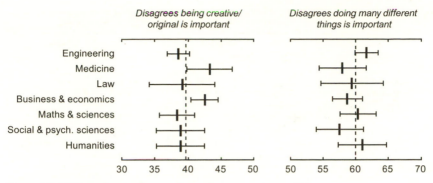

Figure 6.6: NFC, preference for novelty and new experiences (%).
Source: ESS, male graduates, 17 European countries, cumulative data for 2002, 2004, 2006, and 2008.

We considered six additional questions in the above figures that, although ignored by Thorisdottir et al., arguably speak to the same five components.[14] These additional questions in the ESS confirm the results: engineers find it particularly likely that a terror attack will happen in the next twelve months, indicating a strong threat perception; display a strong preference for authoritarian schooling; and are economically to the right on questions about redistribution and welfare, albeit less so than economics graduates.

ESS data on the third personality feature identified earlier, namely preference for a clear in-group/out-group distinction, make engineers stand apart even from the other disciplines with right-wing inclinations. We measured this trait by looking at respondents' attitudes toward immigration, a set of questions that polarizes disciplines like no other (figure 6.7). Economics students and even more so law graduates are less rigid on immigration, while engineers seem eager to preserve the integrity of their national community (even if not in the name of "tradition"). Social scientists and humanities graduates are by contrast particularly liberal on immigration.

These results hold up in a number of statistical robustness tests. We conducted regressions on all questions in which we measured the impact of different disciplines with dummy variables and included controls for

14 Here and in what follows, we have included all ESS questions of potential relevance to avoid cherry-picking. We have also investigated questions on individuals' satisfaction with their country and economy, on personal success and recognition, on happiness, on feelings of failure, etc., which are not directly relevant to NFC but could have measured different disciplines' propensities to be frustrated. They yielded no systematic results.

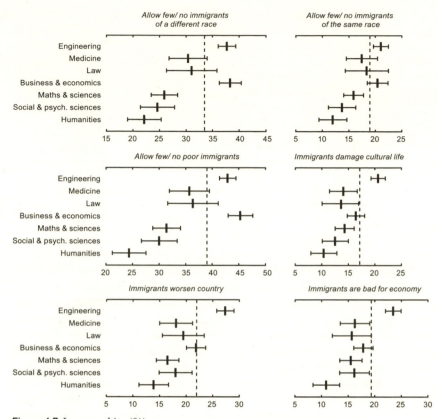

Figure 6.7: In-group bias (%).
   Source: ESS, male graduates, 17 European countries, cumulative data for 2002, 2004, 2006, and 2008.

employment status, age, family status, income group, and country.[15] The dependent variables were coded both as dichotomous responses and as answers on a continuous scale, using logistic and linear regression methods, respectively. The results are essentially the same as those shown in the figures, including for the significance of the engineers variable. A large survey of German students broken down by discipline confirms our ESS findings in that German engineering students are moderately right wing, anti-immigration, and tough on crime but less economically conservative than students in some other disciplines (Simeaner et al. 2007).

15 We ran separate regressions for each discipline (i.e., including a dummy only for the discipline at hand) to be able to measure the impact of each dummy relative to the general average outcome of male graduates.

One could suspect that our measures of psychological traits drawn from a European population may be relevant for understanding Western-born radicals but not graduates in Muslim countries. Muslims in the developing world might have different reasons for choosing their discipline of study; given strong family bonds and the high prestige of engineering programs, parental pressure, for example, might play a more important role than preferences. Al-Qaida ideologue Anwar Al-Awlaki, for example, complained that his father pressured him to become an engineer.[16] One could suspect relative deprivation to be more important than mind-set in explaining engineers' strong presence in Muslim world Islamist militancy.

As we argued in chapter 2, however, in Muslim countries medical studies are generally as prestigious (and time-consuming and costly) as engineering. High-achieving students hence should have a reasonably free choice between these two degrees. We already know that doctors are more frequent among peaceful Islamists and less overrepresented among the violent variety. Might this have to do with different "types" of young Muslims choosing one over the other discipline?

There is some evidence for this from a survey conducted by Riaz Hassan to record religious and social attitudes in Iran, Egypt, Kazakhstan, Pakistan, and Turkey in the mid-2000s. Among 1,744 male graduates in the survey, 69 were identified as engineers and 27 as doctors. A re-analysis of Hassan's data shows that for 25 questions that cover attitudes to Islam as a social and political system, engineers fall on the conservative/Islamist side in 18 cases, doctors only in 11.[17] Engineers' response biases relative to other graduates are significant in three cases, all of which are in an Islamist direction. The numbers are small and the survey contains no ESS-style questions that would allow us to tap into personality traits. But it provides some evidence that the general population of engineers in the Islamic world, just as in the West, harbors conservative attitudes oriented toward social order. The differences between doctors and engineers further confirm that social context cannot provide the full story.

ENTER WOMEN

We can follow another route to test for the robustness of our results. This requires introducing a remarkable fact. In addition to male graduates in the social sciences and humanities, there is another group that manifests

16 *New York Times*, 8 May 2010, www.nytimes.com/2010/05/09/world/09awlaki.html? pagewanted=2&ref=middleeast.
17 We thank Riaz Hassan for sharing his raw data; 20 of the 25 questions we used are documented in detail in his work (2008: 50–53).

TABLE 6.1
Presence of women among militants in extremist groups

Left-wing groups	%	Right-wing and Islamist groups	%
Pre-1917 Bolsheviks	10	Islamists	1.0
Spartacus League (Germany)	18	Nazis	0.7
Rote Armee Fraktion (Germany)	47	German and Austrian neo-Nazis	4.6
Red Brigades (Italy)	23	Extreme right in United States	7
U.S. left-wing militants	27	Extreme right in Italy	7
FARC (Colombia)	~30	Extreme right in Russia	3.6

Sources: Our databases in chapters 1, 3, and 5; Evans Clements 1997: 1, 22; Handler 1990; Smith and Morgan 1994; Weinberg and Eubank 1988: 538; "Colombia's Female Fighting Force," BBC News, 4 January 2002.

an *inverse* distribution to that of the engineers: women. The ratios of female militants that we have been able to assemble for a number of groups show that the left-wing group with the lowest share of women still boasts a higher share than the highest shares of any right-wing or Islamist group (table 6.1).[18] Even the 1 percent female share among militant Islamists might be an overestimate, as at least 4 of the 8 women in our samples of Islamist radicals have played a subordinate role in their networks, which they joined because they were spouses of or otherwise related to male jihadis.

Women's negligible presence among right-wing and Islamist extremists vis-à-vis the presence of engineers tallies also with the fact that almost everywhere in the world engineering is the most male-dominated discipline.[19] Conversely, female representation among humanities and social sciences students is much stronger, in line with their stronger representa-

18 Smith and Morgan (1994: 52–53) report that in their sample of 75 right-wing U.S. extremists who were indicted for terrorist-related activities, only five were females. "In almost all of these cases, the women were married to active members of violent elements of the extreme right. Only two played major roles in terroristic violence: Margaret Jean Craig performed the surveillance on Allen [*sic*] Berg prior to his assassination, and Deborah Dorr, along with her husband, was a leader of the Order II." Handler (1990) reports similar results.

19 On a lighter note, this cleavage also matches tastes in fantasy and mythology found among right-wing and Islamist militants (see chapter 4), who are typically male and whom popular culture associates with socially inept, technically oriented nerds.

tion among leftist groups. It hence is not surprising that the only Western engineering programs in which females have a strong presence are those with a strong social or humanitarian component.[20]

We are not the first to detect this pattern of female militancy. It is amply documented—with reference to many countries and groups active at one time or another over the last hundred years—by Weinberg and Eubank (2011). Their conclusions could not be clearer. Women have been, first of all, active participants through all four waves of terrorist violence from the Russian People's Will and Socialist Revolutionaries through the contemporary Tamil Tigers and Hamas. Second, the tasks women have performed in these organizations have varied substantially, often based on political and religious considerations.

By and large women have become leaders of left-wing or revolutionary terrorist groups in Europe as well as in North and South America (2011: 39). The authors point out that this is not due to being exposed to Western values, as one might suspect; in fact, women have been active, and often in leadership roles, also among the Sri Lankan Tamil Tigers, the Indian Maoists known as Naxalites, and the Nepalese People's Liberation Army. While this is what we find in left-wing groups, the situation on the right is very different:

> women have largely been missing from the ranks of neo-fascist, neo-Nazi, and violent racial supremacist groups. And, so far as we are aware, women have rarely participated in the "death squads" that were prevalent in Central and South America during the 1970s. These rightist groups typically stressed the traditional child-bearing role of women and emphasized the manliness and therapeutic benefits of violence. (40)

Lastly,

> for those groups claiming inspiration from Islamist ideas—Hamas, PIJ, Al Qaeda in Mesopotamia—... beyond their roles as suicide bombers women have not been prevalent in the religiously-inspired terrorist groups. They are rarely if ever leaders and even the roles of recruiters and "handlers" are usually the tasks of male members of the organization. (40)

Similar patterns are confirmed by a variety of other studies (Cunningham 2003; Eager 2008; Henshaw 2013). Discrimination, one could suspect, may contribute to this pattern, as extremists could be keeping women out of their ranks, so their absence would not result from women's choice and would not therefore mean that women have a mind-set more averse

20 *New York Times*, 27 April 2015, http://mobile.nytimes.com/2015/04/27/opinion/how-to-attract-female-engineers.html?referrer=.

than that of men to right-wing or Islamist extremism. There could be women clamoring to join who are not given the chance to do so.

For right-wing radicalism this is unlikely, for even without organizational barriers holding women back, their political preferences are less extreme than men's: in a study that pooled results from twenty-four elections in Western Europe, controlling for age, education, and social class, "being male increases the probability of an individual being an extreme right voter by more than 50 percent.... This finding supports results from existing national studies that found that right-wing extremist parties have consistently attracted a considerably higher number of male voters than female voters" (Arzheimer and Carter 2006: 428).[21] Recent studies show that European women generally vote less frequently for extremist parties, but this effect is more pronounced for right-wing ones (Harteveld et al. 2013).

For Islamist radicalism it is harder to establish whether the low presence of militant women is a choice due to women's antithetic proclivities rather than to discrimination. We know that there is discrimination. The BBC, for instance, reports that "Ayman al-Zawahiri [Al-Qaida's leader] rejects the participation of women in armed actions. His wife, Omayma, directed an open letter last December to Muslim women urging them to support Jihad by all means other than physical fighting. 'It is not easy for women ... and it is forbidden for her to move without being accompanied by male relatives and jihad requires mobility,' she argued."[22]

However, women have been allowed to join Islamist groups in ancillary roles and, sometimes, as suicide attackers. In the latter role they have been active especially in the Chechen conflict and in Palestine.[23] Proportionally, however, they have never committed more than 10 percent of a group's suicide attacks, despite the operational advantages that female

21 For similar findings the authors also refer to a study by Hans-Georg Betz (1994: 142–49).

22 This attitude that allows women's participation only in ancillary roles or in martyrdom operation might be relaxing somewhat. Hassan Abu Haniya, an Amman-based analyst of Islamist groups, told the BBC in 2010 that "While the traditional jihadists limit women's participation in jihad to supporting militant men in activities such as nursing, teaching, and moral support, the new ideologues have begun to mention female participation in armed actions in their literature recently" (7 October 2010, www.bbc.co.uk/news/world-middle-east-11484672).

23 Suicide bombers of both genders are not typically proper militants, let alone leaders. They follow a separate "career" path—a "shortcut to paradise"—and volunteer specifically for martyrdom. "They don't want to gradually earn their entry to paradise by participating in operations against the Americans. They want martyrdom immediately," said Abu Qaqa al-Tamini, a former officer of Saddam's regime, interviewed by *Time* magazine under this pseudonym, who specializes in organizing suicide attacks and claims to have coordinated thirty of them on behalf of both camps of the insurgency (Gambetta 2006: 311).

bombers enjoy—a much lower rate than that among non-Islamist groups such as the Sri Lankan Tamil Tigers or the Kurdistan Workers' Party (Schweitzer 2006: 8). In Palestine itself the vast majority of women suicide attackers belonged to secular and left-leaning groups; until 2006 only one of them came from Hamas (Schweitzer 2006: 26).

Women have been part of Islamist groups in supporting roles but only of the larger and territorial ones, which want to maintain a domestic side to support their male fighters. A prominent example is that of the Islamic State (ISIS), which has been accepting recruits of all sorts from around the world:[24] "Women and girls appear to make up about 10% of those leaving Europe, North America and Australia to link up with jihadi groups, including Islamic State." Their motives, however, differ and seem less bellicose than those of men: "In most cases, women and girls appear to have left home to marry jihadis, drawn to the idea of supporting their 'brother fighters' and having 'jihadist children to continue the spread of Islam', said Louis Caprioli, former head of the French security agency Direction de la Surveillance du Territoire."[25] Outside of domestic duties women have only been allowed to join all-female police brigades operating in Iraq and Syria, with the task of enforcing sharia law among other women.[26]

We cannot say for certain whether, if allowed to fight on a par with men and to take leadership roles, women would not join Islamist militancy in greater numbers; what we can say is that given what they can do now, their presence remains negligible among smaller underground non-territorial groups, and even in larger territorial groups there are still fewer

24 11 August 2014, www.huffingtonpost.com/2014/11/08/foreign-fighters-iraq-syria_n_6116440.html.
25 29 September 2014, www.theguardian.com/wrld/2014/sep/29/schoolgirl-jihadis-female-islamists-leaving-home-join-isis-iraq-syria. The article also reports that "France has the highest number of female jihadi recruits, with 63 in the region—about 25% of the total—and at least another 60 believed to be considering the move. Counter-terrorism experts in the UK believe about 50 British girls and women have joined Isis, about a tenth of those known to have travelled to Syria to fight. Many are believed to be based in Raqqa, the eastern Syrian city that has become an Isis stronghold. Those identified by researchers at the International Centre for the Study of Radicalisation at Kings College London are mainly aged between 16 and 24. Many are university graduates, and have left behind caring families in their home countries. At least 40 women have left Germany to join Isis in Syria and Iraq in what appears to be a growing trend of teenagers becoming radicalised and travelling to the Middle East without their parents' permission."
26 In a manifesto on the role of women circulated by ISIS militants in 2015 the emphasis remains "on the importance of motherhood and family support—in this sense, IS is no different from any other jihadist group. It is fundamentally misogynist and, within its interpretation of Islamism, the role of women is 'divinely' limited." "Women of the Islamic State: A Manifesto on Women by the Al-Khanssaa Brigade," translation and analysis by Charlie Winter for the Quilliam foundation, www.quilliamfoundation.org/wp/wp-content/uploads/publications/free/women-of-the-islamic-state3.pdf.

women than there are in left-wing groups, while their presence in leadership roles is simply nonexistent.

If the contrast between women's and engineers' distribution across the radical spectrum reflects their respective underlying traits, we should find women to differ systematically from both engineers and males in general in the ESS sample. Women should have preferences more in line with those of humanities and social science graduates. In the same ESS waves we used for men, we found that, contrary to our conjecture, women graduates score higher than men on four out of twenty-one items: they deem family and religious tradition, and living in a safe environment, as more important than do men; they discount the value of creativity more, and more of them think immigrants are bad for the economy. These differences are small but significant. (They also fear terror attacks slightly more than do men and are slightly more opposed to accepting immigrants of the same ethnicity, but insignificantly so; in their expectation toward the government to provide safety, they are identical to men.)

On *all other measures* that we presented for male graduates, women do indeed score lower than men do and, a fortiori, much lower than engineers: they are less tolerant of inequality, have a weaker preference for order and hierarchy, are less opposed to gay freedom, and more tolerant of immigrants in all other respects. The difference with regard to men in the predicted direction is significant for thirteen items and is robust to including demographic control variables.[27]

For the four measures in which women score higher than men, one could explain their attitudes as having to do with their family and labor market roles and their greater potential exposure to violent harassment rather than with the underlying traits that separate left and right preferences. However, even without belittling this evidence to the contrary, on balance our conjecture—that women's profile on the relevant traits, while close to that of students of humanities and social science, is the reverse of that of engineers—seems confirmed.

One More Trait: "Simplism"

There is a fourth trait that we have not mentioned so far that could incline its bearers toward the extreme right but that political psychology researchers have not discussed. Political scientists Seymour Martin Lipset

---

27 Of course, if we control also for discipline of study then the difference between men and women becomes smaller and less frequently significant. But we cannot infer from that that therefore the relation that interests us is spurious: this is because the more frequent presence of women in certain disciplines is itself a plausible measure of their character traits, as we discuss in the next section.

and Earl Raab first attributed to right-wing extremists what they called *simplism*: the "unambiguous ascription of single causes and remedies for multifactored phenomena" (1971: 7). A penchant to seek simple and unambiguous explanations of the social world and its ills is a cognitive trait that could be part of the NFC galaxy.

It stands to reason that extremists of all stripes, not just right-wingers, in order to do what they do, need a considerable degree of cognitive naïveté concerning how the world works, especially about the causes of the state of affairs that particularly incenses them—think of imperialist plots, Jewish conspiracies, or Bilderberg Conference world domination plans. Simplism is also reflected in beliefs concerning how the status quo can be changed. The RAF and the Red Brigades, for instance, pursued their campaign of assassinating members of the elite on the fanciful expectation that this would lead to brutal state repression, which in turn would spur the working class to surge in an impetus of revolutionary rage.

At the opposite political extreme, we find the same imaginary "clockwork" reasoning in British militant David Copeland's explanation of why he bombed—with self-built nail-laced devices—a gay pub, a supermarket, and a Bangladeshi neighborhood over a thirteen-day campaign in April 1999, which killed three people and left over a hundred wounded. A member of the British National Party (BNP), a self-declared neo-Nazi sympathizer, and the son of an engineer, Copeland is now in jail for life. He told the police: "My main intent was to spread fear, resentment and hatred throughout this country, it was to cause a racial war." He said, "If you've read The Turner Diaries, you know in the year 2000 there'll be the uprising and all that, racial violence on the streets. My aim was political. It was to cause a racial war in this country. There'd be a backlash from the ethnic minorities, then all the white people will go out and vote BNP."[28]

New evidence suggests that a feature arguably related to simplism, overconfidence in one's beliefs, is indeed stronger on the right than on the left, and that Lipset and Raab's conjecture might be correct. Ortoleva and Snowberg (2014) developed a theoretical model that predicts that (1) overconfidence in one's beliefs leads to ideological extremeness, and that (2) "ideological extremeness has a substantially higher covariance with overconfidence for those to the right of center than for those to the left of center." Both predictions are borne out by their empirical analysis (22–23 and table 5).

Is simplism present also among Islamist extremists? Psychologist Bernhard Fink and evolutionary biologist Robert Trivers argue that "cognitive simplicity" is particularly powerful among religiously motivated suicide bombers (Fink and Trivers 2014; see also Triandis 2008). Although there

28 "The Nailbomber," BBC Panorama, 30 June 2000.

are no systematic data to prove this, anecdotal evidence abounds. The assassins of Egyptian president Anwar Sadat believed that his regime would quickly crumble after his killing, allowing them to establish an Islamic state (Beattie 2000: 276). Michael C. Finton, an American convert to Islam with a criminal record accused in a 2009 Illinois bomb plot, believed that he could bring down the U.S. government by blowing up a building.[29] But the example of simplism that best fit our era is found in a videotaped testimony by Saajid Badat, a thirty-three-year-old British Muslim convicted in London in 2005 for a plot to bring down an American Airlines flight from Paris to Miami with explosives hidden in his shoes. In his testimony, played before a federal jury in New York, Badat recounts that when he met the Al-Qaida founder, "[bin Laden] said that 'the American economy is like a chain. If you break one link of the chain, the whole economy will be brought down.'" Bin Laden expected that a new operation after the September 11 attacks would "ruin the aviation industry and in turn the whole economy will come down."[30]

Is simplism also a feature of engineers? For all their technical superiority engineers can be surprisingly naïve when it comes to political issues. U.S. research has shown that students in the pure sciences have more sophisticated and less closed views of knowledge than do students in engineering (understood as an "applied science"); those in soft, social scientific fields have the most open-ended view of knowledge as uncertain and dependent on their own reasoning ability (Paulsen and Wells 1998; Jehng, Johnson, and Anderson 1993).

One might object that scientists, who are largely absent from all forms of violent political activism, are just like engineers in their focus on "hard" natural laws. Yet they differ in that they are more oriented toward answering fundamental questions than practical ones and are in principle engaged in creating new knowledge at a frontier at which truth is uncertain, and thus more accustomed to a gradual and deliberative type of inquiry. Scientists learn to ask questions, while engineering students, like followers of text-based religions, rely more strongly on answers that have already been given. In our ESS sample we found that engineers strongly believe that science can solve environmental problems, much more so than the scientists themselves do.

This cognitive feature could make engineers less adept at dealing with the confusing causality of the social and political realms, as well as the compromise and circumspection that these entail. It is striking that engineers, according to the ESS data, find politics "too complex to understand"

29 *New York Times*, 27 September 2009; www.nytimes.com/2009/09/28/us/28springfield .html?ref=us&pagewanted=print..
30 *The Guardian*, 24 April 2012, www.theguardian.com/world/2012/apr/24/shoe -bomber-osama-bin-laden-9-11.

much more so than anyone else, including the two other right-wing disciplines (economics and law), which find politics easier to grasp. Perhaps their penchant for joining violent groups rather than peaceful Islamist parties (see chapter 3) is a draconian way in which a small minority of engineers deals with the puzzling complexity of the piecemeal and messy democratic process.

The ordered, hierarchical, and corporatist view of society—akin to a well-maintained machine—that we mentioned in chapter 4 could gel with the engineering mentality, seeking clear answers to closed-end problems. There is indeed an understanding of "science" ('ilm in Arabic) among radical Islamists that is much closer to applied engineering: Roy (1990) argues that Islamists' understanding of modern science, and its compatibility with Islam, is facile and secondhand, as a set of fixed, indisputable truths, not as an open quest for knowledge. Wiktorowicz reports that salafists claim to eliminate human bias by literalist interpretation of sacred texts and "frequently exhibit the arrogance of scientific certitude.... It is as though Muslims posit questions to a computer run by divine software. Ipso facto, all alternative conclusions are misguidance" (2006: 214).

An extreme case illustrating the "arrogance of scientific certitude" is Bekkay Harrach, whom we met in chapter 1, a German Moroccan student of engineering who went to Afghanistan in 2007 to train for jihad, joined Al-Qaida, and died in a bombardment of the Bagram air base in 2010. He had released some videos that can still be viewed on YouTube:[31] in one of them he presents, neatly written out on a blackboard, two simple mathematical formulas that produce curves that represent the fight between the West and Al-Qaida, aiming to "prove" that the latter will inevitably prevail.[32]

---

31 www.youtube.com/watch?v=OaYghPA8gIU.

32 Even former Iranian president Mahmoud Ahmadinejad, who was among Ayatollah Khomeini's frontline supporters who overthrew the Shah in 1979 and holds a PhD in transport engineering, seems to rely on similar "science" for explaining the political world. In a speech given in early September 2007 aimed against elements inside Iran who were pressing for compromise in the nuclear standoff with the West over fears that the United States could launch a military strike, Ahmadinejad said: "In some discussions I told them 'I am an engineer and I am examining the issue. They do not dare wage war against us and I base this on a double proof.' ... I tell them: [First] 'I am an engineer and I am a master in calculation and tabulation. I draw up tables. For hours, I write out different hypotheses. I reject, I reason. I reason with planning and I make a conclusion. They cannot make problems for Iran. [Second] I believe in what God says. God says that those who walk in the path of righteousness will be victorious. What reason can you have for believing God will not keep this promise?'" (AFP, 3 September 2007).

A 2015 New York Times profile describes Ayelet Shaked, a female justice minister in Israel from the far right who has studied computer engineering and ran on an anti-Arab platform, as monosyllabic, action-oriented, "very calculated and not very sensitive," and reports that she is criticized for her "simplistic approach to complex problems"; New

The evidence for simplism is too scattered for firm conclusions, but it is a plausible complement to familiar arguments based on NFC.

Traits and Disciplines

In line with the findings in political psychology, we have argued that right-wing political preferences are influenced by specific personality traits, and that these traits are as strong among engineers as they are weak among graduates in the humanities and social sciences. Our argument rests on two assumptions, which, in our focus on extremist behavior and psychological traits, we have not discussed thus far: first, that among the wider population on which we have poll data different disciplines indeed cluster across the political spectrum as expected; and second, that it is indeed the underlying traits that push graduates of different disciplines toward different ends of the political spectrum—that is, that disciplines are only "proxies" for the traits we have identified.

To test these assumptions, we used ESS data on self-declared political preferences, measured on a 0 to 10 left to right scale recorded by the ESS, broken down by discipline. The distribution is reported in figure 6.8: in line with our expectations, economics, law, and engineering are more to the right than the average of the whole sample while social sciences and humanities graduates are more to the left. Students of science and medicine, which are closer to the average in the personality traits investigated above, have no systematic presence on either left or right. U.S. data from surveys of male students and faculty in 1969 and 1984 confirm all findings, with the exception that law students have more of a presence on the left (Carnegie 1984).[33] A 2000 survey of Canadian professors also found that engineers are the least liberal, followed by faculty in business studies, while humanities and social science professors had the most leftist attitudes (law, medicine, and sciences were not included; Nakhaie and Brym 1999). Data on German students reveal similar patterns (Simeaner et al. 2007).

Women in the ESS data, too, match the expectation and are more to the left by a small but significant margin (their score is 4.9 versus 5.1 for men). There is also at least one piece of evidence linking Muslim world engineers with conventional right-wing politics: a 1948 survey of 3,890

York Times, 16 May 2015, www.nytimes.com/2015/05/16/world/middleeast/ayelet-shaked -israels-new-justice-minister-shrugs-off-critics-in-her-path.html?_r=0.

Neither of these two politicians is a violent militant, but both are engineers who are considered political extremists by many observers.

33 Data of the 1969 survey can be obtained at ICPSR, at the University of Michigan, www.icpsr.umich.edu/.

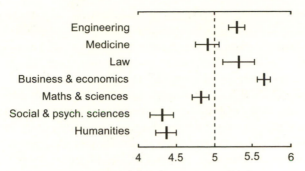

Figure 6.8: Average score left-right spectrum (ESS; 0 = very left, 10 = very right).
Source: ESS, male graduates, 17 European countries, cumulative data for 2002, 2004, 2006, and 2008.

Cairo University students recorded the highest sympathies for fascist ideology among engineering students—9 percent, followed by 7 percent among science students and 5 percent among students in agriculture and medicine (Botman 1984: 70).[34]

Regressions on the left-right score as (continuous) dependent variable, with full controls for demographic factors, confirm the findings. Logistic regressions with the presence of extreme left- and right-wing attitudes as dependent variable yield further information: first, engineering is the only discipline that has a statistically significant and positive effect on an individual's likelihood to reach position 10 on the scale, that is, the very right.[35] This is some evidence of a small, but extreme, sub-population among engineers that is relatively larger than that among other disciplines. Second, social science and humanities are statistically significant predictors of an individual's presence on the extreme left, while engineering and economics are statistically significant predictors of an individual's *absence* from the extreme left.[36]

But to which extent is a bias toward one or the other political camp just an unexplained corollary of discipline, and to which extent is the statistical impact of discipline a reflection of the discipline-specific traits

34 At the same time, the discipline of science has the highest share of individuals with no political affiliation (12 percent) while engineering has the lowest (3 percent).
35 Coefficients for law and economics/business graduates are both smaller and not significant.
36 This is the case whether the radical left is defined as including only position 0 or both positions 0 and 1 on the scale (law is significant at $p < .1$ as a predictor of absence when the broader definition of radical leftism is used, although with a coefficient comparable to that of engineering).

that we have identified? Do traits, in other words, "do the work" in explaining various disciplines' ideological biases?

The evidence we have supports the latter claim. When we control for the fourteen NFC-related variables, the logit coefficient for the engineers' dummy variable is reduced from .27 to .17. Almost the same reduction obtains if we control for in-group preferences, while a smaller reduction (to .25) results if we include the measure for disgust (the question about gays).[37] If we include all trait variables together, the dummy for engineers is reduced to .11. This means that, statistically speaking, the various traits account for about 60 percent of what makes engineers more rightist. The difference between the engineering dummies in the estimates with and without full controls for traits is highly significant. Similar results apply for social sciences and for humanities, where about half of the leftward bias seems to be explained by the full list of traits, and the difference between coefficients again is highly significant. Replicating the same tests for only women graduates produces very similar results regarding the impact of the three disciplines on political attitudes and the role of traits in explaining this impact of disciplines.[38]

In all of the regressions, we also controlled for six or more demographic variables (age, education, income, marital status, etc.). Leaving all these out of our estimates hardly increases the discipline coefficients. This implies that the impact of the trait variables on the discipline coefficients is not just a function of "throwing in" more controls, as other control variables reduce the coefficient of the discipline dummies much less strongly and systematically. In conclusion, the test shows that the combined traits we identified appear to account for much of the link between disciplines and political attitudes.[39]

The fact that the effect related to the discipline is largely absorbed by the traits leads us to a further question: are the traits innate, that is, do they make individuals both choose a particular discipline *and* gravitate toward a particular political behavior? Or are they acquired in the course of studying a particular subject—in which case the discipline would be the proper underlying cause of political behavior and personality traits only a transmission mechanism (or "intervening variable")?[40]

37 Including the two ESS variables measuring simplism, however, results in no noticeable reduction of the dummy coefficient.

38 The only exception is that for female engineers, where the measures of in-group preference and disgust do not reduce the impact of the engineering dummy (while NFC measures have a strong impact).

39 No individual questionnaire item has a particularly large effect in terms of reducing the engineer dummy's coefficient. This is arguably a sign that none of the individual items by itself sufficiently captures larger concepts like "need for closure."

40 Friedrich von Hayek, in 1952, made a strong case for the peculiarity of the engineering mentality, which in his view is the result of an education that does not train them to

To properly address this issue, one would have to follow the same individuals over time as they pass through university. The ESS data provide snapshots in time and therefore cannot address this question. There is, however, a growing body of literature, to which we referred at the onset of this chapter (see footnote 1), arguing for and offering some evidence that political attitudes could be inherited (Alford, Funk, and Hibbing 2005; Verhulst, Eaves, and Hatemi 2012). There is also indirect evidence that individuals who already possess a given mind-set are attracted to specific disciplines. Ladd and Lipset, drawing on the large 1969 Carnegie survey, not only document the above-mentioned political biases among U.S. faculty and students; they also show that "un-socialized" students in the first four semesters of study already exhibit these biases (1975: 74–75). In their study, no other variable predicts ideological leanings as powerfully as discipline.

Even deeper biases are documented by Block and Block (2006), who show that personality differences that distinguish liberals and conservatives in adulthood were already present when the same individuals were in nursery school: "Preschool children who 20 years later were relatively liberal were characterized as: developing close relationships, self-reliant, energetic, somewhat dominating, relatively under-controlled, and resilient. Preschool children subsequently relatively conservative at age 23 were described as: feeling easily victimized, easily offended, indecisive, fearful, rigid, inhibited, and relatively over-controlled and vulnerable" (734). We cannot say to what extent the traits we have identified—disgust, need for closure, in-group preference, and simplism—overlap with this somewhat disorienting list of attributes. But as psychologists generally deem our triplet of traits to be similarly fundamental personality features, this reinforces our belief that disciplines select minds rather than shape them.[41]

---

understand individuals and their world as the outcome of a social process in which spontaneous behaviors and interactions play a significant part. Rather, it fosters in them a script in which a strict "rational" control of processes plays the key role (1952: 94–102): this would make them on the one hand less adept at dealing with the confusing causality of the social and political realms and the compromise and circumspection that these entail, and on the other hand inclined to think that societies should operate in an orderly fashion, akin to well-functioning machines—akin to the hierarchical and corporatist view of society among Islamists and right-wingers that we discussed in chapter 4. "It is not surprising," Hayek prophetically concluded, "that many of the more active minds among those so trained sooner or later react violently against the deficiencies of their education and develop a passion for imposing on society the order which they are unable to detect by the means with which they are familiar" (1952: 102).

41 A strong indication that different disciplines sort people with different innate attributes was discovered by Simon Baron-Cohen. Among the relatives of 641 Cambridge students in math, engineering, and physics there were 6 cases of autism while only 1 case was reported for 652 control cases studying literature (Baron-Cohen et al. 1998). In another study of a sample of 919 families with a child with autism, 28.4 percent had either a

Why should our traits have an affinity to engineering as a discipline—why should individuals who possess the traits be attracted to it in the first place? Although it is not possible to investigate this directly, in line with our discussion of "simplism" we can surmise that individuals with NFC and a craving for order are attracted to engineering as a discipline that provides concrete, unambiguous answers and recoil from the open-ended project of natural science and the ambiguities of humanities and social sciences. The latter should be more attractive to individuals who tolerate ambiguity and disorder, traits associated with the left.

Conclusions

Our findings about disciplines, personality traits, and political preferences are remarkably consistent. The outstanding result we obtained is that *the distribution of traits across disciplines mirrors almost exactly the distribution of disciplines across militant groups* we examined in chapter 5. As we can see from the summary tables (6.2a and 6.2b), engineers are present in groups in which social scientists, humanities graduates, and women are absent, *and* engineers possess traits—proneness to disgust, need for closure, in-group bias, and (at least tentatively) simplism—in a measure that the other two groups do not and indeed usually lack more than any other group of graduates. The evidence indicates that there are specific traits that are more frequent among particular disciplines, are associated with specific social and political attitudes, and as a result drive individuals to different types of political radicalism (see figure 6.9).

Our survey analysis suggests that engineers are not necessarily "traditional" in the sense of wanting to preserve customs and religion. Instead, as a result of the psychological traits identified, they tend to dislike deviance from their societies' broader norms and boundaries, whether embodied by gays or foreigners. While economically conservative, they are

---

father or grandfather who was an engineer, compared to only 15 percent in a control group of families (Baron-Cohen et al. 1997). Although not necessarily autists, engineers are more likely to be high on the autism spectrum disorder. It is plausible—though not established in the literature—that autism with its need for predictability and routines is related to high need for closure. There is at least one confirmed case of a young Western convert to Islam with Asperger syndrome who has joined ISIS; according to his mother, daily Islamic rituals and the clear answers of radical Islam provided him with the certainty he craved (*Politiken*, 22 March 2015, http://politiken.dk/magasinet/interview/ECE2597450/dr-var-han-min-skatterfis-udraabt-til-martyr/). A study of 140 jihadist volunteers who had traveled from Denmark to Syria by February 2014 identified 20 individuals with serious behavioral issues and 8 with diagnosed disorders. The former group includes two jihadis with autistic symptoms, while the latter includes one individual with an autism spectrum disorder diagnosis (Weenink 2015: 24–25).

TABLE 6.2A
Presence of traits by types of extremists, and intensity of traits by discipline

Traits	Presence of traits by ideology			Intensity of traits		
	Islamists	Right-wingers	Left-wingers	Engineers	Social science, humanities	Women
Proneness to disgust	Yes	Yes	No	High	Low	Low
Need for closure	Yes	Yes	No	High	Low	Low
In-group bias	Yes	Yes	No	High	Low	Low
Simplism	Yes	Yes	?	High	Low	?

TABLE 6.2B
Presence of disciplines of study and of women by type of extremists

	Islamists	Right-wingers	Left-wingers
Engineers	Yes	Yes	No
Social Science/Human	No	No	Yes
Women	No	No	Yes

less so than business and economics graduates, who also self-report right-wing political attitudes. This apparent anomaly is in fact consistent with evidence in the political psychology literature that the link between right-wing self-identification and tolerance of inequality is incidental and less deep-seated than the links between being on the right and the need for order, norm maintenance, and security—aspects of NFC on which engineers score more consistently than all other disciplines.[42]

42 Thorisdottir et al. (2007), for example, find that acceptance of inequality is linked to right-wing attitudes only in Western Europe, not in Eastern European countries, possibly because the latter have a stronger "tradition" of egalitarianism. Carney et al. (2008) find that cultural conservatism is more strongly linked to low openness to new experience and high conscientiousness among U.S. respondents than is the case with economic conservatism. Using data from 51 countries, Malka et al. (2014) similarly find that valuing conformity, security, and tradition predicts only cultural aspects of conservatism, not economic ones.

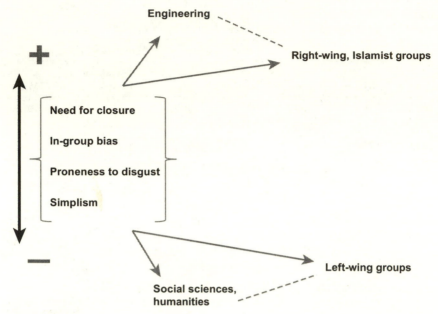

Figure 6.9: Our argument.

The general personality traits and aspects of right-wing ideology on which engineers score highly fit the profile of Islamist ideology from chapter 4 remarkably well: a desire to keep society clean or purify it, a preference for social order, and rigid in-group/out-group distinctions. Our data are not fine-grained enough to weigh the relative importance of disgust, need for closure, in-group preferences, or simplism. Although we believe that all play a role, on balance the evidence for NFC is strongest.

Reinforcing our belief in the importance of traits, graduates of social sciences and humanities—disciplines whose associated traits present a mirror image of those among engineers—are practically absent among the ideological groups that are the most attractive to engineers. Conversely, these disciplines are strongly represented among extremist groups at the opposite, leftist end of the ideological spectrum, where order, hierarchy, and social boundaries are challenged rather than defended, and where there are few or no engineers. Finally, the disciplines that have a less clear-cut profile in terms of traits, such as science and medicine, consistently do not appear strongly on either side of the political spectrum.[43]

---

43 Lawyers, who have a strong presence among the extreme right in the West but are on the right side on only some traits, are the only partial exception. Their level of political activity in the West is generally high, however.

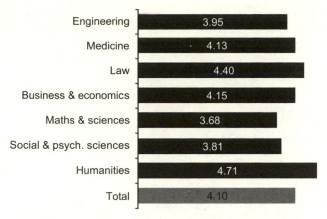

Figure 6.10: Average degree of religiousness by disciplines (ESS).
Note: 0 = "not at all religious"; 10 = "very religious."
Source: ESS, male graduates, 17 European countries, cumulative data for 2002, 2004, 2006, and 2008.

Apart from simplism, which might to a smaller extent affect extremists on all fronts, the relations between traits, disciplines, and forms of political extremism that we uncovered are almost uncannily perfect.

A question of much importance that we have not addressed in this chapter is whether engineers are attracted by Islamism, and perhaps by right-wing ideologies, because they are more strongly religious. What originally made the overrepresentation of engineers among Islamist radicals particularly puzzling was to find individuals with a secular technical education in the ranks of strictly religious groups. We have seen that radical engineers, even when they have a choice, prefer religious over secular groups and that this might be true among right-wing groups in the United States. While original Nazism was not a religious movement, it too left more space for religiousness than the revolutionary left. One of Nazism's chief ideologues, Alfred Rosenberg, proposed a racially inspired "positive Christianity"—hailing, among other things, Jesus as an Aryan resisting Jewish dominance—as a national belief system in Germany (Steigmann-Gall 2003).

The evidence for personal religiousness is mixed. The 1984 Carnegie poll data show that engineering students and faculty in the United States are indeed not only much more right wing but also much more religious. Yet in the ESS sample they are significantly *less* religious (together with scientists and social scientists, see figure 6.10). German student polls also show engineers as rather areligious (Simeaner et al. 2007). In Hassan's Muslim world data, engineers also score below average (albeit insignificantly) on indicators of personal religiousness.

Does this matter? It does, in the sense of *ruling out religiosity as a fundamental cause of engineers' radicalization*. Religiosity is typically a personal rather than a political affair, and other research shows that it is not a driver of radicalism. A Gallup poll taken in 2006 from ten different Muslim countries indicated that individuals who were critical of the United States and approved of the 9/11 attacks reported about as high religiosity and mosque attendance as those who did not (Esposito and Mogahed 2007). Similarly, drawing on Pakistani poll data, Shapiro and Fair report that "religiosity writ large is a poor predictor of support for militant organizations" (2009: 102). Many Islamist militants are not particularly religious before joining radical networks and become "born again" Muslims in the course of radicalization (Sageman 2004). Wiktorowicz even reports that religiously grounded individuals are *less* likely to be radicalized into militant Islamist groups in the UK (2004b: 18, 20).

This evidence deflates the importance of religiosity in explaining engineers' overrepresentation. It is more likely to be Islamism's vision of social order combined with the well-regulated daily routines that attracts engineers—and if we strip Islamism of religious dogma, what is left looks even more like right-wing ideology.[44] Religion happens to be part of the established order in the Muslim world (and, arguably, in the United States) but is much less so in Western Europe.

44 This argument is also in accord with the understanding of conservatism from the political psychology literature: "Although what is understood as conservative differs across time, the geographic locations and socio-political contexts, the function of conservative worldview seems to remain the same: opposition to social change and preference for social hierarchy" (Golec de Zavala, Cisłak, and Wesołowska 2010: 523, referring to Jost et al. 2003).

Conclusions

WHAT HAVE WE LEARNED ABOUT VIOLENT EXTREMISTS GENERALLY AND
Islamist extremists in particular that we did not know before pursuing
our puzzle?

The evidence we found is ample enough to revive the theory of relative
deprivation and frustrated expectations as a fundamental explanation of
why people form and join extremist movements. The theory emerges
from our analyses not just stronger but with sharper contours than it had
previously, when it was employed with a broader brush to explain differences between countries or within countries at different times rather
than, as we do here, to explain differences in extremist groups' educational composition. As we have argued in chapters 2 and 3, the theory's
predictions match the variations we uncovered in the profile of the members of Islamist radical groups across time and space, as the proportion
of graduates reflects, inversely, shifts in economic opportunity of the
regions from which they originate: on the one hand, there is no overrepresentation of graduates in the West and in much of Asia, where they
fared well professionally. The profile of extremists from Saudi Arabia—
the only MENA country to experience a shortage of engineers—similarly
reflects their society, with a smaller overrepresentation of graduates and
no elite bias among them. In all these areas violent Islamism has attracted
proportionally more marginal individuals with lower educational and
professional qualifications, with a good share of drifters and petty criminals among them. On the other hand, we find a significant overrepresentation of graduates, especially from elite degrees, among the violent Islamist radicals originating from other MENA countries, where they had to
endure a severe shortage of professional opportunities. Engineers, and to
a smaller extent doctors, stand out among them because when economic
development ground to a halt in the late 1970s and early 1980s, they fell
from the highest perch in terms of expectations and formed or joined Islamist movements that in previous decades had been led by lower-status
graduates.

The sources of frustrated expectations are not rooted in sheer materialism, however. Our claim is not that individuals take extreme risks for
highly uncertain returns out of raw self-interest—that would be contradictory. The fuel flows rather from the feeling of being unjustly deprived
of a status for which they and their families worked hard and sacrificed,

and to which they felt entitled to aspire, and, grander still, from the lack of opportunity to prove one's worth in shaping the future one's country— the nationalistic pride that autocratic Middle Eastern regimes had injected in massive doses in their elite graduates was soured by economic failure. Exacerbated by the regimes' rampant corruption, the broken promises galled the first generation of extremists who, before they evolved into a roaming international jihadi movement aiming their weapons at the West, tried unsuccessfully to challenge the oppressive establishments of their countries.

Middle East regimes would discover that promoting higher education does not promote social acquiescence. On the contrary, the highly educated can suffer the most in economic downturns, become more socially upset, *and* have better means to do something about it. The first generation of violent Islamist radicals in the 1970s was replete with highly educated individuals. Even if the rank and file is eventually filled by marginal individuals with little to lose, the first emergence of a menacing radical Islamist movement owes much to the elite graduates. Relative deprivation does not of course exclude other motives to join rebellions—motives that propel the absolutely deprived and the socially troubled to seek emancipation from and order in their insecure lives through the higher social purposes afforded by the ideology of extremist groups. Signs of "proletarization" have been apparent in radical Islamist groups now for a while, as we noted in chapter 1. Still, these motives seem to take effect in a second stage, after groups have been formed and their goals and ideology have taken shape.

Relative deprivation is not, however, an exhaustive explanation of engineers' overrepresentation. Engineers continue to be vastly overrepresented among radical Islamists in both the West and South Asia despite not being exposed to the same relative deprivation as their peers in the Middle East. The fact that, especially with the events of post-9/11 and the Iraq war, radicalization has been occurring in Western countries suggests that better economic chances (as well as opportunities for democratic expression) no longer suffice to prevent it and that the movement has now found its own momentum and draws its resources from new channels. Still, it continues to attract engineers.

Individual cases embodying this pattern, several of which we mentioned in the course of the book, continue to emerge. As we were finishing the book, the Pakistani army released the news in late 2014 that "in an intelligence-borne operation, top Al-Qaeda commander Adnan El Shukrijumah was killed by the forces in a raid in Shinwarsak, South Wazirastan." The FBI, which had offered a $5 million reward for his head, claims that he "took over as the chief of al-Qaeda's 'external operations council' in 2010—a post once held by the alleged mastermind of the 9/11 attacks,

Khalid Sheikh Mohammed." Adnan, the son of an imam, moved to the United States as a child and later earned a degree in computer engineering; he could easily have had a good career in the United States.[1]

Among 485 Western jihadis who went to fight in Syria and Iraq in 2013–14 (and whose biographies were collected by us as well as the International Centre for the Study of Radicalisation [ICSR] at King's College London), we found 28 men with university exposure and 8 of them in engineering—28.5 percent, or twice as many as we would expect given the general male student population.

So why are engineers not only proportionally more prone than all other graduates to join Islamist extremists but also to do so even where the economic situation is not so dire? And there is more: we found evidence that engineers are more likely to join violent opposition groups than non-violent ones, to prefer religious groups to secular groups, and to be less likely to defect once they join an Islamist group. None of these findings seems explicable in terms of relative deprivation.

Three of our findings in particular—that the overrepresentation of engineers occurs in vastly different social and economic contexts, that it occurs across many different and unrelated radical groups, and that engineers also predominate among small cells of self-starters in the West—help us reject other theories of extremism. First, network connections by themselves do not explain the overrepresentation of engineers: this cannot be due to a hypothetical jihadi engineer-mutant who started the whole process, which then spread through his engineer-dominated network of friends and trusted contacts. Network connections also fail to explain why engineers are less likely, and social scientists and humanities students much more likely, to drop out of radical organizations.

Next, the patterns of overrepresentation show the limits of social movement theories that, in order to explain the emergence of rebel movements, invoke "political opportunity structures" and "political entrepreneurs" able "to frame discontent" by drawing on local cultural resources (Snow et al. 1986; Tarrow 1998; Tilly 2004; Wiktorowicz 2004a, 2004b)—in this case an Islamic rhetoric of probity, offering a narrative of social and political renovation through tradition. Were it not for the emergence of Islamism as a credible narrative for political opposition to authoritarian and corrupt establishments we would not have the kind of radical groups that have arisen. But the concepts of social movement theory cannot account

---

1 www.bbc.com/news/world-south-asia-30358259; http://nation.com.pk/national/07-Dec
-2014/military-kills-top-qaeda-leader-wanted-by-us.

for the uneven success of Islamist activism across different categories of people and, by implication, the influence that the membership of groups has on their militant strategies and persistence. As we argued in the preface, they cannot explain why among larger dissatisfied populations certain agents were the first to become radicalized or were more prone to join, or stay the course. They fail to account for the different trajectories of engineers relative to those who pursued other elite degrees and cannot explain the dynamics of small, cell-based organizations among which engineers predominate and that are uprooted from the wider social and institutional context on which social movement theory typically focuses.

Another theory of extremists' profile purports that it would be determined by recruiters' choices, that it would be in other words demand driven. Recruiters would prefer more educated members and, among them, those possessing skills that are useful for the fight they pursue. Recruiters do have such preferences and actively pursue them. We saw in chapter 1 that recruiters can in fact search, according to MI6, in "schools and colleges where young people may be very *inquisitive* but *less challenging*"[2] and that people with engineering and information technology degrees might be more likely to have these traits. Still, our evidence suggests that recruiters' preferences do not account for engineers' overrepresentation: in groups in which members are selected by recruiters, engineers are *less* frequent than they are in groups in which members are *self-recruited*—a good indication that the overrepresentation of engineers is supply driven, that is, it reflects engineers' stronger willingness to join radical groups. Recruiters can enroll only those who want to be enrolled. In left-wing movements, too, they may have a preference for engineers but get hardly any.

As none of the existing theories of political violence could account for the engineers' puzzle, our next step was to try to find out whether there might be something peculiar about engineers and extremism and whether this is the case regardless of Islam. We broke this question down into two parts: Do engineers show a penchant to join other violent movements fighting for *any* ideology, or do they have discriminating ideological tastes? To find answers we investigated the educational composition of more than a dozen violent right- and left-wing groups in chapter 5. We found that engineers are nearly absent among left-wing groups: these are dominated by graduates in the humanities and the social and psychological sciences, of whom we had found barely any among Islamist radicals. By contrast, we

2 *Sunday Times*, 10 July 2005.

found a sizable presence of engineers among right-wing extremists: the only other notable trace of engineers' prominence outside of Islamist violent groups is among neo-Nazis and white supremacists in Germany, Russia, and the United States; this is all the more striking given the generally low level of education among members of such groups, especially those created after World War II. The engineers' absolute number is tiny but still disproportionate relative to that of other graduates. Conversely, humanities and social sciences graduates are systematically absent from right-wing groups (as they are from Islamist radicalism). Overall, there is a remarkable correspondence between right- and left-wing militancy on the one hand and type of degree on the other, and this near perfect correlation is found across a variety of groups in different countries and at different times.

This finding shows, first of all, that the "love affair" between engineers and extremism, while particularly marked in the Islamist case, is not peculiar to it. Next, just by knowing that someone is a university graduate one cannot guess what kind of an extremist one could become—graduates generally can become extremists of all sorts, right, left, and Islamist. But by knowing the *type* of graduate one can guess, with near perfect accuracy in the case of some disciplines, which type of extremism a graduate is attracted to or repulsed by—even if the share of cases pondering radical action among all disciplines remains tiny. Engineers possess not so much a proclivity to extremism as such but to extremism of a certain type.

In the case of MENA countries, relative deprivation and ideological propensity worked together: the former selected elite graduates and the latter boosted the share of engineers among them. In this regard our book shows exactly how the interaction between social conditions and personal characteristics, about which countless scholars have speculated, can work. But in the West and some developed Asian countries, as well as among right-wing extremists, ideological propensity *alone* has sufficed—defying our own prior beliefs—to tempt a disproportionate share of engineers to radicalize.

Finally, this evidence suggests that ideology matters—different types of people are attracted to different ideologies; or, to put it differently and in line with a core claim of political psychology, different ideologies meet the cognitive and emotional needs of different people. Once we compare the tenets of the ideologies we discover that, in fact (chapter 4), right-wing extremism has much more in common with Islamist radicalism than with left-wing extremism, which is consistent with finding engineers among right-wing radicals and not left-wing ones, where other degrees dominate. Radical Islamist movements share a large majority of their fundamental ideological tenets with the radical right, including nostalgia for a lost past, a focus on tradition, a preference for order and hierarchy, and an obsession with rigid identity boundaries. By contrast, radical Islam has only a few generic traits of ideological rigidity in common with the extreme left. We also found intriguing signs that, like identical twins separated at birth whose proclivities continue to be governed by the same genome (e.g., Wright 1998), right-wing and Islamist extremists share an array of values, tastes, and beliefs: values such as antimodernism, opposition of cultural decadence, and pursuit of purity, whether racial or religious; tastes in iconography; and an antiscientific menu of superstitious beliefs.

The near perfect match we found between types of degree and types of extremists is a strong indication that the degree is an approximate reflection of underlying character traits that sort people at once into certain degrees *and* into different ends of the political spectrum. It is hard to imagine any systematic social or institutional factors that could neatly apportion individuals into different types of groups in the wide variety of historical contexts investigated in this book. The surmise that character or mind-set matters is strengthened by another near perfect match between group membership and ideology: while we found that among the militants of right-wing and Islamist movements women are virtually absent, in left-wing groups women are a sizable minority, often in leadership roles—a fact that we argue is not only due to differences in recruitment strategy. All these findings imply that the traits that shape people's predilection for one or another type of extremism should also be nonoverlapping, present only among members of one side and weak or absent among those of the other.

The most plausible sorting features that we identified in chapter 6 are three character traits that, according to much research in political psychology, incline people toward the right generally: proneness to disgust, need for closure, and strong in-group bias. Using multinational survey data, we found solid evidence not only that these traits are more frequent among engineers than among those pursuing other degrees but also, symmetrically, that they are weakly present among graduates in the social sciences and the humanities, who are typically found at the other end of the political spectrum. They are also stronger among men than they are among women, consistent with women's presence in extremist movements of the left and not of the right. Finally, the traits account for much of the difference in reported left/right positions between graduates of different disciplines.

We do not have direct evidence that the same traits that favor right-wing extremism are also those that favor Islamist extremism. Ours is a surmise supported by piecemeal evidence and, deductively, by the ideological overlap between right-wing extremists and Islamist extremists: since we know that these traits satisfy the former, it is likely that they satisfy the latter, and this jointly explains why we find engineers in both but not on the left. In fact, when present these traits match the core tenets of both right-wing and Islamist ideology: proneness to disgust is related to the strong reaction to perceived corruption of customs and a desire for social and sexual purity. In-group bias is related to a marked aversion for those who are different, be they immigrants, ethnic others, or infidels. The most multifaceted of these traits, need for closure (NFC), is related to a strong preference for hierarchy and social order and an aversion to change, which can reach the extreme of longing for a mythical past.

One of the main components of NFC, intolerance of ambiguity, was a key concept of *The Authoritarian Personality*, a famous study by Theodor Adorno, Else Frenkel-Brunswik, and others published in 1950. Adorno said, in a statement that remains as pertinent today as it was sixty-five years ago, that "Intolerance of ambiguity is the mark of an authoritarian personality." Adorno and his colleagues believed that these traits were induced by socialization and fomented by fascist groups on otherwise tabula rasa minds. Increasing evidence emerging from contemporary political psychology, however, suggests that politically relevant traits are innate rather than acquired.

Regardless of whence these traits come, our conclusions confirm Jost et al.'s contention (2003, 2007) that there is a continuous left-right spectrum and that core traits on one side of the spectrum are the inverse of those at the other. To this fundamental claim of political psychology we add both methodologically and substantively.

Methodologically, our findings do not rely on reported voting and political attitudes but on the link between socially important and potentially costly *behaviors*, namely the choice of degree and the choice of militancy. We extend political psychology's empirical predictions around core personality traits, usually applied to more sedate political views, to the violent—and directly observable—extremes. As a result, if we accept that degrees are proxies of traits, then the contention of political psychology comes out much strengthened, linked not only to mundane "progressive" and "conservative" positions but to much more extreme ideologies as well as *actions*.

In our analysis of left and right, we also diversify the field far beyond the two typical representatives in the political psychology literature: U.S. conservatives and liberals. Next, by introducing a third case, namely the ideology of radical Islamism, and showing how close it is to that of right-wing extremists, we further validate the core claim of political psychology that different ideologies attract different types because ideologies meet different needs. In this, we move beyond the Western-centered findings of political psychology not just to other ideologies but also to other regions of the world.

Substantively, our findings identify which aspects of ideology really matter in sorting into different political extremes people with different traits—for example, preference for social order, aversion to change, and intolerance of out-group members—while other features of ideology that vary within right-wing groups between United States and Europe, or between Islamism and the secular right, are revealed as context dependent. Among these, one feature is the view of the state, vehemently opposed by U.S. right-wing groups and staunchly supported by their European counterparts. But religiosity is perhaps the most surprising varying feature—it seems organic to all Islamists and to many U.S. right-wing extremists but is ignored by their European counterparts. The thirst for order in personal and social life can be satisfied by different means.

BIBLIOGRAPHY

Abdel Jabber, Tayseer. 1993. "Inter-Arab Labor Movements: Problems and Prospects." In Said El-Naggar, ed., *Economic Development of the Arab Countries: Selected Issues*. Washington, D.C.: International Monetary Fund, 145–62.

Abdollahyan, Hamid, and Hooshang Nayebi. 2009. "Conceptualizing Occupational Prestige: An Empirical Case Study from Iran." *Asian Journal of Social Science* 37 (2), 192–207.

Abrahamian, Ervand. 1980. "The Guerrilla Movement in Iran, 1963–1977." *MERIP Reports* 86, 3–15.

———. 1989. *The Iranian Mojahedin*. New Haven: Yale University Press.

Abuza, Zachary. 2003. *Militant Islam in Southeast Asia: Crucible of Terror*. Boulder, CO: Lynne Rienner.

———. 2006. "Education and Radicalization: Jemaah Islamiyah Recruitment in South East Asia." In James J. F. Forest, ed., *The Making of a Terrorist: Recruitment, Training and Root Causes*. Westport, CT: Praeger Security International, 66–83.

Afari, Janet, and Kevin B. Anderson. 2005. *Foucault and the Iranian Revolution: Gender and the Seductions of Islamism*. Chicago: University of Chicago Press.

Akkache, Ahmed. 1990. "Ingenieurs et Emploi: Quelques Donnees sur l'Algerie." In Longuenesse, *Batisseurs et Bureaucrates*, 147–54.

Alford, John R., Carolyn L. Funk, and John R. Hibbing. 2005. "Are Political Orientations Genetically Transmitted?" *American Political Science Review* 99 (2), 153–67.

Altemeyer, Bob. 1998. "The Other 'Authoritarian Personality.'" In L. Berkowitz, ed., *Advances in Experimental Social Psychology*. Orlando, FL: Academic Press, 47–92.

Altunbas, Yener, and John Thornton. 2011. "Are Homegrown Islamic Terrorists Different? Some UK Evidence." *Southern Economic Journal* 78 (2), 262–72.

Al-Zawahiri, Ayman. 2001. *Knights under the Prophet's Banner*. London: Al-Sharq al-Awsat.

Amass, Ty. 2004. "Empirical Evaluation of Political Ideology as Social Cognition." Honors thesis, Politics Department, New York University.

Amodio, David, John Jost, Sarah Master, and Cindy Yee. 2007. "Neurocognitive Correlates of Liberalism and Conservatism." *Nature Neuroscience* 9 September. www.nature.com/neuro/journal/v10/n10/pdf/nn1979.pdf.

Angrist, Joshua D. 1995. "The Economic Returns to Schooling in the West Bank and Gaza Strip." *American Economic Review* 85 (5), 1065–87.

Antifaschistisches Autorenkollektiv. 1996. *Drahtzieher im Braunen Netz: Ein Aktueller Überblick über den Neonazi-Untergrund in Deutschland und Österreich*. Hamburg: Konkret Literatur Verlag.

Apter, David E. 1965. *The Politics of Modernization*. Chicago: University of Chicago Press.

Arab Republic of Egypt. 1996. "*Development of Education in Arab Republic of Egypt*." Report presented to International Conference on Education, Geneva, Switzerland.

Arjomand, Said Amir. 1986. "Iran's Islamic Revolution in Comparative Perspective." *World Politics* 38 (3), 383–414.

Arzheimer, Kai, and Elisabeth Carter. 2006. "Political Opportunity Structures and Right-wing Extremist Party Success." *European Journal of Political Research* 45, 419–43.

Ashour, Omar. 2009. *The De-radicalization of Jihadists: Transforming Armed Islamist Movements*. London: Routledge.

Atran, Scott, Lydia Wilson, Richard Davis, and Hammad Sheikh. 2014. "The Devoted Actor, Sacred Values, and Willingness to Fight: Preliminary Studies with ISIL Volunteers and Kurdish Frontline Fighters." Paper presented to the Strategic Multilayer Assessment of ISIL in Support to SOCCNET, Washington, D.C.

Aust, Stefan. 2008. *The Baader Meinhof Complex*. London: The Bodley Head.

Ayubi, Nazih. 1993. *Political Islam: Religion and Politics in the Arab World*. London: Routledge.

Azam, Ahmad Jamil. 1997. "The Islamic Action Front Party." In Hani al-Hourani and Hussain Abu Ruma, eds., *The Islamic Movements and Organizations in Jordan*. Amman: Al-Urdun Al-Jadid Research Center/Sindbad Publishing House, 91–140 (in Arabic).

Bahgat, Gawdat. 1999. "Education in the Gulf Monarchies: Retrospect and Prospect." *International Review of Education* 45 (2), 127–36.

Bahman, Nirumand, ed. 1990. *Im Namen Allahs: Islamische Gruppen und der Fundamentalismus in der Bundesrepublik Deutschland*. Dreisam-Verlag: Köln.

Bakker, Edwin. 2006. "Jihadi Terrorists in Europe." Security Paper 2. Clingendael: Netherlands Institute of International Affairs.

Baron-Cohen, Simon, Sally Wheelwright, et al. 2001. "The Autism-Spectrum Quotient (AQ): Evidence from Asperger Syndrome/High-Functioning Autism, Males and Females, Scientists and Mathematicians." *Journal of Autism and Developmental Disorders* 31 (1), 5–17.

Baron-Cohen, Simon, Patrick Bolton, Sally Wheelwright, et al. 1998. "Autism Occurs More Often in Families of Physicists, Engineers, and Mathematicians." *Autism* 2, 296–301.

Baron-Cohen, Simon, Sally Wheelwright, Carol Stott, et al. 1997. "Is There a Link between Engineering and Autism?" *Autism* 1, 153–63.

Bartlett, Jamie, Jonathan Birdwell, and Michael King. 2010. *The Edge of Violence: A Radical Approach to Extremism*. London: Demos.

Batatu, Hannah. 1982. "Syria's Muslim Brethren." *MERIP Reports* 110, 12–20, 34, 36.

Beattie, Kirk J. 2000. *Egypt during the Sadat Years*. London: Palgrave Macmillan.

Benmelech, Efraim, and Claude Berrebi. 2007. "Attack Assignments in Terror Organizations and the Productivity of Suicide Bombers." NBER Working Papers 12910, National Bureau of Economic Research.

Benmelech, Efraim, Claude Berrebi, and Esteban F. Klor. 2010. "Economic Conditions and the Quality of Suicide Terrorism." NBER Working Papers 16320, National Bureau of Economic Research.

Bergen, Peter, and Swati Pandey. 2005. "The Myth of the Madrassa." *New York Times*, 15 June.

———. 2006. "The Madrassa Scapegoat." *Washington Quarterly* 29 (2), 117–25.

Berman, Eli, Michael Callen, Joseph Felter, and Jacob Shapiro. 2011. "Do Working Men Rebel? Insurgency and Unemployment in Afghanistan, Iraq, and the Philippines." *Journal of Conflict* Resolution 55 (4), 496–528.

Berrebi, Claude. 2007. "Evidence about the Link between Education, Poverty, and Terrorism among Palestinians." *Peace Economics, Peace Science and Public Policy* 13 (1), article 2. RAND Corporation, Berkeley Electronic Press.

Best, Shedrack. 1999. "The Islamist Challenge: The Nigerian Shiite Movement." In Monique Mekenkamp, Paul van Tongeren, and Hans van de Veen, eds., *Searching for Peace in Africa: An Overview of Conflict Prevention and Management Activities*. Utrecht: European Platform for Conflict Prevention and Transformation.

Betz, Hans-Georg. 1994. *Radical Right-Wing Populism in Western Europe*. Houndmills: Macmillan.

Bjorgo, Tore, and John Horgan, eds. 2009. *Leaving Terrorism Behind: Individual and Collective Disengagement*. New York: Routledge.

Block, Jacob, and Jeanne H. Block. 2006. "Nursery School Personality and Political Orientation Two Decades Later." *Journal of Research in Personality* 40 (5), 734–49.

Boroumand, Ladan, and Roya Boroumand. 2002. "Terror, Islam, and Democracy." *Journal of Democracy* 13 (2), 5–20.

Botman, Selma. 1984. "Oppositional Politics in Egypt: The Communist Movement, 1936–1954." PhD diss., Harvard University.

Bueno de Mesquita, Ethan. 2005. "The Quality of Terror." *American Journal of Political Science* 49 (3), 515–30.

Cantori, Louis. 1997. "Islam's Potential for Development." *The World & I*, 12, 9 January.

Capoccia, Giovanni. Forthcoming. "Institutional Change and Constitutional Tradition: Responses to 9/11 in Germany." In Martha Crenshaw, ed., *The Consequences of Counterterrorist Policies in Democracies*. New York: Russell Sage.

Carnegie Foundation. 1984. National Survey of Higher Education. www.thearda.com/Archive/Files/Descriptions/NSHEF84.asp.

Carney, Dana R., John T. Jost, Samuel D. Gosling, and Jeff Potter. 2008. "The Secret Lives of Liberals and Conservatives: Personality Profiles, Interaction Styles, and the Things They Leave Behind." *Political Psychology* 29 (6), 807–40.

Carvalho, Jean-Paul. 2009. "A Theory of the Islamic Revival." Working Paper. Department of Economics, University of Oxford.

Cederman, Lars-Erik, Nils B. Weidmann, and Kristian Skrede Gleditsch. 2011. "Horizontal Inequalities and Ethnonationalist Civil War: A Global Comparison." *American Political Science Review* 105 (03), 478–95.

Chang, Timothy, and Daphne Chang. 2000. "The Role of the Myers-Briggs Type Indicator in Electrical Engineering Education." Working Paper, International

Conference on Engineering Education, Taipei. www.ineer.org/Events/ICEE2000/Proceedings/papers/MD6-2.pdf.

Chapkovski, Philipp. 2012. "'We Should Be Proud Not Sorry': Apologetic Neo-Stalinist Literature in Contemporary Russia." Paper presented at the Symposium on Narratives of Suffering in Post–Cold War Europe, Alexanteri Institute, Finland.

Chehabi, Houchang E. 1990. *Iranian Politics and Religious Modernism: The Liberation Movement of Iran under the Shah and Khomeini.* Ithaca: Cornell University Press.

Chirumbolo, Antonio. 2002. "The Relationship between Need for Cognitive Closure and Political Orientation: The Mediating Role of Authoritarianism." *Personality and Individual Differences* 32 (4), 603–10.

Chirumbolo, Antonio, and Luigi Leone. 2008. "Individual Differences in Need for Closure and Voting Behaviour." *Personality and Individual Differences* 44 (5), 1279–88.

Chirumbolo, Antonio, Alessandra Areni, and Gilda Sensales. 2004. "Need for Cognitive Closure and Politics: Voting, Political Attitudes and Attributional Style." *International Journal of Psychology* 39 (4), 245–53.

Cikara, Mina, Emile Bruneau, et al. 2014. "Their Pain Gives Us Pleasure: How Intergroup Dynamics Shape Empathic Failures and Counter-Empathic Responses." *Journal of Experimental Social Psychology* 55, 110–25.

Combatting Terrorism Center. 2006. *The Islamic Imagery Project: Visual Motifs in Jihadi Internet Propaganda.* West Point: United States Military Academy.

Cornand, Jocelyne. 1990. "Le Rôle des Ingenieurs dans le Secteur Privé en Syrie: Le Cas du Textil." In Longuenesse, *Batisseurs et Bureaucrates,* 187–200.

Crowson, Michael, Stephen J. Thoma, and Nita Hestevold. 2005. "Is Political Conservatism Synonymous with Authoritarianism?" *Journal of Social Psychology* 145 (5), 571–92.

Cunningham, Karla J. 2003. "Cross-Regional Trends in Female Terrorism." *Studies in Conflict & Terrorism* 26 (3), 171–95.

Cunningham, Robert, and Yasin Sarayrah. 1993. *Wasta: The Hidden Force in Middle Eastern Society.* Westport, CT: Praeger.

Davies, James C. 1962. "Toward a Theory of Revolution." *American Sociological Review* 27 (1), 5–19.

Demiralp, Seda. 2006. "The Rise of Islamic Capital and the Decline of Islamic Radicalism in Turkey." Paper presented at the annual conference of the Midwest Political Science Association, Chicago.

Diwan, Ishac, and Maurice Girgis. 2002. *Labor Force and Development in Saudi Arabia.* Paper prepared for the Symposium on the Future Vision for the Saudi Economy" organized by the Ministry of Planning, Riyadh, Kingdom of Saudi Arabia.

Duckitt, John. 2006. "Differential Effects of Right Wing Authoritarianism and Social Dominance Orientation on Outgroup Attitudes and Their Mediation by Threat from and Competitiveness to Outgroups." *Personality and Social Psychology Bulletin* 32 (5), 684–96.

Eager, Paige Whaley. 2008. *From Freedom Fighters to Terrorists.* London: Ashgate.

Eccleshall, Robert, Vincent Geoghegan, Richard Jay, Michael Kenny, Iain Mackenzie, and Rick Wilford. 1994. *Political Ideologies: An Introduction*. 2nd ed. London: Routledge.

Elster, Jon. 1999. *Alchemies of the Mind*. Cambridge: Cambridge University Press.

Eschenhagen, Paul. 2004. *Antisemitismus als verbindendes Element zwischen Rechtsextremisten und radikalen Islamisten*. Munich: GRIN Verlag.

Esposito, John L., and Dalia Mogahed. 2007. "Battle for Muslims' Hearts and Minds: The Road Not (Yet) Taken." *Middle East Policy* 14 (1), 27–41.

Evans Clements, Barbara. 1997. *Bolshevik Women*. Cambridge: Cambridge University Press.

Fabei, Stefano. 2003. *Il Fascio, la Svastica e la Mezzaluna*. Milano: Mursia.

Fahmy, Ninette S. 1998. "The Performance of the Muslim Brotherhood in the Egyptian Syndicates: An Alternative Formula for Reform?" *Middle East Journal* 52 (4), 551–62.

Fair, Christine C. 2010. "Students Islamic Movement of India and the Indian Mujahideen: An Assessment." *Asia Policy* 9, 101–19.

Federico, Christopher M., and Grace M. Deason. 2011. "Uncertainty, Insecurity, and Ideological Defense of the Status Quo." In Michael A. Hogg and Danielle L. Blaylock, eds., *Extremism and the Psychology of Uncertainty*. London: Wiley-Blackwell, 197–211.

Federico, Christopher M., Agnieszka Golec, and Jessica L. Dial. 2005. "The Relationship between the Need for Closure and Support for Military Action against Iraq: Moderating Effects of National Attachment." *Personality & Social Psychology Bulletin* 31 (5), 621–32.

Fenzi, Enrico. 2006. *Armi e Bagagli: Un Diario dalle Brigate Rosse*. 3rd ed. Milano: Costlan.

Ferracuti, Franco, and Francesco Bruno. 1981. "Psychiatric Aspects of Terrorism in Italy." In I. L. Barak-Glantz and C. R. Huff, eds., *The Mad, the Bad and the Different: Essays in Honor of Simon Dinitz*. Lexington, MA: Lexington Books.

Fink, Bernhard, and Robert Trivers. 2014. "Cognitive Simplicity and Self-Deception Are Crucial in Martyrdom and Suicide Terrorism." *Behavioral and Brain Sciences* 37 (4), 366–67.

Finkel, Steven E., and James B. Rule. 1986. "Relative Deprivation and Related Psychological Theories of Civil Violence." In Kurt Lang and Gladys Engel Lang, eds., *Research in Social Movements, Conflicts and Change*. London: JAI Press.

Flora, Peter. 1983. *State, Economy, and Society in Western Europe 1815-1975. A Data Handbook in two Volumes*. Vol. 1, *The Growth of Mass Democracies and Welfare States*. Frankfurt: Campus.

Focquaert, Farah, et al. 2007. "Empathizing and Systemizing Cognitive Traits in the Sciences and Humanities." *Personality and Individual Differences* 43 (3), 619–25.

Foran, John. 2005. *Taking Power: On the Origins of Third World Revolutions*. Cambridge: Cambridge University Press.

Franceschini, Alberto, Pierre V. Buffa, and Franco Giustolisi. 1988. *Mara, Renato e Io: Storia dei Fondatori delle BR*. Milan: Mondadori.

Galleni, Mauro. 1981. *Rapporto sul terrorismo*. Milan: Rizzoli.

Gambetta, Diego. 2006. Epilogue to the paperback edition. In Gambetta, ed., *Making Sense of Suicide Missions*. Oxford: Oxford University Press, 301–33.

———. 2010. "Heroic Impatience." *The Nation*, 4 March. www.thenation.com/article/heroic-impatience.

Gartenstein-Ross, Daveed, and Laura Grossman. 2009. *Homegrown Terrorists in the U.S. and the U.K.: An Empirical Examination of the Radicalization Process*. Washington, DC: Foundation for the Defense of Democracies.

Gerber, Alan S., Gregory A. Huber, David Doherty, Conor M. Dowling, and Shang E. Ha. 2010. "Personality and Political Attitudes: Relationships across Issue Domains and Political Contexts." *American Political Science Review* 104, 111–33.

Gerges, Fawaz. 2006. *Journey of the Jihadist: Inside Muslim Militancy*. Orlando, FL: Harcourt.

Gobe, Eric. 2001. *Les Ingénieurs Maghrébins dans les Systèmes de Formation*. Tunis: Institut de recherche sur le Maghreb contemporain de Tunis.

Goldziher, Ignaz. 1981. *Introduction to Islamic Theology and Law*. Princeton: Princeton University Press.

Göle, Nilufer. 1990. "Ingenieurs Islamistes et Etudiantes Voile en Turquie: Entre le Totalitarisme et l'Individualisme." In Gilles Kepel and Yann Richard, eds., *Intellectuels et Militants de l'Islam Contemporain*. Paris: Editions du Seuil, 167–92.

Golec de Zavala, Agnieszka, Aleksandra Cisłak, and Elżbieta Wesołowska. 2010. "Political Conservatism, Need for Cognitive Closure and Intergroup Hostility." *Political Psychology* 31 (4), 521–41.

Greenberg, Jeff, and Eva Jonas. 2003. "Psychological and Political Orientation: The Left, the Right, and the Rigid: Comment on Jost et al." *Psychological Bulletin* 129, 376–82.

Gurr, Ted. 1970. *Why Men Rebel*. Princeton: Princeton University Press.

Haddad, Yvonne, John Voll, John Esposito, Kathleen Moore, and David Sawan. 1991. *The Contemporary Islamic Revival: A Critical Survey and Bibliography*. Westport, CT: Greenwood.

Hafez, Mohammed. 2003. *Why Muslims Rebel: Repression and Resistance in the Islamic World*. Boulder, CO: Lynne Rienner.

Hanafi, Sari. 1990. "La Formation des Ingénieurs en Syrie et son Adaptation aux Besoins de la Societé." In Longuenesse, *Batisseurs et Bureaucrats*, 171–85.

———. 1997. *La Syrie des Ingénieurs: Une Perspective Comparée avec l'Egypte*. Paris: Editions Karthala.

Handler, Jeffrey. 1990. "Socioeconomic Profile of an American Terrorist: 1960s and 1970s." *Terrorism* 13 (3), 195–213.

Hansen, Hans Thomas. 2002. Introduction to Julius Evola, *Men among the Ruins: Postwar Reflections of a Radical Traditionalist*. Rochester, VT: Inner Traditions.

Harteveld, Eelco, Stefan Dahlberg, Andrej Kokkonen, and Wouter van der Brug. 2013. "The Gender Gap in Voting: Extremity, Ambiguity and Social Cues." ECPR working paper.

Hasan, Noorhaidi. 2006. *Laskar Jihad: Islam, Militancy, and the Quest for Identity in Post–New Order Indonesia*. Ithaca: Southeast Asia Program Publications, Cornell University Press.

Hassan, Riaz. 2008. *Inside Muslim Minds*. Melbourne: Melbourne University Press.

Hatemi, Peter, Sarah Medland, Robert Klemmensen, Sven Oskarsson, et al. 2014. "Genetic Influences on Political Ideologies: Twin Analyses of 19 Measures of Political Ideologies from Five Democracies and Genome-Wide Findings from Three Populations." *Behavior Genetics* 44 (3), 282–322.

Hayek, Friedrich A. 1952. *The Counter-revolution in Science*. Glencoe, IL: The Free Press.

Heaven, Patrick C. L., and Sandra Bucci. 2001. "Right-wing Authoritarianism, Social Dominance Orientation and Personality: an Analysis Using the IPIP Measure." *European Journal of Personality* 15 (1), 49–56.

Hegghammer, Thomas. 2006. "Terrorist Recruitment and Radicalization in Saudi Arabia." *Middle East Policy* 13 (4), 39–60.

———. 2009a. "Jihadi Salafis or Revolutionaries: On Religion and Politics in the Study of Islamist Militancy." In Roel Meijer, ed., *Global Salafism: Islam's New Religious Movement*. London/New York: Hurst/Columbia University Press, 244–66.

———. 2009b. "The Ideological Hybridization of Jihadi Groups." *Current Trends in Islamist Ideology* 9 (18 November).

———. 2013. "The Recruiter's Dilemma: Signalling and Rebel Recruitment Tactics." *Journal of Peace Research* 50 (1), 3–16.

Henry, Clement M., and Robert Springborg. 2001. *Globalization and the Politics of Development in the Middle East*. Cambridge: Cambridge University Press.

Henshaw, Alexis Leanna. 2013. "Why Women Rebel: Understanding Female Participation in Intrastate Conflict." PhD diss., University of Arizona.

———. 2016. "Where Women Rebel." *International Feminist Journal of Politics* 18 (1), 1–22.

Herf, Jeffrey. 1984. *Reactionary Modernism: Technology, Culture, and Politics in Weimar and the Third Reich*. Cambridge: Cambridge University Press.

Heritage Foundation. 1983. "The PLO's Growing Latin American Base." www.heritage.org/research/reports/1983/08/the-plos-growing-latin-american-base.

Hertog Steffen. 2009. "Alan B. Krueger: *What Makes a Terrorist? Economics and the Roots of Terrorism*." *European Sociological Review* 26 (2), 253–58.

———. 2010. *Princes, Brokers, and Bureaucrats: Oil and the State in Saudi Arabia*. Ithaca: Cornell University Press.

Hinze Travis, Joseph Doster, and Joe C. Victor. 1997. "The Relationship of Conservatism and Cognitive-Complexity." *Personality and Individual Differences* 22 (2), 297–98.

Hizb ut-Tahrir. 2002. "List of Those Arrested from Hizb ut-Tahrir." www.hizb-ut-tahrir.org/english/english.html.

Hoffman, Valerie. 1995. "Muslim Fundamentalists: Psychosocial Profiles." In M. E. Marty and R. S. Appleby, eds., *Fundamentalisms Comprehended*. The Fundamentalisms Project. Vol. 5. Chicago: University of Chicago Press, 199–230.

Holmes, Stephen. 2005. "Al-Qaeda, September 11, 2001." In D. Gambetta, ed., *Making Sense of Suicide Missions*. Oxford: Oxford University Press, 131–72.

Horgan, John. 2009. *Walking Away from Terrorism: Accounts of Disengagement from Radical and Extremist Movements*. New York: Routledge.

Hudson, Rex A. 1999. "The Sociology and Psychology of Terrorism: Who Becomes a Terrorist and Why." Report prepared under an Interagency Agreement by the Federal Research Division. Library of Congress, September.

Huneeus, Carlos. 2000. "Technocrats and Politicians in an Authoritarian Regime: The 'ODEPLAN Boys' and the 'Gremialists' in Pinochet's Chile." *Journal of Latin American Studies* 32 (2), 461–501.

Hunter, Shireen T., ed. 1988. *The Politics of Islamic Revivalism: Diversity and Unity*. Bloomington: Indiana University Press.

Huntington, Samuel. 1996. *The Clash of Civilizations and the Remaking of World Order*. New York: Simon and Schuster.

Ibrahim, Saad Eddin. 1980. "Anatomy of Egypt's Militant Islamic Groups: Methodological Note and Preliminary Findings." *International Journal of Middle East Studies* 12 (4), 423–53.

———. 1982. "Egypt's Islamic Militants." *MERIP Reports*, no. 103, February, 5–14.

———. 1996. "Reform and Frustration in Egypt." *Journal of Democracy* 7 (4), 125–35.

Inbar, Yoel, David A. Pizarro, and Paul Bloom. 2008. "Conservatives Are More Easily Disgusted than Liberals." *Cognition & Emotion* 23 (4), 714–25.

Inbar, Yoel, David A. Pizarro, Ravi Iyer, and Jonathan Haidt. 2012. "Disgust Sensitivity, Political Conservatism, and Voting." *Social Psychological and Personality Science* 3 (5), 537–44.

Inbar, Yoel, David A. Pizarro, Joshua Knobe, and Paul Bloom. 2009. "Disgust Sensitivity Predicts Intuitive Disapproval of Gays." *Emotion* 9 (3), 435–39.

Institute of International Education. 2005. *Open Doors Online*. http://opendoors .iienetwork.org/?p=69694.

International Crisis Group (ICG). 2004. *Islamism in North Africa II: Egypt's Opportunity*. Cairo/Brussels: ICG.

———. 2005. "Understanding Islamism." Cairo/Brussels: ICG. www.crisisgroup .org/en/regions/middle-east-north-africa/north-africa/037-understanding -islamism.aspx.

Iqbal, Farrukh. 2006. *Sustaining Gains in Poverty Reduction and Human Development in the Middle East and North Africa*. Washington, D.C.: World Bank.

Iribarren, Florencio Domínguez. 1998. *ETA: Estrategia organizativa y actuaciones, 1978–1992*. Bilbao: Universidad del País Vasco.

Iyer, Ravi, Spassena Koleva, Jesse Graham, Peter Ditto, and Jonathan Haidt. 2012. "Understanding Libertarian Morality: The Psychological Dispositions of Self-Identified Libertarians." PLoS ONE 7 (8). www.plosone.org/article/info% 3Adoi%2F10.1371%2Fjournal.pone.0042366.

Jacobson, Michael. 2010. "Terrorist Dropouts: Learning from Those Who Have Left." *Policy Focus* 101 (January).

Jäger, Herbert, Gerhard Schmidtchen, and Lieselotte Süllwold. 1981. *Analysen zum Terrorismus, Vol. 2, Lebenslaufanalysen*. Opladen, Germany: WDV.

Jarausch, Konrad H. 1986. "The Perils of Professionalism: Lawyers, Teachers, and Engineers in Nazi Germany." *German Studies Review* 9 (1), 107–37.

Jehng, John-Chang J., Scott D. Johnson, and Richard C. Anderson. 1993. "Schooling and Students' Epistemological Beliefs about Learning." *Contemporary Educational Psychology* 18 (1), 23–35.

Jordanian Ministry of Higher Education. 2005. Enrollment statistics. www.mohe .gov.jo (in Arabic).

Jost, John T., and David M. Amodio. 2011. "Political Ideology as Motivated Social Cognition: Behavioral and Neuroscientific Evidence." *Motivation and Emotion* 36 (1), 55–64.

Jost, John T., and Jaime L. Napier. 2011. "The Uncertainty-Threat Model of Political Conservatism." In Michael A. Hogg and Danielle L. Blaylock, eds., *Extremism and the Psychology of Uncertainty*. London: Wiley-Blackwell, 90–111.

Jost, John T., Christopher M. Federico, and Jaime L. Napier. 2009. "Political Ideology: Its Structure, Functions, and Elective Affinities." *Annual Review of Psychology* 60 (1), 307–37.

Jost, John T., Arie Kruglanski, Jack Glaser, and Frank Sulloway. 2003. "Political Conservatism as Motivated Social Cognition." *Psychological Bulletin* 129 (3), 339–75.

Jost, John T., Jaime L. Napier, Hulda Thorisdottir, Samuel D., Gosling, Tibor P. Palfai, and Brian Ostafin. 2007. "Are Needs to Manage Uncertainty and Threat Associated with Political Conservatism or Ideological Extremity?" *Personality and Social Psychology Bulletin* 33 (7), 989–1007.

Kahana, Ephraim. 2007. "Covert Action: The Israeli Experience." In Loch K. Johnson, ed., *Strategic Intelligence: Understanding the Hidden Side of Government*. Vol. 3. Westport, CT: Praeger Security International.

Kanai, Ryota, Tom Feilden, Chris Firth, and Geraint Rees. 2011. "Political Orientations Are Correlated with Brain Structure in Young Adults." *Current Biology* 21 (8), 677–80.

Karshenas, Massoud. 1994. "Structural Adjustment and Employment in the Middle East and North Africa." Working Paper 9420. Cairo: Economic Research Forum.

Karvar, Anousheh. 2003. "L'Idéal Technocratique des Ingénieurs à l'Épreuve de la Construction de l'État: Maghreb, Machrek, Indochine au XXᵉ Siècle." *Revue des mondes musulmans et de la Méditerranée* 101–2, 199–211.

Keddie, Nikkie. 1983. "Iranian Revolutions in Comparative Perspective." *American Historical Review* 88 (3), 579–98.

Kemmelmeier, Markus. 1997. "Need for Closure and Political Orientation among German University Students." *Journal of Social Psychology* 137 (6), 787–78.

Kepel, Gilles. 1985. *Muslim Extremism in Egypt: The Prophet and Pharaoh*. Berkeley: University of California Press.

———. 1993. *The Prophet and Pharaoh: Muslim Extremism in Egypt*. Berkeley: University of California Press.

———. 2002. *Jihad: The Trail of Political Islam*. London: I. B. Tauris.

Khatchadourian, Raffi. 2007. "Azzam the American: The Making of an Al Qaeda Homegrown." *New Yorker*, 22 January.

Khosrokhavar, Farhad. 2005. *Suicide Bombers: Allah's New Martyrs*. Ann Arbor, MI: Pluto Press.

King, Michael, and Donald M. Taylor. 2011. "The Radicalization of Homegrown Jihadists: A Review of Theoretical Models and Social Psychological Evidence." *Terrorism and Political Violence* 23 (4), 602–22.

Kolinksy, Eva 1988. "Terrorism in West Germany." In Juliet Lodge, ed., *The Threat of Terrorism*. Boulder, CO: Westview, 75–76.

Kossowska, Malgorzata, and Alain Van Hiel. 2003. "The Relationship between Need for Closure and Conservative Beliefs in Western and Eastern Europe." *Political Psychology* 24 (3), 501–18.

Krueger, Alan B. 2007. *What Makes a Terrorist? Economics and the Roots of Terrorism*. Princeton: Princeton University Press.

Krueger, Alan B., and Jitka Maleckova. 2003. "Education, Poverty and Terrorism: Is There a Causal Connection?" *Journal of Economic Perspectives* 17, 119–44.

Kruglanski, Arie W., and Shira Fishman. 2006. "The Psychology of Terrorism: 'Syndrome' versus 'Tool' Perspectives." *Terrorism and Political Violence* 18 (2), 193–215.

Kruglanski, Arie W., and Edward Orehek. 2011. "The Need for Certainty as a Psychological Nexus for Individuals and Society." In Michael A. Hogg and Danielle L. Blaylock, eds., *Extremism and the Psychology of Uncertainty*. London: Wiley-Blackwell, 3–18.

Kruglanski, Arie W., Xiaoyan Chen, Mark Dechesne, Shira Fishman, and Edward Orehek. 2009. "Fully Committed: Suicide Bombers' Motivation and the Quest for Personal Significance." *Political Psychology* 30 (3), 331–57.

Kurzman, Charles. 2003. "The Qum Protests and the Coming of the Iranian Revolution, 1975 and 1978." *Social Science History* 27 (3), 287–325.

Kurzman, Charles, and Erin Leahey. 2004. "Intellectuals and Democratization, 1905–1912 and 1989–1996." *American Journal of Sociology* 109 (4), 937–86.

Kuwaiti Ministry of Education. 2001. *National Report*. Presented to the 46th session of the International Conference on Education, Geneva. www.ibe.unesco.org/International/ICE/natrap/Kuwait_Scan_4.pdf.

Labévière, Richard. 2000. *Dollars for Terror: The United States and Islam*. New York: Algora Publishing.

Ladd, Carll E., Jr., and Seymour M. Lipset. 1972. "Politics of Academic Natural Scientists and Engineers." *Science* 176, 1091–1100.

———. 1975. *The Divided Academy: Professors and Politics*. New York: McGraw-Hill.

Lappin, Elena. 2002. "Atta in Hamburg." *Prospect*, 20 September.

Laryš, Martin, and Miroslav Mareš. 2011. "Right-Wing Extremist Violence in the Russian Federation." *Europe-Asia Studies* 63 (1), 129–54.

Leach, Colin Wayne, Aarti Iyer, and Anne Pedersen. 2007. "Angry Opposition to Government Redress: When the Structurally Advantaged Perceive Themselves as Relatively Deprived." *British Journal of Social Psychology* 46 (1), 191–204.

Lee, Alexander. 2011. "Who Becomes a Terrorist?: Poverty, Education, and the Origins of Political Violence." *World Politics* 63 (2), 203–45.

Lee, Martin. 2002. "The Swastika and the Crescent." *Southern Poverty Law Center Intelligence Report* Spring (105). www.splcenter.org/get-informed/intelligence-report/browse-all-issues/2002/spring/the-swastika-and-the-crescent?page=0,0.

Lipset, Seymour M., and Earl Raab. 1971. *The Politics of Unreason: Right-wing Extremism in America, 1790–1970*. London: Heinemann.

Lobmeyer, Hans Günter. 1995. *Opposition und Widerstand in Syrien*. Hamburg: Deutsches Orient-Institut.

Loboda, Luke. 2004. "The Thought of Sayyid Qutb." BA thesis, Ashland University. www.ashbrook.org/wp-content/uploads/2012/06/2004-Loboda-The-Thought -of-Sayyid-Qutb-PDF.pdf.

Longuenesse, Elisabeth, ed. 1990. *Batisseurs et Bureaucrates: Ingénieurs et Société au Maghreb et au Moyen-Orient: Table-ronde CNRS tenue à Lyon du 16 au 18 mars 1989*. Etudes sur le monde arabe, no. 4. Lyon: Maison de l'Orient.

———. 2000. "Les Syndicats Professionnels en Jordanie, Enjeux de Société et Lutte Nationale." GREMMO Working Paper (Groupe de recherches et d'études sur la Méditerranée et le Moyen-Orient). http://halshs.archives-ouvertes.fr/ halshs-00111075/en/.

———. 2007. *Professions et Société au Proche-Orient: Déclin des Élites, Crises des Classes Moyennes*. Rennes: Presses Universitaires de Rennes.

Lyttelton, Adrian. 1973. *The Seizure of Power: Fascism in Italy, 1919–1929*. London: Widenfeld and Nicolson.

Maegerle, Anton. 2006. "Die iranische Rechtsextremisten-Connection." *Vierteljahresheft Tribüne. Zeitschrift zum Verständnis des Judentums*. Heft 178. www .doew.at/thema/re_iran/maegerle.html.

Malaysian Department of Statistics. 2002. Population and Housing Census. www .statistics.gov.my/english/frameset_news.php?file=pressedu.

Malka, Ariel, Christopher J. Soto, Michael Inzlicht, and Yphtach Lelkes. 2014. "Do Needs for Security and Certainty Predict Cultural and Economic Conservatism? A Cross-National Analysis." *Journal of Personality and Social Psychology* 106 (6), 1031–51.

McAdam, Doug. 1986. "Recruitment to High-Risk Activism: The Case of Freedom Summer." *American Journal of Sociology* 92 (1), 64–90.

McAdam, Doug, Sidney Tarrow, and Charles Tilly. 2001. *Dynamics of Contention*. Cambridge: Cambridge University Press.

McGregor, Ian, Kyle A. Nash, and Mike Prentice. 2011. "Religious Zeal after Goal Frustration." In Michael A. Hogg and Danielle L. Blaylock, eds., *Extremism and the Psychology of Uncertainty*. London: Wiley-Blackwell, 147–64.

McKay, Mary-Jayne. 2009. "The Mastermind." *60 Minutes*. 11 February. www .cbsnews.com/stories/2002/10/09/60II/main524947.shtml.

Merani, Hacène. 2005. "Les Cadres des Entreprises Publiques en Algérie: Des Privilèges au Déclassement." *Revue des mondes musulmans et de la Méditerranée* 105–6, 267–82.

Merolla, Jennifer L., Jennifer M. Ramos, and Elizabeth J. Zechmeister. 2011. "Authoritarianism, 'Need for Closure' and Conditions of Threat." In Michael A. Hogg and Danielle L. Blaylock, eds., *Extremism and the Psychology of Uncertainty*. London: Wiley-Blackwell, 212–27.

Meyersson Milgrom, Eva, and Guillermina Jasso. 2004. "Identity, Social Distance, and Palestinian Support for the Roadmap." CDDRL Working Paper, Stanford University.

Michael, George. 2006. *The Enemy of My Enemy*. Lawrence: University Press of Kansas.

Milani, Mohsen. 1994. *The Making of Iran's Islamic Revolution*. 2nd ed. Boulder, CO: Westview.

Mitchell, Richard. 1969. *The Society of the Muslim Brothers*. London: Oxford University Press.

Moghaddam, Fathali M. 2005. "The Staircase to Terrorism." *American Psychologist* 60 (2), 161–69.

Moore, Clement Henry. 1994. *Images of Development: Egyptian Engineers in Search of Industry*. Cairo: American University in Cairo Press.

Moore, Pete, and Bassel Salloukh. 2007. "Struggles under Authoritarianism: Regimes, States, and Professional Associations in the Arab World." *International Journal of Middle East Studies* 39 (2), 53–56.

Moss, David. 1989. *The Politics of Left-Wing Violence in Italy, 1969–85*. London: Macmillan.

Motadel, David. 2015. "The Swastika and the Crescent." *Wilson Quarterly* (Winter). http://wilsonquarterly.com/stories/the-swastika-and-the-crescent.

Munson, Henry Jr. 1986. "The Social Base of Islamic Militancy in Morocco." *Middle East Journal* 40 (2), 267–84.

Munson, Ziad. 2001. "Islamic Mobilization: Social Movement Theory and the Muslim Brotherhood." *Sociological Quarterly* 42 (4), 487–510.

Myyry, Liisa, and Klaus Helkama. 2001. "University Students' Value Priorities and Emotional Empathy." *Educational Psychology* 21 (1), 25–40.

Nakhaie, Reza M., and Robert J. Brym. 1999. "The Political Attitudes of Canadian Professors." *Canadian Journal of Sociology* 24 (3), 329–53.

Nesser, Petter. 2004. *Jihad in Europe: A Survey of the Motivations for Sunni Islamist Terrorism in Post-millennium Europe*. Norwegian Defence Research Establishment. http://rapporter.ffi.no/rapporter/2004/01146.pdf.

———. 2006. "How Does Radicalization Occur in Europe?" Presentation given at the Second Inter-Agency Radicalization Conference, hosted by the U.S. Department of Homeland Security, Washington, D.C., July. www.mil.no/multimedia/archive/00080/DHS_foredrag_80480a.pdf.

———. 2009. "Joining Jihadi Terrorist Cells in Europe." In Magnus Ranstorp, ed., *Understanding Violent Radicalisation: Terrorist and Jihadist Movements in Europe*. Oxon: Taylor & Francis, 87–115.

Oppenheimer, Andy. 2009. "How Terrorists Acquire Technology and Training: Lessons from the IRA." www.newsecuritylearning.com/index.php/feature/123-how-terrorists-acquire-technology-and-training-lessons-from-the-ira.

Ortoleva, Pietro, and Erik Snowberg. 2014. "Overconfidence in Political Behavior." Working Paper. 25 March. www.columbia.edu/~po2205/papers/Ortoleva_Snowberg_Overconfidence.pdf.

Østby, Gudrun. 2008. "Polarization, Horizontal Inequalities and Violent Civil Conflict." *Journal of Peace Research* 45 (2), 143–62.

Owen, Roger, and Şevket Pamuk. 1998. *A History of Middle East Economies in the Twentieth Century*. London: I. B. Tauris.

Oxford Analytica. 2006. "Middle East: Intra-Regional Trade to Expand Slowly." *In-Depth Analysis*, Oxford, 19 April.

Palestinian Ministry of Higher Education. 2005. Enrollment Statistics. www.mohe .gov.ps (in Arabic).

Paulsen, Michael B., and Charles T. Wells. 1998. "Domain Differences in the Epistemological Beliefs of the College Students." *Research in Higher Education* 39 (4), 365–84.

Pedahzur, Ami. 2005. *Suicide Terrorism*. Cambridge: Polity Press.

Pettigrew, Thomas F., Oliver Christ, Ulrich Wagner, et al. 2008. "Relative Deprivation and Intergroup Prejudice." *Journal of Social Issues* 64 (2), 385–401.

Piazza, James A. 2006. "Rooted in Poverty?: Terrorism, Poor Economic Development, and Social Cleavages." *Terrorism and Political Violence* 18 (1), 159–77.

Rangwala, Glenn. 2005. Palestinian Biographies. http://middleeastreference.org .uk/indexbio.html.

Reader, Ian. 2000. *Religious Violence in Contemporary Japan*. Richmond, Surrey: Routledge Curzon.

Rees, Philip. 1990. *Biographical Dictionary of the Extreme Right since 1890*. New York: Simon and Schuster

Reid, Donald M. 1974. "The Rise of Professions and Professional Organization in Modern Egypt." *Comparative Studies in Society and History* 16 (1), 24–57.

Rhines Cheney, Gretchen, Betsy Brown Ruzzi, and Karthik Muralidharan. 2005. "A Profile of the Indian Education System." Paper prepared for the New Commission on the Skills of the American Workforce, organized by the National Centre on Education and the Economy.

Richards, Alan, and John Waterbury. 1996. *A Political Economy of the Middle East*. 2nd ed., Boulder, CO: Westview.

Ricolfi, Luca. 2005. "Palestinians, 1981–2003." In D. Gambetta, ed., *Making Sense of Suicide Missions*. Oxford: Oxford University Press, 77–129.

Rodinson, Maxime. 1978. "Islam Resurgent?" *Le Monde*, 6–8 December.

———, ed. 1979. *Marxism and the Muslim World*. London: Zed Books.

Rodríguez, José A. 2005. "Terrorist Network: In Its Weakness Lies Its Strength." Working Paper, EPP-LEA, Grupo de Estudios de Poder y Privilegio, Departament de Sociologia i Anàlisi de les Organitzacions, Universitat de Barcelona.

Roets, Arne, and Alain Van Hiel. 2006. "Need for Closure Relations with Authoritarianism, Conservative Beliefs and Racism: The Impact of Urgency and Permanence Tendencies." *Psychologica Belgica* 46 (3), 235–52.

Rose, David. 2004. "9/11: The European Dimension." Unpublished section of contribution to D. Rose, B. Burrough, and N. Zeman. "The Path to 9/11." *Vanity Fair*. September 2004.

Rouadjia, Ahmed. 1990. *Les Frères et la Mosquée: Enquete sur le Mouvement Islamiste en Algérie*. Paris: Karthala.

Roy, Olivier. 1990. "Les nouveaux intellectuels islamistes: Essai d'approche philosophique." In Gilles Kepel and Yann Richard, eds., *Intellectuels et Militants de l'Islam Contemporain*. Paris: Editions du Seuil, 261–83.

———. 1994. *The Failure of Political Islam*. Cambridge, MA: Harvard University Press.

———. 2004. *Globalised Islam: The Search for a New Ummah*. London: Hurst & Co.

Rubin, Barnett R. 1992. "Political Elites in Afghanistan: Rentier State Building, Rentier State Wrecking." *International Journal of Middle East Studies* 24 (1), 77–99.

Rubinstein, Ariel. 2006. "A Sceptic's Comment on the Study of Economics." *Economic Journal* 116 (March), C1–C9.

Ruby, Charles L. 2002. "Are Terrorists Mentally Deranged?' *Analyses of Social Issues and Public Policy* 2 (1), 15–26.

Runciman, Walter G. 1966. *Relative Deprivation and Social Justice: A Study of Attitudes to Social Inequality in Twentieth-Century England.* Berkeley: University of California Press.

Russell, Charles A., and Robert E. Hildner. 1971. "Urban Insurgency in Latin America: Its Implications for the Future." *Air University Review* 22 (6), 54–64.

Russell, Charles A., and Bowman Miller. 1977. "Profile of a Terrorist." *Terrorism* 1 (1), 17–34.

Ruthven, Malise. 1997. *Islam: A Very Short Introduction.* Oxford: Oxford University Press.

Sageman, Marc. 2004. *Understanding Terror Networks.* Philadelphia: University of Pennsylvania Press.

Salert, Barbara. 1976. *Revolutions and Revolutionary.* New York: Elsevier.

Saudi Arabia, Kingdom of. *Annual Statistical Yearbook*, various issues. Riyadh.

Saudi Arabian Ministry of Planning. 1999. *Seventh Development Plan.* Riyadh.

———. 2004. *Eighth Development Plan.* Riyadh.

Saudi Arabian Monetary Agency. 2006. *Forty-Second Annual Report.* Riyadh.

Scahill, Jeremy. 2013. *Dirty Wars.* New York: Nations Book.

Schacht, Joseph. 1982. *An Introduction to Islamic Law.* Oxford: Clarendon Press.

Schulze, Reinhard. 1990. "Zum Hintergrund Islamischer Politischer Bewegungen." In Bahman, ed. 1990. *Im Namen Allahs*, 9–37.Schweitzer, Yoram, ed. 2006. *Female Suicide Bombers: Dying for Equality, Memorandum.* No. 84. Tel Aviv: Jaffee Center for Strategic Studies.

Shapiro, Jacob N., and C. Christine Fair. 2009. "Understanding Support for Islamist Militancy in Pakistan." *International Security* 34 (3), 79–118.

Shepard, William E. 1987. "Islam and Ideology: Towards a Typology." *International Journal of Middle East Studies* 19 (3), 307–35.

Silke, Andrew. 1998. "Cheshire-Cat Logic: The Recurring Theme of Terrorist Abnormality in Psychological Research." *Psychology, Crime & Law* 4 (1), 51–69.

Simeaner, H., S. Dippelhofer, H. Bargel, M. Ramm, and T. Bargel. 2007. *Studiensituation und Studierende an Universitäten und Fachhochschulen: Datenalmanach Studierendensurvey 1983–2007.* University of Konstanz. http://cms.uni-konstanz.de/ag-hochschulforschung/studierendensurvey/.

Singaporean Ministry of Home Affairs. 2003. *White Paper: The Jemaah Islamiyah Arrests and the Threat of Terrorism.* www.mha.gov.sg/Newsroom/speeches/Documents/English.pdf.

Smith, Brent, and Kathryn Morgan. 1994. "Terrorists Right and Left: Empirical Issues in Profiling American Terrorists." *Studies in Conflict and Terrorism* 17 (1), 39–57.

Smith, Heather J., and Daniel J. Ortiz. 2002. "Is It Just Me? The Different Consequences of Personal and Group Relative Deprivation." In Iain Walker and Heather J. Smith, eds., *Relative Deprivation: Specification, Development, and Integration.* Cambridge: Cambridge University Press, 91–115.

Smith, Shawna, Yuan-Ling Chiao, Aaron Johnston, et al. 2003. "Why Are Islamic Militants More Likely to Emerge from Science/Engineering Departments?" Students' Project, Hilary Term, University of Oxford, Department of Sociology.

Snow, David A., E. Burke Rochford, Steven K. Wordon, and Robert D. Benford. 1986. "Frame Alignment Processes, Micromobilization, and Movement Participation." *American Sociological Review* 51 (4), 464–81.

Sonbol, Amira el-Azhary. 1988. "Egypt." In Hunter, *The Politics of Islamic Revivalism,* 23–38.

Springborg, Robert. 1978. "Professional Syndicates in Egyptian Politics, 1952–1970." *International Journal of Middle East Studies* 9 (3), 275–95.

Stark, Rodney, Laurence R. Iannaccone, and Roger Finke. 1996. "Religion, Science, and Rationality." *American Economic Review Papers and Proceedings* 86 (2), 433–37.

———. 1998. "Rationality and the 'Religious Mind.'" *Economic Inquiry* 36, 373–89.

Steigmann-Gall, Richard. 2003. *The Holy Reich: Nazi Conceptions of Christianity, 1919–1945.* Cambridge: Cambridge University Press.

Stern, Jessica. 2003. *Terror in the Name of God: Why Religious Militants Kill.* New York: Ecco/HarperCollins.

Tacchi, Francesca. 1994. "L'Ingegnere, il Tecnico della 'Nuova' Società Fascista." In Gabriele Turi, ed., *Libere Professioni e Fascismo.* Franco Angeli: Milano, 177–216.

Tarrow, Sidney. 1998. *Power in Movement: Social Movements and Contentious Politics.* Cambridge: Cambridge University Press.

Thorisdottir, Hulda, John J. Jost, Ido Liviatan, and Patrick E. Shrout. 2007. "Psychological Needs and Values Underlying Left-Right Political Orientation: Cross-National Evidence from Eastern and Western Europe." *Public Opinion Quarterly* 71 (2), 175–203.

Tilly, Charles. 2004. *Social Movements, 1768–2004.* Boulder, CO: Paradigm.

Tocqueville, Alexis de. [1857] 1988. *The Ancien Régime.* London: J. M. Dent & Sons.

Tourné, Karine. 2005. "Diplômés Chômeurs: L'Expérience de l'Infortune Sociale et les Nouveaux Dispositifs de l'Insertion en Égypte." *Revue des mondes musulmans et de la Méditerranée* 105–6, 91–108.

Triandis, Harry C. 2008. *Fooling Ourselves: Self-deception in Politics, Religion, and Terrorism.* Westport, CT: Greenwood.

Tyler, Tom R., Robert J. Boeckmann, Heather Jean Smith, and Yuen J. Huo. 1997. *Social Justice in a Diverse Society.* Boulder, CO: Westview.

Tzannatos, Zafiris. 2011. "Labour Demand and Social Dialogue: Two Binding Constraints for Creating Decent Employment and Ensuring Effective Utilization of Human Resources in the Arab Region?" Presentation at the Expert Group Meeting on "Addressing Unemployment and Underemployment in the

Islamic Development Bank Member Countries in the Post-Crisis World." Islamic Development Bank Headquarters, 9–10 May.

UNDP. 2003a. *The Arab Human Development Report*. New York: United Nations Development Programme, Regional Bureau for Arab States.

———. 2003b. *National Human Development Report: Saudi Arabia*. Riyadh: United National Development Program/Saudi Ministry of Economy and Planning.

UNESCO. Institute for Statistics. www.uis.unesco.org/Pages/default.aspx.

———. 1990. Statistical Yearbook. Paris: United Nations Educational, Scientific and Cultural Organization.

Van Hiel, Alain. 2012. "A Psycho-Political Profile of Party Activists and Left-wing and Right-wing Extremists." *European Journal of Political Research* 51 (2), 166–203.

Van Hiel, Alain, Mario Pandelaere, and Bart Duriez. 2004. "The Impact of Need for Closure on Conservative Beliefs and Racism: Differential Mediation by Authoritarian Submission and Authoritarian Dominance." *Personality and Social Psychology Bulletin* 30 (7), 824–37.

Verhulst, Brad, Lindon J. Eaves, and Peter K. Hatemi. 2012. "Correlation Not Causation: The Relationship between Personality Traits and Political Ideologies." *American Journal of Political Science* 56 (1), 34–51.

Verhulst, Brad, Peter K. Hatemi, and Nicholas G. Martin. 2010. "The Nature of the Relationship between Personality Traits and Political Attitudes." *Personality and Individual Differences* 49 (4), 306–16.

Victoroff, Jeff. 2005. "The Mind of the Terrorist: A Review and Critique of Psychological Approaches." *Journal of Conflict Resolution* 49 (1), 3–42.

Von Baeyer-Katte, Wanda Claessens, Dieter Claessens, Hubert Feger, et al .1983. *Analysen zum Terrorismus*. Vol. 3. Gruppenprozesse, Opladen, Germany: WDV.

Wagemakers, Joas. 2008. "Framing the 'Threat to Islam': Al-wala' wa al-bara' in Salafi Discourse." *Arab Studies Quarterly* 30 (4), 1–22.

Waltz, Susan. 1986. "Islamist Appeal in Tunisia." *Middle East Journal* 40 (4), 651–70.

Watkins, Kevin. 2011. "Education Failures Fan the Flames in the Arab World." World Education Blog. http://efareport.wordpress.com/2011/02/23/education-failures-fan-the-flames-in-the-arab-world/.

Weenink, Anton W. 2015. "Behavioral Problems and Disorders among Radicals in Police Files." *Perspectives on Terrorism* 9 (2), 17–33.

Weinberg, Leonard. 2003. "Conclusions." In Peter H. Merkl and Leonard Weinberg, eds., *Right-wing Extremism in the Twenty-first Century*. London: Taylor & Francis.

Weinberg, Leonard, and William Lee Eubank. 1988. "Neo-Fascist and Far Left Terrorists in Italy: Some Biographical Observations." *British Journal of Political Science* 18 (4), 531–49.

———. 2011. "Women's Involvement in Terrorism." *Gender Issues* 28 (1–2), 22–49.

Whine, Michael. 1999. "Islamist Organizations on the Internet." *Terrorism and Political Violence* 11 (1), 123–32.

Whitley Jr., Bernard E. 1999. "Right-Wing Authoritarianism, Social Dominance Orientation, and Prejudice." *Journal of Personality and Social Psychology* 77 (1), 126–34.

Wickham, Carrie. 2002. *Mobilizing Islam: Religion, Activism and Political Change in Egypt*. New York: Columbia University Press.

Wiktorowicz, Quintan, ed. 2004a. *Islamic Activism: A Social Movement Theory Approach*. Bloomington: Indiana University Press.

———. 2004b. "Joining the Cause: Al-Muhajiroun and Radical Islam." Paper presented at workshop titled "Roots of Islamic Radicalism," Yale University.

———. 2005. "A Genealogy of Radical Islam." *Studies in Conflict and Terrorism* 28 (2), 75–97.

———. 2006. "Anatomy of the Salafi Movement." *Studies in Conflict and Terrorism* 29 (3), 207–39.

Willis, Michael. 1996. *The Islamist Challenge in Algeria: A Political History*. Reading: Ithaca.

Windolf, Paul. 1990. "Die Expansion der Universitäten 1870–1985: Ein internationaler Vergleich (ZA8175)." Manheim: GESIS, Leibniz Institute for the Social Sciences. www.gesis.org/histat/en/project/tables/88B218B9252B3F60B1DB81CEE5325809.

World Bank. 2008. *The Road Not Traveled: Education Reform in the Middle East and North Africa*. Washington, D.C.: World Bank.

Wright, Lawrence. 2002. "The Man behind bin Laden." *The New Yorker*, 16 September.

———. 2006. *The Looming Tower: Al-Qaeda and the Road to 9/11*. New York: Knopf.

Wright, William. 1998. *Born That Way: Genes, Behavior, Personality*. London: Routledge.

Yazbeck Haddad, Yvonne, John L. Esposito, and John O. Voll. 1991. *The Contemporary Islamic Revival: A Critical Survey and Bibliography*. Westport, CT: Greenwood.

Zaidi, Akbar S. 1986. "Class Composition of Medical Students: Some Indications from Sind, Pakistan." *Economic & Political Weekly* 21 (40), 1756–59.

Zewail, Ahmed. 2010. "Reflections on Arab Renaissance." *Cairo Review of Global Affairs*. www.aucegypt.edu/gapp/cairoreview/Pages/articleDetails.aspx?aid=22.

INDEX